W9-BKV-594

This book examines the effects of the English Reformation on the full spectrum of lay religion from 1540 to 1580 through an investigation of individuals and parishes in Gloucestershire.

Rather than focusing on either the acceptance of Protestantism or the demise of the traditional Catholic religion, as other historians have done, this book considers all shades of belief against the backdrop of shifting official religious policy. The result is the story of responses ranging from stiff resistance to eager acceptance, creating a picture of the religion of the laity which is diverse and complex, but also layered, as parishes and individuals expressed their faith in ways which reflected the institutional or personal nature of their piety. Finally, while the book focuses on Gloucestershire, it reveals broad patterns of beliefs and practices which could probably be found all over England.

Cambridge Studies in Early Modern British History

THE ENGLISH REFORMATION
AND THE LAITY

Cambridge Studies in Early Modern British History

Series editors

ANTHONY FLETCHER
Professor of History, University of Essex

JOHN GUY
Professor of Modern History, University of St Andrews

and JOHN MORRILL
Reader in Early Modern History, University of Cambridge, and Vice Master of Selwyn College

This is a series of monographs and studies covering many aspects of the history of the British Isles between the late fifteenth century and early eighteenth century. It includes the work of established scholars and pioneering work by a new generation of scholars. It includes both reviews and revisions of major topics and books which open up new historical terrain or which reveal startling new perspectives on familiar subjects. All the volumes set detailed research into broader perspectives and the books are intended for the use of students as well as of their teachers.

For a list of titles in the series, see end of book

THE ENGLISH REFORMATION
AND THE LAITY

Gloucestershire, 1540–1580

CAROLINE LITZENBERGER

West Virginia University

 CAMBRIDGE
UNIVERSITY PRESS

PUBLISHED BY THE PRESS SYNDICATE OF THE UNIVERSITY OF CAMBRIDGE
The Pitt Building, Trumpington Street, Cambridge CB2 1RP, United Kingdom

CAMBRIDGE UNIVERSITY PRESS
The Edinburgh Building, Cambridge, CB2 2RU, United Kingdom
40 West 20th Street, New York, NY 10011–4211, USA
10 Stamford Road, Oakleigh, Melbourne 3166, Australia

First published 1997

Printed in the United Kingdom at the University Press, Cambridge

Typeset in Sabon 10/12 pt [CE]

A catalogue record for this book is available from the British Library

Library of Congress Cataloguing in Publication data

Litzenberger, C. J.
  The English Reformation and the laity: Gloucestershire, 1540–1580
/ Caroline Litzenberger.
    p.   cm. – (Cambridge studies in early modern British history)
  Includes bibliographical references and index.
  ISBN 0 521 47545 7 (hardback)
  1. Reformation – England – Gloucestershire.   2. Gloucestershire
(England) – Religion.   I. Title.   II. Series.
  BR375.5.G56L57 1997   274.24′106–dc21   97–1361   CIP

ISBN 0 521 47545 7 hardback

In memory of my daughter,
Alison
(November 1970–May 1986)

CONTENTS

FIGURES

TABLES

ACKNOWLEDGMENTS

I owe thanks to the many people who have supported me at various stages during the project which has culminated in this book. This work has been aided significantly by financial support received from an Overseas Research Student Award, a Trinity College Overseas Student Bursary, an American Friends of Cambridge University Scholarship and a Cambridge Overseas Trust Scholarship. In addition, I would like to thank the managers of the Lightfoot Scholarship, Archbishop Cranmer, Eddington and Dealty Funds for their generous support. The last phase of this project was supported by grants from the West Virginia University Faculty Senate and the West Virginia Radiological Consultants Association, and I am grateful for their generosity. Also, while I was completing this work I had an opportunity to participate in the National Endowment for the Humanities Summer Institute on Society and Religion in Early Modern England, and I am thankful for the intellectual stimulation and substantive suggestions I received from that experience. I would also like to thank the Gloucestershire Record Office for giving permission to publish the illustrations from Gloucestershire churches which appear in the body of the text. The cover illustration is printed with permission from the Folger Shakespeare Library, and I would like to thank Drs Jesse Lander and Richard McCoy for their generous advice in helping me to locate a suitable image.

In fact, I have been fortunate to benefit from the helpful and knowledge-able suggestions of numerous historians. Most significantly, whatever strengths the work possesses are primarily a result of the guidance, criticism and encouragement I have received from Professor Patrick Collinson. He has managed to be simultaneously affirming and challenging, and this work is the better because of that. I am also indebted to Drs Eamon Duffy, Diarmaid MacCulloch, Marjorie McIntosh, John Morrill and Ann Weikel for their encouragement and support. I discussed the methodologies employed in the analysis of Gloucestershire wills with Dr John Dawson of the Cambridge Centre for Literary and Linguistic Computing and with members of the Cambridge Group for the History of Population and Social

Structure, especially Jim Oeppen, Dr Roger Schofield and Dr Richard Wall, and their assistance was invaluable. I have also had the good fortune to be a part of a large and vibrant group of early modernists at Cambridge, many of whom have been very helpful to me. In this regard I would like to thank both past and present members, including David Crankshaw and Drs John Craig, Steve Hindle, Michael Frearson, Anthony Milton, Beat Kümen, Susan Wabuda and Alex Walsham. More particularly, I would like to thank Drs Lynn Botelho, Patrick Carter, Barendina Galloway, Judith Maltby and Kate Peters, who each read portions or all of this work. I am most grateful for their thoughtful comments and criticisms. Of course, any errors which remain are solely my own.

My research has necessarily required extensive access to the records held by the Gloucestershire Record Office, and I would particularly like to thank David Smith, County Archivist, Kate Haslam, Search Room Supervisor and Assistant County Archivist, and the other members of the Search Room staff for their professional, efficient and good-humoured support of my work. Thanks are also due to Godfrey Waller, supervisor of the Manuscripts Room in the Cambridge University Library, who worked with the staff of the Gloucestershire Record Office to facilitate my access to the Gloucestershire wills on microfilm. I would further like to express my gratitude to the staffs of the Gloucester City Library Gloucestershire Collection, the British Library, the Institute of Historical Research, the Public Record Office in Chancery Lane, the Folger Shakespeare Library, the West Virginia University Library, the University of Pittsburgh Library, the Honnold/Mudd Library of the Claremont Colleges and the University of Washington Library for their assistance.

In addition, a number of people have provided special support and encouragement. In this regard I wish to thank the history faculty of West Virginia University and the participants and leaders of the NEH Summer Institute on Society and Religion in Early Modern England. I have also been heartened by the extraordinary support of a number of individuals, including Dr Eric Carlson, Dr Eileen Groth, Kate Loggan, Dr Margaret Minor, Dr Kenneth Parker, the Revd John Scannell, Dr Alice Scannell, and Patty and Dale Walhood. In addition, I want to express special 'thank yous' to the Reverend Vivienne Faull for her hospitality, and to Bill and Barbara Larson for their generosity and friendship. I am also most grateful for the support I have received from my mother, Pat Wiles, from my brother and sisters, and especially from my son, Brian Litzenberger; they have all had faith in me throughout this process. Finally, I would like to thank Jane Larson for her companionship, patience and helpful editorial suggestions as I laboured to complete this work. It has been a long haul and I have been truly blessed.

ABBREVIATIONS AND CONVENTIONS

ABBREVIATIONS

A&M	J. Foxe, *The Acts and Monuments of John Foxe*, ed. G. Townsend (London, 1846), 8 vols.
APC	*Acts of the Privy Council*, new ser., ed. J. R. Dasent (London, 1894), 32 vols.
BL	British Library
Brigden, *London*	S. Brigden, *London and the Reformation* (Oxford, 1989)
Cardwell, *Annals*	*Documentary Annals of the Reformed Church of England*, ed. E. Cardwell (London, 1839), 2 vols.
Cardwell, *Synodalia*	*Synodalia: a Collection of Articles of Religion, Canons, and Proceedings of Convocations*, comp. E. Cardwell (Oxford, 1842), 2 vols.
CCC	Corpus Christi College
'Chantry Certificates'	J. Maclean, ed., 'Chantry Certificates, Gloucestershire (Roll 22)', *TBGAS* 8 (1883–4), pp. 229–308
Clark, *Society*	P. Clark, *English Provincial Society from the Reformation to the Revolution: Religion, Politics and Society in Kent 1500–1640* (Hassocks, Sussex, 1977)
Commission	*The Commission for Ecclesiastical Causes with the dioceses of Bristol and Gloucester, 1574*, ed. F. D. Price (Bristol and Gloucestershire Archaeological Society, Records Section, vol. X, Gateshead, 1972)
Dickens, *Reformation*	A. G. Dickens, *The English Reformation*, 2nd edn (London, 1989)
DNB	*Dictionary of National Biography*, ed. Sidney Lee (London, 1885–1900)

Duffy, *Stripping*	E. Duffy, *The Stripping of the Altars: Traditional Religion in England, c. 1400–c. 1580* (New Haven, CT, and London, 1992)
E	Exchequer classes, Public Record Office
EHR	*English Historical Review*
Garrett, *Marian Exiles*	C. H. Garrett, *The Marian Exiles: A Study in the Origins of Elizabethan Puritanism* (1938; reprint Cambridge, 1966)
GBR	Gloucester Borough Records
GCL	Gloucester City Library
GRO	Gloucestershire Record Office
GRO Wills	GRO, Gloucestershire Wills
Haigh, *Reformations*	C. Haigh, *English Reformations: Religion, Politics and Society under the Tudors* (Oxford, 1993)
'History of Gloucester'	GRO, D327, Furney MS
HJ	*Historical Journal*
Hooper, *Early Writings*	*The Early Writings of Bishop Hooper*, ed. S. Carr (Cambridge, 1843)
Hooper, *Later Writings*	*Later Writings of Bishop Hooper*, ed. C. Nevinson (Cambridge, 1852)
HWRO	Hereford and Worcester Record Office
HWRO Wills	HWRO, Diocese of Worcester Wills
JBS	*Journal of British Studies*
JEH	*Journal of Ecclesiastical History*
L&P	*Letters and Papers, Foreign and Domestic of the Reign of Henry VIII*, ed. J. S. Brewer (1864; reprint, New York, 1965), 21 vols.
Latimer, *Sermons*	H. Latimer, *Sermons and Remains of Hugh Latimer*, ed. G. E. Corrie (Cambridge, 1845)
Liturgical Services	*Liturgical Services: Liturgies and Occasional Forms of Prayer*, ed. W. K. Clay (Cambridge, 1847)
LPS	*Local Population Studies*
MacCulloch, *Suffolk*	D. MacCulloch, *Suffolk and the Tudors: Politics and Religion in an English County, 1500–1600* (Oxford, 1986)
Narratives	*Narratives of the Days of the Reformation*, ed. J. G. Nichols (Camden Society, vol. LXXVII, London, 1859)
Original Letters	*Original Letters Relative to the Reformation*, trans. and ed. H. Robinson (Cambridge, 1846) 2 vols.

P&P	*Past & Present*
Powell, 'Beginnings'	K. G. Powell, 'The Beginnings of Protestantism in Gloucestershire', *TBGAS* 90 (1971), pp. 141–57
Powell, 'Social Background'	K. G. Powell, 'The Social Background of the Reformation in Gloucestershire', *TBGAS* 92 (1973), pp. 96–120
Prayer Books	*The First and Second Prayer Books of Edward VI* (Everyman's Library, 1910; reprint, London and New York, 1960)
Primus, *Vestments*	J. H. Primus, *The Vestments Controversy: an Historical Study of the Earliest Tensions with the Church of England in the Reigns of Edward VI and Elizabeth* (Amsterdam, 1960)
PRO	Public Record Office
REED	*Records of Early English Drama: Cumberland, Westmorland, Gloucestershire*, ed. A. Douglas and P. Greenfield (Toronto, Buffalo and London, 1986)
Reformation Revised	*The English Reformation Revised*, ed. C. Haigh (Cambridge, 1987)
TBR	Tewkesbury Borough Records
Tewkesbury	*Tewkesbury Churchwardens' Accounts, 1563–1624*, ed. C. Litzenberger (Gloucestershire Record Series, vol. VII, Gloucester, 1994)
SCJ	*Sixteenth Century Journal*
STC	Short Title Catalogue Number
TBGAS	*Transactions of the Bristol and Gloucestershire Archaeological Society*
TRP	*Tudor Royal Proclamations, The Early Tudors (1485–1553)*, ed. P. L. Hughes and J. F. Larkin (New Haven, CT, and London, 1964), 3 vols.
VAI	*Visitation Articles and Injunctions of the Period of the Reformation*, ed. W. H. Frere and W. M. Kennedy (Alcuin Club Collections, vol. XV, London and New York, 1910), 3 vols.
Verey, *Gloucs.*	D. Verey, *Buildings of England: Gloucestershire*, 2nd edn (Harmondsworth, 1976), 2 vols.

'Visitation Booke'	'A True Copy of Bishop Hooper's Visitation Booke, Made by Him. AD 1551, 1552', Dr Williams's Library, Morice MS 31L, Item 3
Watt, *Cheap Print*	T. Watt, *Cheap Print and Popular Piety* (Cambridge, 1991)
Whiting, *Blind Devotion*	R. Whiting, *The Blind Devotion of the People* (1989; reprint, Cambridge, 1991)
Wilkins, *Concilia*	A. Wilkins, ed., *Concilia Magnae Britanniae et Hiberniae ab anno MDXLVI ad annum MDCCXVII* (London, 1737), 4 vols.
'Wills as Propaganda'	J. Craig and C. Litzenberger, 'Wills as Religious Propaganda: the Testament of William Tracy', *JEH* 44 (1993)
Zurich Letters	*The Zurich Letters Comprising the Correspondence of Several English Bishops and Others with some of the Helvetian Reformers*, trans. and ed. H. Robinson (Cambridge, 1845), 3 vols.

A NOTE ON TRANSCRIPTION

In quotations and titles the original spelling has been retained except for the pairs of letters, i and j, and u and v, which have been changed to adhere to modern usage. Additionally, dates have been standardised in the old style but with the year beginning on January 1; standard abbreviations have been silently expanded and punctuation has been added where necessary to clarify meaning. Also, details of the origin and context of the data have been noted in each case. In this way, details from the original document have been preserved in the extracted information in anticipation of future use in later stages of analysis.

Introduction

In the summer of 1551, in the middle of the reign of Edward VI, the churchwardens of St Michael's, Gloucester, paid two labourers 4s 'for the cariege of yerthe owte of the churche' to lower the floor where the altar had stood and prepare the place for the new wooden communion table required by Edwardian Protestantism. Two years later St Michael's installed a new altar, having paid 6s 8d to 'the halyer for xiij lodes of earthe for [raising] the said altur' as required by the return to Catholicism under Mary I, Edward's half-sister and successor. Here we see a local parish responding promptly and conscientiously to the requirements of the successive religious policies of the Crown. This return to Catholicism may have been the most abrupt and dramatic policy shift, but since the early 1530s official policy in England had swung back and forth between various forms of the old and the new religion. In that earlier decade, the break with Rome, the prohibition of selected traditional beliefs and practices, and the dissolution of the monasteries signalled a move away from the theology and discipline of the pre-Reformation church. Meanwhile, the centrality of scripture in preaching, worship and piety determined the nature of the newly emerging Henrician Church. This was not, however, the beginning of a steady move toward Protestantism akin to the inexorable rise of the waters behind a dam after the flood gates have been closed, but more like the ebb and flow of the waters of an ocean, at least until the 1570s. Hence, the religious world of the English laity was periodically disrupted, sometimes in sudden and wrenching ways. One month people were being urged to make pilgrimages to shrines which housed holy relics; the next month the relic was gone. One Easter they were to erect and watch the Easter sepulchre; the next year that practice was prohibited. One Sunday the service was in Latin and the next week it was in English. Altars were removed, floors lowered, wall paintings whitewashed and elaborate vestments eliminated. Then after a few short years, the floors were raised, altars put back, and elaborate vestments resurrected. The process of removal and simplification would then be repeated again in another few years, but this time changes would be introduced more slowly and, at least at first, less definitively. Thus, from the early 1530s to the early 1580s (from the middle of the reign of Henry VIII to the middle of the reign of Elizabeth I), the laity experienced a series of major upheavals. Some would welcome the new religion each time it was promoted; others would rejoice in every swing back toward the old. The anguish experienced by those who were trying to be obedient subjects and faithful Christians must have been excruciating.

Both Tessa Watt and Christopher Haigh have asserted that lay religion during this period was complex, as indeed it was.[1] When individuals are required to deal with change they respond in a variety of ways very similar to the responses one might have to a death: there is denial, resistance and anger before there can be acceptance. Of course, people's responses to change varied dramatically, depending on their experience, knowledge, preferences and personalities. In the case of religious change this is especially true. Thus some parishioners were delighted by the introduction of aspects of Protestantism, while others regretted the loss of traditional religion. Meanwhile, still others were angry and impatient, feeling that reform never went far enough. In addition, as the experiences of continuing shifts in official religion gave way to sustained periods with a particular set of beliefs and practices, people became more familiar with the new and began to accept it more readily. Such acceptance would, however, take time.

Only by investigating the religion of the laity can we see clearly how official policies played in the pews, and historians of the English Reformation are only now beginning to address such issues as we move into what might be described as the 'third phase' in the recent historiography of religion in sixteenth-century England. The first phase began with A. G. Dickens's work on pre-Elizabethan Protestantism and Patrick Collinson's examination of Elizabethan Puritanism. These provided the impetus for a number of local studies of the promotion of Protestantism which concentrated on diocesan administrations and the local gentry, while exploring the means of advancement of the new religion, and the speed and effects of such reform.[2] This approach, with its concentration of the identification of

---

[1] Haigh, *Reformations*, pp. 18, 285–95, *passim*; Watt, *Cheap Print*, pp. 324–8, *passim*.

[2] A. G. Dickens, *Lollards and Protestants in the Diocese of York 1509–1559* (1959; reprint, London, 1982); Dickens, *Reformation*; P. Collinson, *The Elizabethan Puritan Movement* (1967; reprint, Oxford, 1990); J. E. Oxley, *The Reformation in Essex to the Death of Mary* (Manchester, 1965); R. B. Manning, *Religion and Society in Elizabethan Sussex: a Study of the Enforcement of the Religious Settlement, 1558–1603* (Leicester and Bristol, 1969); Clark, *Society*; J. F. Davis, *Heresy and Reformation in the South-East of England, 1520–1559* (Royal Historical Studies, London and Atlantic Highlands, NJ, 1983); W. J. Sheils, *The Puritans in the Diocese of Peterborough, 1558–1610* (Northampton Record Society, vol. XXX, Northampton, 1979).

Protestants was challenged by Christopher Haigh in his study of the Reformation in Lancashire. His subsequent debate with Professor Dickens concerning the speed and catalysts of reform ushered in the second historiographical phase.[3] However, even this later phase was dependent on a clear delineation being made between Protestants and Catholics, and it is difficult to characterise accurately the actions, let alone the faith, of either individuals or parishes in terms of such strict dichotomies.

Of course, recent historians did not invent the concept of religious dichotomies. Rather, they have followed the lead of religious leaders in sixteenth-century England. Reformers referred to the pope as Antichrist and labelled as superstitious the traditional public rituals and private acts of piety. Meanwhile, those promoting the old faith characterised many of the beliefs and practices of the new religion as heretical. Defining or representing the self by demonising the 'Other' may have been an aspect of the developing awareness of the individual in early-modern England, but its institutional antecedents can be found in early Christianity.[4] Then, as the church developed, so too did the need for a clearer definition of orthodox belief. One of the primary means of achieving this goal was to define orthodoxy in terms of what it was not and to label that 'Other' as heresy.[5] As the reformers strove to re-establish the purity of the early 'true' church, they, along with the defenders of traditional religion, also adopted this strategy. Historians, it may be said, have merely been accepting and using the religious paradigms perceived and described by the articulate proponents of the various orthodoxies within sixteenth-century English religion. However, these rigid religious divisions do not necessarily reflect the faith actually practised in homes, parishes and even cathedrals across England, and more current historiography reflects that reality.

Moving beyond the Haigh–Dickens debate, historians are now investigating the impact of the Reformation more generally by exploring a myriad of topics and admitting the possibility of a more complex picture of the past. In particular, the ways in which the new religion and society acted

[3] C. Haigh, *Reformation and Resistance in Tudor Lancashire* (Cambridge, 1975). The debate between Haigh and Dickens is defined in two articles: A. G. Dickens, 'The Early Expansion of Protestantism in England 1520–1558', *Archiv für Reformationsgeschichte* 78 (1987), pp. 187–222; C. Haigh, 'The Recent Historiography of the English Reformation', *HJ* 25 (1982), pp. 995–1007, also printed in *Reformation Revised*, pp. 19–33. Cf. J. J. Scarisbrick, *The Reformation and the English People* (Oxford, 1984); Whiting, *Blind Devotion*.

[4] S. Greenblatt, *Renaissance Self-Fashioning from More to Shakespeare* (London and Chicago, IL, 1980), pp. 1–114, *passim*.

[5] For further discussion of the interplay between heresy and orthodoxy in early Christianity, see W. Bauer, *Orthodoxy and Heresy in Earliest Christianity*, ed. R. A. Kraft and G. Kodel (Philadelphia, PA, 1971). For further discussion of the use of the constructs of heresy and orthodoxy in defining belief systems, see L. R. Kurtz, 'The Politics of Heresy', *American Journal of Sociology* 88 (1983), pp. 1085–115.

upon and transformed each other has increasingly attracted the attention of scholars, as have the dynamics of the implementation of the new faith and the nature of Marian and Elizabethan Catholicism and its traditional pre-Reformation antecedent.[6] This study enters the historiographical discussion at this point, but re-directs the focus. Rather than asking about the progress of Protestantism or the effects of reform on pre-Reformation lay piety, it examines the existing faith in its many shapes and forms, allowing for a wide range of religious beliefs.

This work focuses on the people and parishes of one particular western county, Gloucestershire, and by so doing it is able to accommodate and describe in detail a much more diverse and complex religious scene than could be depicted by a study encompassing the entire kingdom. Furthermore, it reveals much that can be attributed to human nature and to the inefficiencies inherent in the enforcement of the established religion throughout the realm. Thus, while personalities and specific religious beliefs of key individuals, including bishops, priests and lay leaders, certainly influenced particular responses to individual policies, and the conservative nature of most of the residents of Gloucestershire created a climate which was generally resistant to the new religion, similar broadly complex patterns of beliefs and practices could probably be found all over England. Each county or region might have found its religious centre at a different point along the spectrum of beliefs, but diversity rather than uniformity would be the watchword of lay religion in England, at least during the forty to fifty years of tumultuous change which characterised the English Reformation.

The successive swings in official policy between traditional and reformed religion, and the conflicting characteristics of the bishops of Gloucester would have had some impact on the laity of the diocese, both corporately and individually. Gloucestershire has nearly the same boundaries as the diocese of Gloucester, which was created in 1541 and endowed with income derived from the dissolution of the monasteries, most notably from St Peter's Abbey in the city of Gloucester. Over the next forty years of dramatic change in official religious policy, the diocese had four bishops with similarly diverse sets of beliefs and administrative styles: the con-

---

[6] D. Cressy, *Bonfires and Bells: National Memory and the Protestant Calendar in Elizabethan and Stuart England* (London, 1989); Watt, *Cheap Print*; C. Haigh, 'The Continuity of Catholicism in the English Reformation', *P&P* 93 (1981), pp. 37–69, also printed in *Reformation Revised*, pp. 176–208; C. Haigh, 'The Church of England, the Catholics and the People' in *The Reign of Elizabeth I*, ed. C. Haigh (1984; reprint, Basingstoke and London, 1991), pp. 195–219; J. Bossy, 'The Character of Elizabethan Catholicism', *P&P* 21 (1962), pp. 39–59; J. Bossy, *The English Catholic Community, 1570–1850* (London, 1975); P. McGrath, 'Elizabethan Catholicism: a Reconsideration', *JEH* 35 (1984), pp. 414–28; Duffy, *Stripping*.

forming and conformable John Wakeman, former prior of Tewkesbury Abbey; the radical and energetic Zwinglian Protestant, John Hooper; the highly respected Catholic, James Brookes; and the scholarly, conservative and enigmatic Richard Cheyney. Elsewhere in the realm the laity would similarly have felt the effects of the varied beliefs and talents of individuals serving on the episcopal bench.[7] However, the piety and practices of individuals and parishes would not necessarily have conformed to the directives or religious preferences of their superiors.

During the years following the publication of the key historical works by Professors Dickens and Collinson, many historians have done research on particular regions of England.[8] However, religion in sixteenth-century Gloucestershire has received little attention.[9] Three studies have concentrated on John Hooper, Bishop of Gloucester from 1551 to 1553, while three others have examined isolated aspects of the nonconforming laity. F. D. Price focused on Bishop Hooper and his diocesan administration.[10] Following on from Price, two other historians have also concentrated on Hooper, this time in an examination of his theology.[11] To the degree that

[7] For further discussion of the episcopate and the Reformation, see P. Collinson, 'Episcopacy and Reform in England in the Later Sixteenth Century', in *Studies in Church History*, ed. G. J. Cuming (Leiden, 1966), vol. III, pp. 91–125; R. B. Manning, 'The Crisis of Episcopal Authority during the reign of Elizabeth I', *JBS* 11 (1971), pp. 1–25; R. Houlbrooke, 'The Protestant Episcopate 1547–1603: the Pastoral Contribution', in *Church and Society in England, Henry VIII to James I*, ed. F. Heal and R. O'Day (London, 1977), pp. 78–98.

[8] Brigden, *London*; MacCulloch, *Suffolk*; M. C. Skeeters, *Community and Clergy: Bristol and the Reformation c. 1530–c. 1570* (Oxford, 1993); Whiting, *Blind Devotion*.

[9] The social and political history of the county during the sixteenth century has similarly been neglected, the concentration being on the town rather than the county and focusing on either the late-medieval period or the late sixteenth century and beyond: R. A. Holt, 'Gloucester: an English Provincial Town during the Later Middle Ages' (unpublished PhD thesis, University of Birmingham, 1987); R. A. Holt, 'Gloucester in the Century after the Black Death', in *The English Medieval Town: a Reader in English Urban History, 1200–1540*, ed. R. A. Holt and G. Rosser (London and New York, 1990), pp. 141–59; P. Clark, '"The Ramoth-Gilead of the Good": Urban Change and Political Radicalism at Gloucester 1540–1640', in *The English Commonwealth, 1547–1640*, ed. P. Clark, A. G. R. Smith and N. Tyack (Leicester, 1979), pp. 167–87.

[10] F. D. Price, 'The Commission for Ecclesiastical Causes for the Dioceses of Bristol and Gloucester, 1574', *TBGAS* 59 (1937), pp. 61–184; F. D. Price, 'Gloucester Diocese under Bishop Hooper', *TBGAS* 60 (1938), pp. 51–151; F. D. Price, 'An Elizabethan Church official – Thomas Powell, Chancellor of Gloucester Diocese', *The Church Quarterly Review* 128 (1939), pp. 94–112; F. D. Price, 'The Administration of the Diocese of Gloucester 1547–1579' (unpublished BLitt thesis, University of Oxford, 1939); F. D. Price, 'The Abuses of Excommunication and the Decline of Ecclesiastical Discipline under Queen Elizabeth', *EHR* 225 (1942), pp. 106–15; F. D. Price, 'Elizabethan Apparitors in the Diocese of Gloucester', *The Church Quarterly Review* 134 (1942), pp. 37–55; F. D. Price, 'Bishop Bullingham and Chancellor Blackleech: a Diocese Divided', *TBGAS* 91 (1972), pp. 175–98. (A copy of Price's thesis is also available for consultation in the Gloucestershire Record Office.)

[11] W. M. S. West, 'John Hooper and the Origins of Puritanism' (a summary in English of the unpublished PhD thesis with the same title from the University of Zurich), Dr Williams's

lay religion has been investigated in the diocese, the scholars involved have focused exclusively on either radical Protestantism or Catholicism. Thus Kenneth Powell looked at the activities of radical Protestant lay people before 1540, and Patrick McGrath and Francis Moore then concentrated on Elizabethan Catholicism, beginning in the 1560s.[12] The present work is broader than these in two ways: it looks at all aspects of lay religion, and it examines the entire period from the 1530s to the 1580s.

Furthermore, this study approaches some sources in innovative ways. As with most local studies of early-modern English religion, this work uses parish, diocesan and state records, plus observations of surviving parish buildings and decorations dating from the sixteenth century. However, it relies more heavily than most on the analysis of lay people's wills, both elite and non-elite. Additionally, the methodology used to examine the wills is both innovative and complex.[13] Sixteenth-century English wills were typically divided into three sections, each of which may contain clues to the religion of the testator: the bequest of the soul, the bequest of the body, and the bequest of goods or possessions. Analyses of the religious implications of the last two types of legacies are fairly straightforward. Soul bequests (which are also called religious preambles or statements of faith) must be approached with care. During the past two or three decades historians have been quite concerned about the reliability of the religious information contained in these documents. In particular, they have focused on the influence of the scribes who wrote the wills and on the implications of the use of pre-existing formulaic preambles. It is now evident that scribes often offered testators a choice of formulas from which to chose, thus minimising scribal influence and control in many instances. In addition, we now recognise that the twentieth-century need for originality in order to authenticate self-expression did not exist in the sixteenth century. Rather, Renaissance ideas of authorship pertained, and a testator would have been making a stronger statement of belief by choosing a formula others would recognise and understand than by creating his or her own idiosyncratic preamble. Historians have also had difficulty with sampling and categor-

---

Library, MS P.4851; W. M. S. West, 'John Hooper and the Origins of Puritanism', *The Baptist Quarterly* 15 (1954), pp. 346–68; 16 (1955), pp. 22–46, 67–88; D. G. Newcome, 'The Life and Theological Thought of John Hooper, Bishop of Gloucester and Worcester, 1551–1553' (unpublished PhD thesis, University of Cambridge, 1990).

[12] Powell, 'Beginnings'; Powell, 'Social Background'; P. McGrath, 'Gloucestershire and the Counter-Reformation in the Reign of Elizabeth I', *TBGAS* 88 (1969), pp. 5–28; F. A. Moore, '"The Bruised Reed" (Is. 42:3): a Study of the Catholic Remnant in England, 1558–1603, with Special Reference to Gloucestershire' (unpublished MPhil thesis, University of London, 1990).

[13] See Appendix A for a more complete discussion of the methodology used in this study.

ising wills, and the methodology developed for this study is concerned with that aspect of their analysis.

For this investigation of lay beliefs in Gloucestershire a systematic sample of approximately 2,600 wills was selected, which was of sufficient size to be substantially representative of all those who wrote wills between 1540 and 1580 in the county. The preamble texts were analysed to determine the salvation theology they expressed. Over 300 different preamble texts were identified and consolidated under seventeen distinct descriptive headings. These headings were subsequently combined into three general categories: traditional or Catholic; evangelical or Protestant; and ambiguous. The ambiguous group comprised those statements of faith which could have been used in good conscience by anyone without distorting their salvation theology. The word, 'ambiguous' was chosen to reflect the fact that allowing for multiple meanings seems to have been the goal of many who employed preambles from this category. Finally, the codified preambles, further identified by date, region and sex, were analysed statistically to identify trends and determine the significance of observed differences. The results of the analysis of the wills were then used in combination with detailed studies of selected parishes and broader research into state and diocesan court records and other miscellaneous documents to produce a representation of lay religion in sixteenth-century Gloucestershire.

This study, then, uses the story of religious change in one county to gain insight into the experience of the laity of Tudor England through multiple shifts in official policy; most notably by looking at all the laity, no matter what their religious preferences. Frequently the spotlight of historical interest has been directed exclusively at Protestantism, neglecting other aspects of sixteenth-century religion, which have then been lost in the shadows. In particular, the survival of traditional religion has been hidden from view, while the light has been so bright that it flattened the image, obscuring the variations inherent in the multiple manifestations of the new religion. A similar problem has emerged when the centre-stage has been dominated by those who preferred the old religion. A further difficulty arises when one assumes that clear distinctions can be drawn between different religious preferences. Using such sharp distinctions hampers the accuracy of representations of the past, in that it requires religion to be trimmed of its complexities and diversities in order to fit into such strictly delineated categories. It is difficult accurately to characterise the actions, let alone faith, of either individuals or parishes using such a rigid black and white paradigm. We must find ways to accommodate myriad shades of grey, as this study attempts to do. The present work also explores the reflexive, recursive ways in which the new religion and society acted upon

and transformed each other. In so doing, it shows that lay religion during
the English Reformation was both complex and diverse, and that, while it
changed over time, it did not necessarily change in the ways desired by
those in authority.

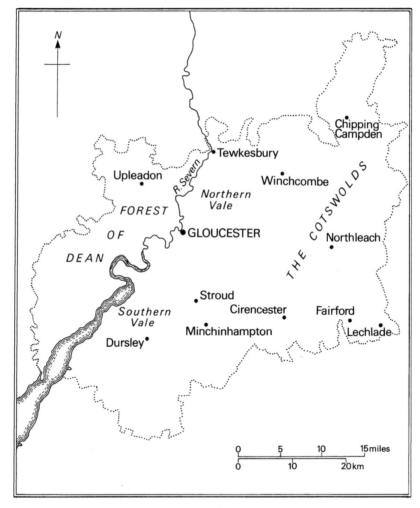

Figure 1.1   Map of Gloucestershire

1

Setting the scene

As a part of the process of ecclesiastical change in the early 1540s, a number of new dioceses were founded. The old diocesan structure had included the huge dioceses of Lincoln and York, as well as other only slightly more manageable sees such as Worcester. In the space of two years after the dissolution of the monasteries, six new dioceses were carved out of the larger sees and endowed with previous monastic holdings: Bristol, Chester, Oxford, Peterborough, Westminster and Gloucester. Bristol was created a year after the others, from portions of Bath and Wells, Salisbury and Gloucester. Both Oxford and Peterborough had been archdeaconries in the diocese of Lincoln. Westminster, which was a diocese for only ten years, was part of the diocese of London both before and after its separate existence. Chester was created out of Lichfield and York.[1] The diocese of Gloucester, most of which had been a deanery in the diocese of Worcester, was established by letters patent on 3 September 1541.[2] The new diocese was nearly contiguous with Gloucestershire.[3] The abbey church of the former monastery of St Peter, Gloucester, became the cathedral, and the former home of the abbot became the bishop's palace.[4]

The geography of the county and diocese of Gloucester was distinctive and varied, and influenced both politics and religion. It is bounded on the west by the Forest of Dean, while on the east, green hillsides cut by narrow valleys and fast-flowing streams rise sharply from the valley floor toward the undulating hills of the Cotswolds. In between lies the flat, fertile Vale of the Severn, with its shimmering river twisting gradually out of sight to the south-west like a silver ribbon. The county is long and narrow, stretching

---

[1] D. M. Smith, *Guide to Bishop's Registers of England and Wales: a Survey from the Middle Ages to the Abolition of Episcopacy in 1646* (London, 1981), pp. 40, 89, 163, 167, 202, 260.

[2] BL, Cotton MS, Appendix ix, fo. 2; translated in R. Atkins, *The Ancient and Present State of Glostershire* (1712; reprint, Wakefield, 1974), pt. I, pp. 44–52.

[3] See Figure 1.1.

[4] M. C. Skeeters, 'The Creation of the Diocese of Bristol', *TBGAS* 103 (1985), pp. 175–8; Smith, *Guide to Bishop's Registers*, p. 95.

from north-east to south-west for a distance of approximately fifty-six miles and measuring just twenty-two miles across its narrow mid-section from north-west to south-east.

Occupying the north-west portion of the county, the Forest of Dean drops precipitously to the River Wye and Herefordshire in the north and west, and slopes gently toward the Severn to the south and east. Established as a royal forest shortly after the Conquest, it was an isolated and proto-industrial region of rolling woodlands, interspersed with pasture, coal and iron mines, iron foundries, and charcoal-producing facilities in the sixteenth century.[5] John Leland, who visited in 1540, described the Forest:

The soyle . . . for the most part is more fruitfull of wood and grasse then of corne, and yet there is good corne sufficient for the inhabitants of it. The ground is fruitfull of iron mines, and divers forges be there to make iron.[6]

William Camden, writing approximately forty-five years later, described the Forest as 'covered with thick woods . . . The soil is a deep clay, fit for the growth of oaks; the hills, full of iron-ore, colour the several springs that have their passage through them. Here are several furnaces for the making of iron.'[7] The central geological feature of the region is a synclinal basin covering a large coal field surrounded by deposits of iron ore, which provided the basis for the development of free mining and the establishment of numerous bloomery furnaces in the area by 1500.

Rights of common inherent in a royal forest, combined with the free-miners' legal system, had created a general sense of isolation from the rest of the county.[8] During the first half of the sixteenth century the Crown moved to increase its control over rights of common, both by granting those rights to inhabitants of neighbouring communities, and by permitting the enclosure of plantations to promote the growth of timber. Forest land could now be fenced for a maximum of seven years, rather than the previous three. This was designed to encourage the growth of timber, a

---

[5] Charcoal was used to fire the furnaces for processing iron ore.

[6] J. Leland, *The Itinerary of John Leland the Antiquary*, 3rd edn, ed. T. Hearne (Oxford, 1769), vol. IV, part. II, p. 83; also printed in Leland, *The Itinerary*, ed. L. T. Smith (London, 1908), vol. II, p. 64.

[7] W. Camden, *Britannia: or a Chorographical Description of Great Britain and Ireland*, 4th edn, trans. and ed. E. Gibson (London, 1772), vol. I, p. 280. The 'furnaces' were used to process the iron ore, employing a procedure in which the iron ore was converted directly into 'a lump of pasty malleable iron' which could then be shaped as desired. C. E. Hart, *The Industrial History of Dean* (Newton Abbot, 1971), p. 8. This bloomery process was slow to be replaced in the Forest, with the first blast furnace not being introduced until the 1590s. A. R. H. Baker, 'Changes in the Later Middle Ages,' in *A New Historical Geography of England before 1600*, ed. H. C. Darby (Cambridge, 1976), p. 231.

[8] C. E. Hart, *Royal Forest: A History of Dean's Woods as Producers of Timber* (Oxford, 1966), p. 7; Hart, *Industrial History*, pp. xxii–iii; C. E. Hart, *The Commoners of the Forest of Dean* (Gloucester, 1951), pp. xiii–xiv.

vanishing resource desperately needed for the construction of ships. By the middle of the sixteenth century the woods had been reduced from approximately 50,000 to between 15,000 and 20,000 acres. In 1559, in a further attempt to preserve timber for ship-building, an act was passed which prohibited the use of large trees within fourteen miles of either the Wye or Severn for charcoal-making, thus curtailing that activity. These changes resulted in conflict and violence between inhabitants of the Forest and representatives of the Crown.[9] The sense of separation and independence from outside authority also made the Forest attractive to 'people of very lewd lives and conversation', further increasing the region's insularity and reputation. In 1430, some inhabitants of Tewkesbury complained to the Crown that people living in the Forest of Dean were refusing to obey the law.[10] Thus, by the early sixteenth century, the region was effectively beyond the reach of external authorities, a factor which would later hamper the implementation and enforcement of both the law in general and official religious policy in particular.

If the Forest rises from the west bank of the Severn, the eastern edge of the Severn Valley is equally well defined. There the escarpment, which defines the edge of the Cotswolds, rises abruptly from the valley floor. The Cotswolds were dominated by the cloth-making industry in the fifteenth and sixteenth centuries, while the broad, gently rolling hills which extend for some distance to the east of the edge were noted primarily for sheep-farming. In describing the hundred of Berkeley just south of the city of Gloucester, John Smyth of Nibley declared,

> one part . . . [stands] high in the wolds, and the other in the vale at the foot of those hills . . . By reason of which scituation [*sic*], many hundreds, even thousandes of springs breake forth at the sydes, knees, and feet of those hills, begettinge divers delicate small rivers, neither knowinge want of water in sommer, nor so increasinge their chanell in winter, that the trade of clothinge which heere aboundeth, is neither in drought nor wett wether hindred: A principall cause of the multitude of tuckmills, and fullinge mills, which heere abound.[11]

The valleys formed by those streams were the portions of the county with the highest concentration of such mills. As Smyth indicated, those small but dependable rivers were ideally suited to drive fulling mills. Their

[9] T. S. Willan, *The Inland Trade: Studies in English Internal Trade in the Sixteenth and Seventeenth Centuries* (Manchester, 1976), p. 25; Hart, *Commoners*, pp. 11, 12; Hart, *Royal Forest*, pp. xx, xxiii, 71.

[10] C. E. Hart, *The Free Miners of the Royal Forest of Dean and Hundred of St Briavels* (Gloucester, 1953), p. 2; J. Thirsk, 'The Farming Regions of England', in *The Agrarian History of England and Wales, 1500–1640*, ed. J. Thirsk (Cambridge, 1967), vol. IV, p. 71; Hart, *Commoners*, p. 11n.

[11] J. Smyth, *A Description of the Hundred of Berkeley in the County of Gloucester and of its Inhabitants*, ed. J. Maclean (The Berkeley Manuscripts, vol. III, Gloucester, 1885), p. 4.

rate of flow was virtually constant and the drop in elevation produced reliable water power for numerous mills to operate downstream from each other along the rivers' narrow valleys. Thus, major cloth-making centres grew up in the areas around Stroud, Painswick, Minchinhampton, Nailsworth, Dursley and Wotton-under-Edge, all located in or near those small valleys. During the sixteenth century, the 'Stroud-water' area along the Frome, in particular, grew to dominate Gloucestershire cloth-making. Equally reliable, but with less total potential power, because of their more gradual descent, were the streams which flowed to the east, providing power for mills near Northleach, Cirencester, Chipping Camden and Bibury.[12]

Lying in the flat between the Forest and the Cotswolds, the Vale itself was noted primarily for dairying, mixed farming, and apple and pear orchards.[13] The valley and the banks of the Severn were also the sites of two of the largest market towns in the county, Tewkesbury and Gloucester, and a parish in each of these towns has contributed significant detail to the depiction of lay religion in sixteenth-century Gloucestershire, which is the focus of this volume. Thus, those towns and parishes deserve special scrutiny.

The river Severn provided both Gloucester and Tewkesbury with a ready-made avenue for transporting barley, malt, wheat and peas, as well as some manufactured goods, from the region to markets outside the county, and for bringing wine, foodstuffs and, increasingly, raw materials into the area.[14] Tewkesbury was nearly surrounded by water, situated as it was at the confluence of the Severn and Avon rivers approximately ten miles up-river from Gloucester, and owed much of its sixteenth-century livelihood to fishing and its leather-working industry, as well as to water-borne trades. Clearly, the rivers were its life-blood. The Severn was also important to Gloucester, but that city was bounded primarily by walls, not water. When John Leland visited the latter, he found it 'antient, well builded of tymbre, and large, and strongly defended with walles, where it is

---

[12] For a thorough discussion of the siting of mills in Gloucestershire, see J. Tann, 'Some Problems of Water Power – a Study of Mill Siting in Gloucestershire', *TBGAS* 84 (1965), pp. 53–77. See also R. Perry, 'The Gloucestershire Woollen Industry, 1100–1690', *TBGAS* 66 (1945), pp. 49–137; J. Tann, *Gloucestershire Woollen Mills* (Newton Abbot, 1967), pp. 15–28, *passim*. The location of cloth-making centres is further defined by the list of those fined for attempting to sell defective cloth in London between 29 September 1561 and 21 September 1562. The list included individuals from Berkeley, Cirencester, Dursley, Gloucester, Kingswood, Minchinhampton, Moreton Valence, North Nibley, Northleach, Painswick, Rodborough, Stroud and Wotton-under-Edge. G. D. Ramsay, 'The Distribution of the Cloth Industry in 1561–1562', *EHR* 57 (1942), pp. 361–9.

[13] F. V. Emery, 'England *circa* 1600', in *A New Historical Geography of England before 1600*, ed. H. D. Darby (Cambridge, 1976), p. 262; J. Thirsk, 'The Farming Regions of England', p. 68.

[14] T. S. Willan, *Inland Trade*, pp. 19–20.

not well fortified with the deepe streame of Severne water. In the wall be 4. gates by east, west, north and south . . . [However,] the beauty of the towne lyeth in 2. Crossing streets.'[15] The town owed its layout to its original foundation in AD 96–8 as the Roman *colonia* of Glevum, although it fell into ruin after the Roman withdrawal and did not regain its former prominence until the tenth century.[16] Gloucester differed from Tewkesbury in its size, with approximately 950 households in 1563 compared with 396 in Tewkesbury, and in the greater number of churches within the town: eleven, compared with Tewkesbury's one.[17]

The single parish of St Mary's in Tewkesbury, along with the parish of St Michael's in Gloucester, two parishes which appear at first glance to have had much in common, will receive special attention in this discussion of the Reformation in Gloucestershire. Prior to the dissolution of the monasteries, Tewkesbury Abbey was the proprietor of St Mary's church, while St Peter's Abbey in Gloucester was patron of the living of St Michael's, and from 1540 both were in the gift of the Crown.[18] Also, the two parishes seem to have been fairly affluent, maintaining their buildings and furnishings in spite of the increasingly onerous financial demands of changing religious policy. Although both were urban parishes, their differences nevertheless outweigh their similarities, and thus they provide contrasting views of the Reformation at the parish level. As one of several parishes in Gloucester, St Michael's was of medium size and affluent, whereas St Mary's was large and socio-economically diverse, since it was the only parish in the town of Tewkesbury.

Furthermore, interactions between the abbey and the townspeople in Gloucester stood in sharp contrast to those in Tewkesbury. Relations were frequently strained during the century before the dissolution in Gloucester, where the Abbey of St Peter's controlled a considerable portion of the property within the city walls. From the time of the Black Death to the dissolution of the monasteries, the oligarchy of the town continually tried to assert their dominance over the Abbey and over the other religious houses located within the walls: Llanthony Priory, St Oswald's Priory, Blackfriars and Greyfriars. Meanwhile, the religious houses sought to retain control of the town, which led to riots and disturbances outside the abbey gates early in the sixteenth century.[19] In particular, there was a

[15] J. Leland, *The Itinerary*, ed. T. Hearne, vol. IV, part 2, p. 77; also printed in J. Leland, *The Itinerary*, ed. L. T. Smith, vol. II, p. 57.
[16] H. P. R. Finberg, 'The Genesis of the Gloucestershire Towns', in *Gloucestershire Studies*, ed. H. P. R. Finberg (Leicester, 1957), pp. 54–60.
[17] GRO, Furney MS B, p. 28; P. Clark, 'Early Modern Gloucester, 1547–1720', in *The History of the County of Gloucester*, vol. IV, ed. N. M. Herbert (London, 1988), p. 73.
[18] GCL Hockaday Abstracts, vol. CCXIX, 1539; vol. CCCLXIX, 1540, unpaginated.
[19] R. A. Holt, 'Gloucester: an English Provincial Town', pp. 237, 267; R. A. Holt, 'Gloucester

dispute between the town of Gloucester and St Peter's Abbey in 1513 concerning the rights of common, which culminated in 'twoo hundreth persones or ther aboute . . . [making] sondry riotouse assemblies insurrections and affraws within the precincts of . . . [the abbey] and diverse of them . . . soore hurte the servauntes of the said abbott'. The abbot of Winchcombe and the prior of Llanthony were enlisted to resolve the differences.[20] By contrast, the parish of Tewkesbury apparently maintained an amicable relationship with their abbey, having used the west end of their abbey church for parish worship for a significant length of time.[21] None the less, Tewkesbury Abbey towered over the town, not only physically but politically and economically too, dominating nearly every aspect of life. Not only did the parish worship there, but the Abbey controlled a substantial proportion of the rental property in the town as well. Yet, despite the potential for conflict, relations between the town and the Abbey appear to have been amicable.

The high cross at the centre of the city of Gloucester, which Leland had so admired, was the site of St Michael's and the geographical and political centre of Gloucester. The church was situated at the point where the four main streets of the city met and counted among its members many of the city's chief inhabitants. It had been considered a substantial benefice for some time, and given its prominence it is perhaps not surprising that it became something of a model parish during the years of greatest religious change.[22] Hence, the removal and replacing of dirt in the chancel mentioned in the Introduction to this work. The church was large, with a south aisle, a south chapel, which had served as their pre-Reformation Lady Chapel, and a chancel. A porch and a large square tower containing six bells had been added between 1455 and 1472.[23] Additionally, before they

---

in the Century after the Black Death', pp. 155–6; L. E. W. O. Fullbrook-Leggatt, 'Medieval Gloucester', *TBGAS* 66 (1945), pp. 3, 8, 11.

[20] GRO GBR B2/1, fos. 118v–19; GRO GBR B2/1, fos. 206v–7, 229v. The violence which characterised the dispute between the abbey and the town of Gloucester was in contrast to the nature of similar disagreements between the city of Norwich and their Benedictine priory, where, according to Muriel McClendon, such differences were being resolved in the 'royal courts' by the beginning of the sixteenth century. M. C. McClendon, 'The Quiet Reformation: Norwich Magistrates and the Coming of Protestantism, 1520–1575' (unpublished PhD thesis, Stanford University, 1990), p. 64.

[21] GRO GBR B2/1, fo. 1; Holt, 'Gloucester in the Century after the Black Death', p. 155; GRO TBR B2/1, p. 1.

[22] St Michael's, Gloucester, was one of the livings granted to Stephen Gardiner, the future bishop of Winchester, secretary to Henry VIII and Lord Chancellor under Mary, in the mid-1520s. During the same period he was also made archdeacon of Taunton in the diocese of Bath and Wells and a canon of Salisbury. A. B. Emden, *A Biographical Register of the University of Oxford, AD 1501 to 1540* (Oxford, 1974), p. 227.

[23] A. R. J. Jurica, 'Churches and Chapels', in *The History of the County of Gloucester*, ed. N. M. Herbert (London, 1988), vol. IV, p. 307. See Figure 1.2.

Figure 1.2   View of St Michael's Gloucester

were abolished, the parish was home to 'the Fraternytie or Company of the Crafte of Wevers, otherwise called Seynt Annes Service', and a second fraternity 'of certain brethern and sisters' dedicated to St John Baptist. There had been a light before the rood, and a light dedicated to St Katherine as well.[24]

St Michael's coherent response to official change and consistent public conformity was in sharp contrast with the varied responses and very public divisions within the elite of Tewkesbury.[25] Perhaps because of its modest size, St Michael's found it necessary to call on a wide range of parishioners to participate in its leadership, even though the city's elite dominated parish administration. Responsibility for funding and running the parish was spread among a wide circle within the worshipping community. This, in turn, increased the level of commitment to the parish, an allegiance which would prove very important as the leaders contended with the successive

[24] 'Chantry Certificates', p. 255; 'History of Gloucester', p. 426.
[25] For further discussion of responses to reform by the parishes of Tewkesbury and St Michael's, see C. Litzenberger, 'The Coming of Protestantism to Elizabethan Tewkesbury', in *The Reformation in English Towns 1500–1640*, ed. P. Collinson and J. Craig (Basingstoke, 1998), and C. Litzenberger, 'St Michael's, Gloucester (1540–1580): the Cost of Conformity in Sixteenth Century England', in *The Parish in English Life 1400–1600*, ed. K. French, G. Gibbs and B. Kümen (Manchester, 1997).

sets of changes required by the Reformation, but still tried to present a consistent image of conformity to other inhabitants of both the city and the diocese. Hence, while the parish was presented in 1569 for lacking both a curate and the *Paraphrases* of Erasmus, and three years later the curate was disciplined by the bishop for using loaf bread rather than wafers for communion, only two parishioners (neither of whom was involved in the leadership of the parish) were accused of nonconformity between 1541 and 1580.[26] The absence of any other examples of refusal to adhere to official religious policy may indeed indicate that the entire parish adapted uniformly and immediately to each new set of directives, but a much more probable explanation lies in the nature of the parish leadership network. Those in charge may merely have preferred to present a public image of harmony and concord, given their prominence within the city, and may therefore have disciplined nonconformists themselves, rather than exposing the parish to public scrutiny. They seem to have redefined the boundary between public and private so that all or almost all that occurred within the parish, whether it involved relations between parishioners or otherwise public actions or utterances by parishioners, would be defined as private and therefore not subject to intervention by outside authorities. Such a strategy would have been feasible, given the evident unity and cohesiveness of the parish elite.

Little is known of Tewkesbury's response to Edwardian Protestantism or Marian Catholicism, beyond the protestations of John Hiche, schoolmaster, in 1550. He filed a complaint in December of that year in the Court of Requests, which may have been intended to win favour from the authorities for his cause, in which he asserted that he and the curate, Robert Erean, had

to thuttermost of theire powre, witt and discrecion, favored, mainteyned and dyvulged the kinges grace procedynges and of long tyme reproved, oppugned and condemned certen ydolatrous abuses, frequented and used in the Church befor thextirpacyon of the detestable and most abhominable popysshe masse and papisti-call ceremonyes.

From the survey of the clergy conducted by Bishop Hooper in 1551, we know that Erean was learned, well qualified to function as a priest, and a licensed preacher.[27] None the less, Hiche may have been protesting too loudly. There are also hints in the records of a lack of unanimity in Tewkesbury concerning the appropriate response to official religious policy at that time.

Unfortunately, it is difficult to discern with any certainty anything further

---

[26] GRO GDR vol. XI, p. 205; vol. XXVI, p. 63; vol. XXIX, p. 85. For a more complete discussion of the enforcement in Gloucester of the use of wafers for communion, see chapter 7.

[27] PRO Req. 2/19/17; 'Visitation Booke', p. 28.

concerning worship or religious beliefs in Tewkesbury before the 1560s. What emerges, then, is the image of a divided parish and town. The two are linked in the case of Tewkesbury, and that linkage dates from at least the dissolution of the monastery at Tewkesbury, if not before. When the abbey was dissolved (or, more accurately, 'surrendered' to the king), the abbey church was to be demolished. However, the parish had worshipped in the west end of that building 'since time out of mind', and the elite of the town were able to raise the requisite funds to purchase it from the Crown in 1543. This cooperative action between parish and town underlines the reciprocal relationship between those two jurisdictions, which would continue at least through Elizabeth's reign. The churchwardens regularly presented their accounts 'yn the parishe churche . . . [to the] bailiffs of Tewkesbury and to other [of] the burgesies and commonaltie of the same towne then present', while the bailiffs financed alterations to the church house and sold church goods in 1576, and three years later used church lead for gutters on the new boothall or guildhall.[28] However, presentments against the bailiffs by the churchwardens dating from 1563 indicate that relations between the leaders of the town and the parish were not always amicable, and that there was a split between supporters of the old religion and the new.[29]

There were in fact two rival leadership networks in Tewkesbury: one a close-knit group of individuals linked by ties of marriage and kinship, as was the case at St Michael's in Gloucester; the other a looser cluster of people whose main bond seems to have been their preference for the old religion. The former group was not necessarily anxious to introduce a whole-hearted switch to Protestantism in their parish, but they did want to conform to Elizabethan religious policy. In addition to presenting the bailiffs, they also presented the curate for refusing to wear the requisite square cap, a sign of Protestant nonconformity which would emerge, along with the wearing of the surplice, as an issue in the vestments controversy over the next three years.[30] The two groups vied for control through the first half of Elizabeth's reign, with the more conservative circle dominating until the early 1570s, when the balance of power began to swing toward the Protestant group. One indication of the shift can be seen in the pattern of pew rentals. The elite who supported the new religion claimed newly constructed seats at the front of the church, and other leaders who also favoured Protestantism moved into the pews just vacated.[31]

Thus, St Michael's and Tewkesbury responded in very different ways to changes in official religious policy, and the nature of the leadership in each

[28] GRO P329 CW 2/1, pp. 1–72, *passim*; printed in *Tewkesbury*, pp. 1–47, *passim*; GRO TBR A1/1, fos. 11, 12v.
[29] See chapter 6.   [30] Cardwell, *Annals*, p. 193; Primus, *Vestments*, pp. 71–148, *passim*.
[31] GRO P329 CW 2/1, pp. 43–7, 49–50; printed in *Tewkesbury*, pp. 27–30, 31–3.

parish influenced each response. The leadership of St Michael's took care to present an orderly conforming parish to the public, moving as promptly as possible to implement each new policy fully and in an orderly fashion. Tewkesbury, on the other hand, seems to have resisted the pressure to conform, holding out as long as possible before being forced into a measure of compliance in 1576 by visitors representing the Archbishop of Canterbury. Perhaps St Michael's was more favourably disposed towards Protestantism than was Tewkesbury, or perhaps dissension among the leaders inhibited the latter's response.

Lack of a unified approach also characterised Tewkesbury's financial activities, whereas St Michael's was quite steady and methodical. This may have been due to the contrasting nature of each parish's leadership structure. However, other differences may also have contributed. In 1563, St Michael's had 450 communicants, only a quarter as many as Tewkesbury's 1,600.[32] Size and location, in turn, produced other differences. Tewkesbury was much less homogeneous and more complex than St Michael's, as it included all the town's inhabitants, whereas St Michael's was located in a particularly prosperous section of Gloucester, which included the market area, boothall or guildhall, and the homes of some of the city's most prominent leaders. Furthermore, each represented a different type of urban parish. St Michael's was one of eleven parishes in the city of Gloucester, while St Mary's was the only parish in Tewkesbury, factors which contributed to the size and disposition of each.[33] In addition, analysis of the churchwardens' accounts of each parish indicates that Tewkesbury relied on *ad hoc* funding for the extra expenses imposed by religious change, whereas St Michael's found it necessary to modify systematically its income-producing scheme in order to meet special expenses.

An examination of St Michael's churchwardens' accounts from 1546 to 1580 reveals an awareness of the need to plan for anticipated expenses.[34] Regular revenues due to the parish were sufficient to fund its regular activities, plus an occasional maintenance project, such as repairing the

---

[32] Only Cirencester, with 1825 communicants in 1563, was larger. 'Bishop's Returns from the Diocese of Gloucester, 1563'; BL Harleian MS 594, fos. 232v, 225, 248. The parish sizes, given in households rather than communicants for the year 1563, are printed in A. Percival, 'Gloucestershire Village Populations' *LPS* 8 (1972), unpaginated attachment. That article shows Tewkesbury's population in 1551 as 2,600; however, the correct number appears to be 1,600, the count given in 1547 in the chantry certificate, and in 1563 in the bishop's returns. 'Chantry Certificates', p. 281.

[33] For a discussion of similarly contrasting parishes see C. Cross, 'Parochial Structure and the Dissemination of Protestantism in Sixteenth Century England: a Tale of Two Cities', in *The Church in Town and Countryside*, ed. D. Baker (Studies in Church History, vol. XVI, Oxford, 1979), pp. 269–78.

[34] This analysis of St Michael's parish finances is based on their churchwardens' accounts. GRO P154/14 CW 1/1–1/31, *passim*.

tower or the roof. However, liturgical change brought with it substantial additional expenses, which could only be funded by either delaying needed building maintenance or raising supplementary funds. Generally, St Michael's chose to raise additional funds, because they were determined both to maintain their building and to respond promptly and fully to each change in official religion. For instance, the cost of restoring Catholicism between 1553 and 1558 under Mary totalled over £8, which was a daunting sum for a parish where other expenses totalled just under £7 per year, and annual revenues typically did not exceed £8. Hence, the parish not only found it necessary to assess a rate on its members, but was also forced to look elsewhere for further income. It therefore chose to charge outsiders for services freely provided to parishioners, such as the tolling of the bell. The parish also assessed those households which were not paying the parish rate 4d each year to help pay for priests to officiate at worship services in the absence of either a rector or a curate.[35]

By these means the parish of St Michael's, Gloucester seems to have steered a steady course of responsible stewardship through the series of major religious alterations which characterised the middle of the sixteenth century. The leadership responded in a positive manner to each new set of directives, and thus were able to maintain the parish's sound financial condition, while simultaneously preserving the quality of both the worship and the building. St Michael's, with its powerful leaders and compatible worshipping community, was an affluent, conforming and effective parish through the years of religious change.

In contrast to St Michael's, Tewkesbury, which presented a picture of inconsistent policies and resistance to change, does not seem to have planned for anticipated additional expenses. Income was generated sporadically, apparently independent of the financial needs of the parish, and there were several years in which much of the parish's revenue came from a few large, unexplained donations from parishioners. Additionally, Tewkesbury relied heavily on church ales as a source of income, as did many other similar parishes, including the Cotswold parish of Minchinhampton. In fact, church ales were the largest single source of revenue in each of those parishes. At Tewkesbury, ales were sometimes held in years of increased financial need, but on other occasions they occurred in years when expenses were quite low. Of course, ales were also an opportunity to socialise, and given the religious divisions within the congregation, the parish leaders may have chosen to hold them at times when tensions between the factions were particularly high in an attempt to diffuse them.[36] However, ales were an option not

[35] GRO P154/14 CW 1/28.
[36] GRO P329 CW 2/1, pp. 1–72, *passim*; printed in, *Tewkesbury*, pp. 1–47; P217 CW 2/1,

available to St Michael's. An urban parish such as St Michael's, surrounded as it was by other urban parishes in the midst of a city, typically would not have found support from inhabitants of the city outside their parochial boundaries for such a fund-raiser. By contrast, single-parish towns surrounded by rural areas seem to have entered into informal arrangements with neighbouring towns and parishes for their mutual financial support, as parishioners attended each other's ales. Tewkesbury benefited from that custom, and seems not to have been influenced by the authorities' efforts to discourage such practices, as Protestantism became more firmly established and more Calvinist under Elizabeth.[37]

Furthermore, Tewkesbury does not appear to have spent nearly as much on liturgical change as did St Michael's, nor did they accrue nearly as much from the sale of church goods. Whereas St Michael's divided their resources between caring for their buildings and providing for worship, most expenditures at Tewkesbury were for property maintenance or improvements. This was partially due, of course, to the size of their church building. Looking more like a cathedral than a parish church, it was and is a huge structure, cruciform in shape, with an imposing central tower and massive pillars rising to support its high roof in both the nave and chancel.[38] However, the differing needs of the fabric of the two parishes does not fully explain the difference in their allocation of funds. When stated as a sum rather than a proportion of total expenses, Tewkesbury still spent less on liturgy than did St Michael's. Also, unlike St Michael's, which sold church goods in 1550/1 and 1560/1, there is no evidence that Tewkesbury sold theirs before 1576, after being prompted by an archiepiscopal visitation. Additionally, the patterns of revenues and expenses are generally much more erratic for Tewkesbury than for St Michael's.[39]

Thus, the two parishes were quite dissimilar, and provide two distinct and detailed views of parish responses to shifts in official religious policy during the period covered by this study. Their stories, along with glimpses of other Gloucestershire parishes, will provide insight into the range of parochial responses which greeted the changing religious policies of the Tudor monarchs. Further perspective will be gleaned from an analysis of possible regional differences in the laity's responses to the shifting form and content of the official English religion.

pp. 2–67; P154/14 CW 1/1–1/31. See also J. M. Bennett, 'Conviviality and Charity in Medieval and Early Modern England', *P&P* 34 (1992), pp. 19–41.

[37] Cf. C. Burgess and B. Kümen, 'Penitential Bequests and Parish Regimes in Late Medieval England', *JEH* 44 (1993), pp. 610–30.

[38] See Figures 1.3 and 1.4.

[39] See Appendix C for tables and graphs which compare Tewkesbury's revenues and expenditures with figures for St Michael's.

Figure 1.3   View of St Mary's, Tewkesbury

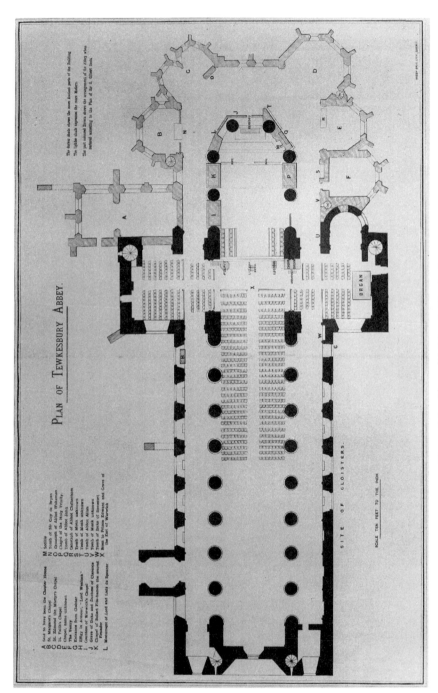

Figure 1.4   Plan of St Mary's, Tewkesbury

2

Gloucestershire in the 1530s

Prior to the founding of the new diocese in 1541, Gloucestershire was marked by the same religious ambivalence that characterised much of the rest of England. On the one hand, there is considerable evidence of the vigour of traditional lay piety among both the elite and the ordinary people. Support for the re-building and re-decoration of local parish churches was continuing and even increasing, and acts of lay piety such as pilgrimages to the Blood of Hailes continued to be popular. On the other hand, there were also signs of the promotion and acceptance of the new religion in public pulpits and private households, as the theological issues which distinguished Protestantism from traditional religion were presented and discussed by all types and conditions of men and women. There were isolated instances of anticlericalism, but for the most part the presentation of the new religion was more positive than that, focusing on issues of faith and doctrine. In Devon and Cornwall, Protestant support may have been motivated primarily by secular concerns, but such was not the case in Gloucestershire.[1] Furthermore, traditional lay piety in that county, as in other areas of England, was thriving. Support for the new religion, while based on theological concerns, was still extremely fragmented and represented a very small proportion of the county's inhabitants. In addition, that percentage would decrease over the next few decades.

The rebuilding of Cotswold churches in the perpendicular style offers convincing evidence of the continued vitality of the pre-Reformation church in England. The assertion that the Protestant Reformation was both welcomed and needed because the late-medieval church had fallen into decay and disrepute among ordinary lay people has been thoroughly laid to rest by a number of historians, and Gloucestershire provides further evidence of this. As was the case in East Anglia, the success of the Gloucestershire clothing industry brought new-found wealth and prestige to a number of towns and individuals, and parish churches were the

---

[1] Whiting, *Blind Devotion*, p. 115.

23

beneficiaries. Examples of such edifices in East Anglia include the parish churches of Long Melford and Lavenham in Suffolk. In general, these munificent actions appear to have been motivated by a desire to do good works, combined with the goal of creating a more beautiful and prestigious worship space.[2]

In Gloucestershire, the only case where the rebuilding or renovation was in response to a need to replace a deteriorating edifice was in North Cerney, where the nave and tower had been gutted by fire between 1465 and 1470.[3] Among the wealthy individuals who contributed to this phenomenon in Gloucestershire, John and Sir Edmund Tame, father and son, towered over the others. Whereas a family wishing to contribute to a parish usually supported the rebuilding of just one church, the Tames contributed to several. John Leland commented that 'Fairford never florished afore the cumming of the Tames onto it'.[4] John Tame was a very successful wool merchant, who chose Fairford parish church as the object of his generosity and good works. He rebuilt the church almost completely during the years just prior to his death in 1500. The tomb of John and his wife, Alice, bears an inscription which evokes the traditional belief in the living and the dead as members of a single community:

Pray for the souls of John Tame Esquire and Alice his wife . . . For Jhus love pray for me, I may not pray nowe pray ye, With a pater noster and an ave, That my paynys relessid may be.

The remarkable survival of these words in brass around the edge of their tomb is matched or perhaps exceeded by the complete set of stained glass windows which were installed when the church was rebuilt, and which then somehow survived the vicissitudes of religious policies over the next 150 years. Even the faces of a number of the images are still intact.

According to Margaret Aston, images in glass were of concern to only the most radical reformers and they generally found only the images of faces to be offensive. In some instances, this led parishioners to whitewash the stained-glass images of the faces of saints, and this may explain the survival of such images at Fairford.[5] The windows which depict the Christian faith from Adam and Eve through the Last Judgment are Flemish in style, probably from the school of Bernard Flower, Henry VII's master glass painter. Arrayed around the nave and chancel of the church, they present the doctrine of traditional Christianity, and are based on the very

[2] G. Hutton and O. Cook, *English Parish Churches* (London, 1976), pp. 117–32; Duffy, *Stripping*, pp. 131–4.
[3] Verey, *Gloucs.*, vol. I, p. 333.
[4] J. Leland, *The Itinerary*, ed. T. Hearne, vol. II, p. 48; also printed in J. Leland, *The Itinerary*, ed. L. T. Smith, vol. I, p. 127.
[5] M. Aston, *England's Iconoclasts: 1. Laws against Images* (Oxford, 1988), pp. 260n, 404.

popular *Biblia Pauperum*. This volume of woodcuts provided the inspiration for religious imagery in Europe as well as in England, including a tomb in Louvain, the carvings which fill the central portal of the Church of St-Maurice, Vienne, and windows in Exeter Cathedral, Tatershall parish church in Lincolnshire and King's College Chapel, Cambridge.[6] At Fairford not only the images but often the grouping of images and the inscriptions were copied from the book. The first window in the sequence depicts the precursors of the incarnation: Eve in the Garden of Eden, Moses with the burning bush, Gideon and the golden fleece, and King Solomon with the queen of Sheba. Those at the east end of the church and in the chapels to either side of the chancel are devoted to the life of Christ. The four evangelists and the four Latin doctors appear on opposite sides of the nave at the west end. Other windows contain images of prophets and apostles, martyrs and enemies of the faith. Yet pre-Reformation survivals at Fairford are not limited to the windows and memorial brasses; there is also an image of Christ of Pity on the west side of the tower just above the roof line.[7] The imagery of Fairford church was, indeed, an elaborate response to the successes brought by cloth-making and the wool trade, a fitting good work for a wealthy and pious Christian prior to the advent of Protestantism. Furthermore, its survival through the years of religious change and iconoclasm is probably a testament to the continued vigilance and traditional faith of the descendants of John Tame, particularly that of his son, Sir Edmund.

The younger Tame became a prominent member of the Gloucestershire gentry. He was married to Agnes, daughter of Sir Edward Greville, another member of the county elite, who probably contributed to the rebuilding of Chipping Campden Church. Sir Edmund served on numerous royal commissions, including that responsible for collecting the subsidy in 1523 and 1524, and was one of those named to attend the king at the time of the Pilgrimage of Grace in 1536. He also served as sheriff in 1524, 1536, 1537 and 1542, and was frequently a member of the commission of the peace.[8] Sir Edmund continued and expanded on the work begun by his father in support of local parishes. First, he completed the rebuilding of the church at Fairford; then, in about 1517, he turned his attentions to Rendcombe

---

[6] A. Henry, 'Introduction', in *Biblia Pauperum: a Facsimile and Edition*, ed. A. Henry (Ithaca, NY, 1987), pp. 35, 37.

[7] Verey, *Gloucs.*, vol. I, pp. 243–7.

[8] *L&P*, vol. III, part 2, no. 3282, vol. IV, part I, nos. 547, 8191, 4085, 6418 (23), 6490 (20), part II, no. 6490 (20), part. III, nos. 6282, 6418, vol. V, no. 1694 (ii), vol. VI, nos. 561 (i), 1189, vol. VII, nos. 149 (37), 1156, vol. XI, nos. 580 (2), 1217 (23), vol. XII, part II, nos. 1008 (18), 1150 (18), vol. XVI, nos. 107 (17), 580 (20), vol. XVII, no. 1154 (75), vol. XIX, part I, no. 273.

parish church, where he was also lord of the manor.[9] As with Fairford, the church at Rendcombe was completely rebuilt; but Sir Edmund did not stop there. As steward of the abbey of Cirencester, he also contributed to the rebuilding of the church there.

The church at Cirencester was remodelled in stages beginning early in the fifteen century, and was one of two such projects in Gloucestershire, where the funding was spread among several families and the parish as a whole also contributed. The other was in Winchcombe. St John the Baptist in Cirencester became the largest parish church in Gloucestershire and one of the largest in the realm through the generosity and good works of many. Henry IV paid for the reconstruction of the tower in thanksgiving for the loyalty of the townspeople, who had captured and executed two men who were plotting treason against him; two prominent merchants and the bishop of Lincoln each built a chantry chapel; and a number of prominent individuals financed the elaborate south porch. Then, between 1516 and the early 1530s, Sir Edmund Tame joined with Sir John Hungerford, several merchants of the town, and a number of Berkeley family members (including Sir Maurice Berkeley and Sir Giles Bridges of Gloucestershire, and Sir William Compton of Warwickshire) to reconstruct the nave, practically from the ground up. Among the merchants, John Pratt, butcher, left £40, and Robert Ricardes, clothier, left £20. As late as 1532, Henry Tapper, grocer, left £10 toward the completion of the rood loft, £4 toward a new organ, hangings for the high altar and vestments for the Lady Chapel, and £20 toward new pews. Shields carrying the arms or merchants' marks of the contributors appear on the pillars in the nave.[10] The project to rebuild Winchcombe parish church is also a remarkable example of cooperation between an abbey and a parish. The abbot erected the chancel, while the parishioners raised £200 to build the nave. 'But', as Leland tells us, 'that summe being not able to performe so costly a work Rafe Boteler Lord Sudeley helped them and finished the worke.' The rebuilt church is distinguished by its lack of a chancel arch and by the line of clerestory windows which continues to the east end of the building. Both features presumably

---

[9] *Verey, Gloucs.*, vol. I, pp. 376–7.

[10] Leland reports that though the Bishop of Durham had promised to contribute, he was 'preventid with deth [and] gave nothing'. However, both his mother and his aunt contributed to the building of the porch. J. Leland, *The Itinerary*, ed. T. Hearne, vol. II, p. 50; also printed in J. Leland, *The Itinerary*, ed. L. T. Smith, vol. I, p. 129; *Verey, Gloucs.*, vol. I, pp. 163–5; D. Verey, *Cotswold Churches* (1982; reprint, Gloucester, 1991), pp. 53–5; K. J. Beecham, *History of Cirencester* (Cirencester, c. 1886), p. 101; J. Maclean, 'The Armory and Merchants' Marks in the Ancient Church of Cirencester', *TBGAS* 17 (1892–3), pp. 268–87.

resulted from the nearly simultaneous reconstruction of the entire edifice.[11]

Other 'wool' churches also rose from the dust of their predecessors in Sudeley near Winchcombe, in Thornbury near Berkeley (the seat of the Duke of Buckingham until his execution in 1521), and in the Cotswold parishes of Northleach, Chipping Campden, Lechlade, Naunton and North Cerney. The most notable of these were in Chipping Campden and Northleach. A group of wealthy wool merchants, probably led by Sir Edward Greville, provided the money at Chipping Campden, while at Northleach a father and son, Thomas and John Fortey, were the key patrons. These two parish churches are noted for the distinctive design of their naves, rather than for their glass, and one master mason appears to have been responsible for both projects. The two are nearly identical with five tall arcades supported by octagonal pillars with concave sides, and very similar capitals, mouldings and other decorative details.[12] Northleach is distinguished, however, by its fine late fifteenth-century porch, which still contains a number of pre-Reformation images, including one of the Blessed Virgin Mary above the entrance. Fairford was not the only Gloucestershire parish which protected its images.

However, as in other regions of England, it was not just the very wealthy parishes which were engaged in projects to improve their buildings, and not all such activity was centred in the Cotswolds. Although in other areas of the diocese the changes were less lavish, buildings and the decorations within them were updated by all sorts and conditions of parishes. Eighteen churches were either built or rebuilt in the late fifteenth or early sixteenth century, and an additional twenty parishes made some significant addition or modification during that same time period.[13] For instance, the north aisle was added at Great Witcombe, the west porch was built at Hartpury, and towers were constructed at Barnwood, Whaddon and Woolstone.[14] A number of churches also built rood screens

[11] J. Leland, *The Itinerary*, ed. T. Hearne, vol. IV, part II, pp. 74–5; also printed in J. Leland, *The Itinerary*, ed. L. T. Smith, vol. II, p. 55; Verey, *Gloucs.*, vol. I, pp. 473–5.

[12] Verey, *Gloucs.*, vol. I, pp. 243, 339.

[13] The other churches which were rebuilt in the fifteenth century included Berkeley, Bourton-on-the-Hill, Didbrook, Hempstead, Westerley and Wormington. The rebuilding at Lechlade began in the fifteenth century but extended into the sixteenth. In addition, Cold Ashton was rebuilt between 1508 and 1540. Verey, *Gloucs.*, vol. I, pp. 125–6, 192, 209–10, 291–2; vol. II, pp. 98, 267, 402, 412–13.

[14] Great Witcombe was located east of Gloucester at the base of the Cotswold 'edge', while Barnwood and Whaddon were adjacent to the city, Hartpury was in the northern vale near the Forest of Dean, and Woolstone was in the Cotswolds. Hartpury was the largest with 280 communicants at the time of Bishop Hooper's visitation in 1551, while Barnwood had 117, and the other three parishes had no more than 70. Verey, *Gloucs.*, vol. II, pp. 96, 256, 265, 402, 412; 'Visitation Booke', pp. 24–6, 31.

and chantry chapels between 1450 and 1540, as Cirencester had done in the course of their rebuilding.[15] Clearly defined worship spaces with the rood screen separating the nave from the chancel and with chapels in the side aisles, all furnished with images, ornaments and lights were essential aspects of conventional pre-Reformation lay piety. In addition, their maintenance was the responsibility of the laity.[16] Thus, continued contributions for maintenance and improvement of such items in Gloucestershire before the religious changes of the 1530s and 1540s, as elsewhere, provide evidence that a substantial portion of the laity continued to view the church in general, and their parish churches in particular, as robust institutions worthy of their generous gifts and continued allegiance.

None the less, not everyone shared the view of the pre-Reformation church held by those munificent donors who demonstrated their faith through their acts of generosity; there were also proponents of the new religion, some of whom publicly expressed their beliefs through the written and spoken word. Others found more physically active ways to demonstrate their dislike of traditional religion and their support for Protestantism. However, these evangelicals generally represented neither the latest of numerous generations of religious dissenters, nor the beginning of a broad, sweeping movement which would rush forward from this time and place in relentless pursuit of full reform of the established church. There was a record of absenteeism from worship in the Forest of Dean dating back to the previous century, and some of those who criticised traditional religion in the 1530s were inhabitants of that remote region.[17] However, there is no direct parish-by-parish connection between those earlier dissenters, who may have been Lollards, and those who favoured the new religion in the 1530s. Furthermore, over the ensuing decades this area would became a safe haven for Catholics, not a hot-bed of radical Protestants. Other early evangelicals could be found in isolated manor houses and parish churches in the Vale of the Severn, both north and south. These included a few priests (some of whom may have given sermons which sparked demonstrations of dissent by lay people), and a few members of the gentry. The latter group probably knew William Tyndale, the Bible translator, and may have been influenced by him, but there is no evidence that he had a following among the inhabitants of the county below the level of the gentry. In fact, he may have merely been one of a number of the elite in the shire attracted to the new religion, rather than the

---

[15] Chedworth, Chipping Sodbury and Evenlode built new pulpits, while Hailes and Berkeley added rood screens in the late fifteenth century. Verey, *Cotswold Churches*, p. 98; Verey, *Gloucs.*, vol. I, pp. 242, 265; vol. II, pp. 99, 155.

[16] Duffy, *Stripping*, pp. 131–41, *passim*.

[17] GCL Hockaday Collections, no. 18, vols. III–XXXX, *passim* (unpaginated).

leader of a circle. Furthermore, that group's influence seems to have been restricted mainly to portions of their own families, and in many cases only to those in their own generation. The extant evidence does not support the depiction of William Tyndale and a group of followers as either the source of a strong, widespread call for reform in Gloucestershire or the beginning of a fast and early acceptance of Protestantism in the county, as some historians have suggested.[18] The humble dissenters in the Forest and their more elite co-religionists in the Vale would prove to be the exception rather than the rule. However, they did gain some prominence, and between 1535 and 1539 they were supported in their efforts by the new, evangelical Bishop of Worcester, Hugh Latimer.

The leading early Protestants in Gloucestershire were Tyndale, the aforementioned translator of the Bible, William Tracy, a member of the county elite, and Latimer. Soon after the introduction of Lutheran ideas in England in the 1520s, some people in Gloucestershire were exposed to this new theology by William Tyndale, a native of the county who had attended both Oxford and Cambridge, and returned to the shire in 1522 to serve as tutor to the young sons of Sir John Walsh of Little Sodbury. Walsh was married to the daughter of Sir Robert Poyntz and counted among his brothers-in-law Sir Anthony Poyntz and Nicholas Weekes, other members of the county elite. Walsh's support of proponents of the new religion was not limited to Tyndale: he was also a patron of John Erley, one of the priests who enjoyed Thomas Cromwell's protection and whose preaching was alleged to have caused considerable disturbance in the cities of Gloucester and Bristol in the 1530s.[19] Tyndale was not able to remain in the Walsh household for very long, as his theology soon brought him into conflict with Dr John Bell, the diocesan chancellor and future bishop. Initially, he was forced to leave the county, and eventually he fled into exile on the continent.[20] However, while he was in the Walsh household, Tyndale had preached in Bristol and in parishes in the southern vale near Berkeley. While in the county he had also met William Tracy, a prominent member of the Gloucestershire gentry and sometime sheriff of the county. The latter served with Sir John Walsh on a number of royal commissions, and would have had occasion to stay with Walsh while carrying out the duties of the commissions. Theological discussions at dinner may well have

---

[18] D. Rollison, *The Local Origins of Modern Society, Gloucestershire 1500–1800* (London and New York, 1992), pp. 84–96, *passim*; D. D. Smeeton, *Lollard Themes in the Reformation Theology of William Tyndale* (Kirksville, MO, 1986), pp. 22–74, *passim*. Cf. P. Collinson, 'William Tyndale and the Course of the English Reformation', *Reformation* 1 (1996), pp. 72–97.

[19] *L&P*, vol. III, no. 3282; vol. IV, nos. 547, 1610 (11), 6248 (11), 6418 (23); vol. VI, no. 1192; Powell, 'Social Background', p. 114.

[20] *A&M*, vol. V, pp. 115–16.

been the basis of Tyndale's later description of Tracy as 'a learned man and better sene in the workes of Sainct Austine xx yeres before he dyed than ever I knew doctoure in Englande'.

In 1531, it was Tracy's turn to provide the leadership for the newly emerging Protestant cause in Gloucestershire, through his will in which he asserted his Protestant faith in four clear and unmistakable paragraphs. It read, in part,

> I commit me unto God . . . trustyng without any doubt or mistrust, that . . . I have and shal have remission of my sinnes and resurrection of body and soul, according as it is written Job xix. I believe that my redemer lyveth, and that in the last day I shal rise out of the earth, and in my flesh shall see my Savior, this my hope is laid up in my bosome.[21]

He went on to assert the efficacy of his faith 'without any other mans woorke or workes', and then very explicitly omitted all bequests to the church so that there would be nothing in his will which might be judged a 'good work'. After his death, the contents of his will were found to be sufficiently offensive to ecclesiastical authorities that the will was refused probate, and an over-zealous diocesan chancellor exhumed Tracy's body and burned it. These actions did not, however, obliterate his declaration of faith.[22] The will was circulated in manuscript form in the early 1530s; two men were imprisoned in the Tower of London in 1531 for (among other things) possessing copies.[23] In 1535, it was printed in Antwerp with commentaries by two noted exiled English Protestants: William Tyndale and John Frith.[24] The printed version appears to have been available to those with similar beliefs shortly thereafter, and was used as a guide in a number of other wills. For instance, in 1537, William Shepard of Mendlesham in the East Anglian county of Suffolk seems to have used the printed edition of 1535 as the basis for his preamble, which appropriated all four paragraphs verbatim, but to which he added his own commentary. For instance, at the end of the Tracy paragraph quoted above, Shepard asserted,

---

[21] *The Testament of Master Wylliam Tracie Esquier/Expounded both by William Tyndale and Jhon Frith* (Antwerp, 1535), STC 24167, sig. Aviii(v); also printed in 'The Testament of Master William Tracy, Esquier, Expounded by William Tyndale', in *Tyndale's Answer to Sir Thomas More's Dialogue etc.*, ed. H. Walter (Cambridge, 1850), p. 279.

[22] Wilkins, *Concilia*, vol. III, pp. 746–7; *L&P*, vol. V, no. 928. The exhumation was authorised, but the burning was not. Ultimately, the chancellor of Worcester, Dr Parker, was required to pay a fine of £300. E. Halle, *Chronicle; Containing the History of England during the Reign of Henry the Fourth and the Succeeding Monarchs to the End of the Reign of Henry Eighth* (1548; reprint, London, 1809), p. 796. Cf. 'Wills as Propaganda', p. 423; Haigh, *Reformations*, pp. 70–87, *passim*.

[23] *A&M*, vol. V, pp. 29–30.

[24] *The Testament of Master William Tracie*, sig. Aiii–iiii; also printed in *Tyndale's Answer*, pp. 271–83.

Here I wold not that men shuld say that I dyspyset other holsome sacramentes or good sermonys. But because I am rude and unlernyd, and know not the scriptur, and therefor loke what Godes Word sayth of theym, that saym do I beleve without any dowte or mystruste.[25]

Over the following several decades, other testators all over England (including some in Gloucestershire) would use portions of Tracy's text, modify them slightly and interject a few of their own words, thus personalizing the text to make it their own. The testament even came to the notice of the Welsh humanist, Sir John Price, who copied it into his commonplace book.[26]

William Tracy was not the only Gloucestershire layman to burn, albeit posthumously, for his beliefs in the early 1530s; his nephew, James Baynham, also died for his faith. James was the youngest son of Tracy's sister, Elizabeth, and Sir Alexander Baynham of Westbury-upon-Severn, head of the most prominent family in the Forest of Dean,[27] and had moved from Gloucestershire to London in the 1520s, become a member of the Inner Temple and married the widow of Simon Fish, the Protestant bookseller. John Foxe described James as knowledgeable in both Latin and Greek, and as being 'an earnest reader of scriptures . . . [and] a great maintainer of the godly'. James was burned at Smithfield on 30 April 1532 for not believing in purgatory and for possessing heretical books, including works by Tyndale and Frith.[28] Significantly, Sir Alexander Baynham did not mention his youngest son in his religiously traditional will, which was dated 20 September 1524.[29]

Whereas, the Protestantism espoused by William Tyndale, William Tracy and James Baynham in the 1520s and early in the 1530s had been at variance with the official religious policies of the Crown, those policies had changed by the mid-1530s as a result of the break with Rome and the ascendancy of supporters of reform to positions of power at court. The shift in policy was first clearly felt in Gloucestershire with the elevation of the reformer, Hugh Latimer, to be bishop of Worcester in 1535.[30] Latimer

---

[25] 'Wills as Propaganda', p. 425.

[26] 'Wills as Propaganda', pp. 427–31; G. Williams, *The Welsh Church from Conquest to Reformation* (rev. edn, Cardiff, 1976), p. 540.

[27] Sir Alexander Baynham served as sheriff of Gloucestershire five times under three kings, as well as on innumerable royal commissions. *L&P*, vol. I, nos. 1176 (iii), 2053 (6ii); vol. II, nos. 713, 1213, 2533, 3297; vol. III, nos. 1248 (vi), 1081, 2415, 3282; vol. IV, nos. 390 (2), 547; GCL Smyth of Nibley Papers, vol. IV, fo. 67; J. Maclean and W. C. Hearne, eds., *The Visitation of the County of Gloucestershire Taken in the Year 1623* (London, 1885), pp. 12–15, 265; C. R. Saunders, 'Social Mobility in the Forest of Dean *c.* 1550–1650' (unpublished DPhil thesis, Oxford Polytechnic, 1989), pp. 226–7; G. Burnet, *The History of the Reformation of the Church of England*, vol. I, ed. N. Pocock (Oxford, 1865), p. 270.

[28] *A&M*, vol. IV, pp. 658, 697–704.   [29] PRO PROB 11/21, fo. 215v.

[30] Most of Gloucestershire was included in the diocese of Worcester until 1541.

had gained notoriety for his preaching in nearby Bristol and Exeter, as well as in London at Paul's Cross and at court. He had also been one of those who had visited James Baynham in the Tower just hours before the latter's death. (After inquiring as to the reasons for Baynham's sentence, he had urged him 'to take his death quietly and patiently'.[31]) None of Latimer's immediate predecessors as bishop had resided in the diocese. Rather, since 1497 the Crown had used the see of Worcester to support its representative to the Papacy, and, as a result, had awarded the bishopric to a series of Italians, none of whom ever came to England.[32] That may have been an effective strategy as long as official religion was not changing. However, once the Crown began to promulgate new policies, it needed someone in residence to implement and enforce them.

Following his elevation to the episcopate, Latimer immediately began to promote his beliefs within the diocese through his own sermons and his patronage of other preachers, three of whom, James Ashe, Anthony Saunders and Hugh Williams alias Rawlyns, held livings in Gloucestershire. Ashe had been the rector of Staunton in the Forest of Dean since the late 1520s, while Saunders had been appointed rector of Winchcombe by Cromwell sometime before November 1534. Rawlyns was one of Latimer's chaplains and served as curate of Holy Trinity, Gloucester. All of Latimer's preachers were reformers who made tours around parts of the diocese expounding the word of God.[33] They preached publicly in the parishes and towns of the diocese, including Tewkesbury, Winchcombe and Gloucester, in the Forest of Dean and in the portion of the Vale of the Severn between the cities of Bristol and Gloucester. Their reception varied, occasionally resulting in complaints (even from their own parishioners), which underscored the continued mixed nature of lay religion in Gloucestershire as elsewhere in the realm. In particular, James Ashe was accused of declaring from his pulpit at Staunton that 'if the King our sovereign lord did not go forth with his laws as he begin, he would call the King Antichrist', and further, 'that the King . . . was nought, the Bishops and Abbots nought, and himself nought too'. William Benet, another of Latimer's chaplains, was accused of asserting during a sermon he gave in Gloucester, 'that if

[31] M. C. Skeeters, *Community and Clergy*, pp. 38–46; W. T. MacCaffrey, *Exeter, 1540–1640: The Growth of an English Town*, (Cambridge, MA, 1958), p. 188; Brigden, *London*, pp. 194–259, *passim*; *A&M*, vol. IV, p. 770; Whiting, *Blind Devotion*, pp. 254–5, 257.

[32] A. G. Chester, *Hugh Latimer: Apostle to the English* (Philadelphia, PA, 1954), p. 103.

[33] S. R. Wabuda, 'The Provision of Preaching during the Early English Reformation: with Special Reference to Itineration, *c.* 1530 to 1547' (unpublished PhD thesis, University of Cambridge, 1991), pp. 104–5, 108; HWRO, 802, BA 2764, p. 153; Powell, 'Beginnings', pp. 147, 149. *L&P*, vol. VIII, no. 171; vol. IX, no. 747; vol. X, no. 1099.

purgatory priests do pray with their tongues till they be worn to the stumps their prayers shall not help souls departed'.[34]

Meanwhile, Anthony Saunders was having trouble at Winchcombe. Not only was he one of Latimer's licensed preachers, he had also been sent to his new cure with explicit instructions from Cromwell 'to preach the word of God and read it to the monks'. However, both the size of the parish and the opposition of the abbot were impeding his efforts, despite the presence and assistance of a schoolmaster of Winchcombe who favoured the gospel. In a letter to Cromwell, dated 2 November 1535, Saunders wrote,

> Whereas you have appointed me to read the pure and sincere word of God to the monks of Winchcombe, to preach in the parish church, which is the abbot's impropried benefice, . . . I have small favor and assistance amongst the Pharisaical papists . . . [The abbot of Hailes] has hired 'a greate Golyas, a sotle Dunys man, yee a greate clerke, as he sayeth,' a Bachelor of Divinity of Oxford, to catch me in my sermons . . . [The bearer of this letter and I] are both in danger of [our] lives.[35]

The abbot seems to have seen Saunders's preaching as having crossed the line into heresy, rather than just supporting the new official religion, and he may have been supported in his judgment by Sir Ralph Boteler, Lord Sudeley, who seems to have continued to favour the old religion.

In the city of Gloucester, meanwhile, in 1537 John Erley and Hugh Williams alias Rawlyns allegedly disturbed the city with their preaching in favour of Protestantism, and in opposition to the swing back toward a more conservative religious policy ushered in by the Act of Six Articles of 1539. Erley, a former friar, enjoyed the support of both Sir John Walsh and Sir Nicholas Poyntz and the protection of both Bishop Latimer and Thomas Cromwell. In 1533, he had preached in the church at Iron Acton (seat of Sir Nicholas Poyntz) at the invitation of the incumbent, and 'the mayor and his brethren' had invited him to preach in the churchyard at Thornbury. He had then been arrested for preaching without a licence at Marshfield and accused of being 'one of Master Latimer's disciples, who had done more hurt in this country than Luther'. Erley would be forced out of the diocese in 1540 following the ascendancy of the conservative John Bell as Latimer's successor as bishop, and would be tried for heresy in Salisbury in 1541. Rawlyns would also be forced to leave the diocese in 1540 following Latimer's resignation as bishop. However, in the 1530s he also benefited from Cromwell's patronage. His parish complained about his behaviour in a letter to Cromwell, and his public utterances in Gloucester, along with those of Erley, were said to have 'set the best of the town "one

---

[34] Discipline for uttering such beliefs would only be initiated after Bishop Latimer's resignation and replacement by his arch-rival, Dr John Bell. *L&P*, vol. X, nos. 1027, 1099; S. R. Wabuda, 'The Provision of Preaching', pp. 104–11; HWRO 802 BA 2764, p. 153.

[35] *L&P*, vol. VIII, no. 171; vol. IX, no. 747.

in another's top"'. Both men were prohibited from further clerical acts within the diocese of Worcester by Cromwell's agent, Thomas Evance, but Rawlyns was reinstated to his cure by Cromwell after Arthur Porter (one of the county elite) wrote on his behalf. Meanwhile, Evance reported that after he took action against the two men, he was able to convince '"divers of the worship of the town" to drink together who had not done so for three quarters of a year'.[36] Partly as a result of the preaching by Latimer's agents, the city's elite had become publicly and vehemently divided, and one of the emblems of that division, if not its primary motivation, was religious preference. In 1535, a similar phenomenon had occurred a short distance to the south in the village of Wotton-under-Edge, where the chief inhabitants reported that 'great troubles are lately risen . . . by reason of divers opinions' primarily pertaining to religious policy.[37]

Bishop Latimer did not limit his campaign against traditional religion to sermons, however; he also moved to discourage the continuing practice of making pilgrimages to shrines, which he viewed as idolatrous. While serving as rector of West Kingston in Wiltshire, he had been troubled by the crowds of pilgrims he had seen pass by his house near the Fosse Way, coming 'by flocks out of the west country to many images, but chiefly to the Blood of Hales'.[38] That particular object of traditional devotion, alleged to be the blood of Christ, had been associated with a number of miracles. In one case, a priest had just used his Easter sermon to try to dissuade his parishioners from making the pilgrimage to the Blood of Hailes and was celebrating the Eucharist. When he uncovered the chalice, its contents, which looked like blood rather than wine, bubbled up to the brim, causing him to realise his error and go on a pilgrimage to Hailes himself. In another case, a baker, his wife and young children had spent the time from Whitsunday to Corpus Christi Day selling bread to the pilgrims at Hailes. As they were leaving, the baker and his wife decided to visit the Blood of Hailes themselves. While they were occupied with their devotions, their horses bolted, smashing the cart in which they had left their children. The children, however, were not hurt, having been protected, so their parents believed, by the miraculous power of the holy relic.[39]

---

[36] HWRO 802 BA 2764, pp. 145–6; *L&P*, vol. VI, nos. 246, 1192; vol. XII, part I, nos. 308, 701, 1147; vol. XII, part II, no. 13; vol. XV, no. 183; GCL Hockaday Abstracts, vol. XXV, 1533 (unpaginated); Powell, 'Beginnings', pp. 143–4; Powell, 'Social Background', pp. 114–15.

[37] *L&P*, vol. X, no. 790.

[38] Latimer, *Sermons*, vol. I, pp. 36–7; vol. II, pp. 363–4. Cf. St Clair Baddeley, 'The Holy Blood of Hayles', *TBGAS* 23 (1900), pp. 276–84.

[39] J. C. T. Oates, 'Richard Pynson and the Holy Blood of Hayles', *The Library*, 5th ser., 13 (1958), pp. 275–6; P. Marshall, 'The Rood of Boxley, the Blood of Hailes and the Defence of the Henrician Church', *JEH* 46 (1995), pp. 689–96; Duffy, *Stripping*, p. 104.

Following Latimer's elevation to the see at Worcester, Hailes was within his diocese and under his authority. Hence, on 28 October 1538, with the assistance of Richard Tracy, son of the Protestant testator, he confiscated the alleged blood, declaring upon examination that while 'it hath a certain unctious moistness, and though it seem somewhat like blood when it is in the glass, yet when any parcel of the same is taken out, it turneth to a yellowness, and is cleaving like glue'.[40] Thus, a relic which had become a particularly popular destination for pilgrims in the early sixteenth century was taken away and destroyed, and with its removal a key object of pre-Reformation lay piety was eliminated. Officially, all objects known 'to be so abused with pilgrimages or offerings' were ordered taken down by the Royal Injunctions of 1538; however, in most dioceses the ecclesiastical hierarchy either turned a blind eye to their continued existence and popularity, or just required that they be hidden from view, as did Archbishop Edward Lee of York. This was not so in the diocese of Worcester.

Latimer stands out as one of the most vigourous proponents of the new religion in England. Even in London, evangelical clerical leadership was weak when compared with that provided by Latimer and his preachers in the diocese of Worcester.[41] While some bishops and priests were ignoring directives for religious change and others were merely destroying vestiges of traditional piety, the ecclesiastcal leadership in the diocese of Worcester were promoting an alternative set of beliefs and practices based on scripture, and encouraging the laity to read the Bible, while simultaneously moving to eliminate the potential objects of all forms of idolatry. Furthermore, through preaching and other pronouncements, Latimer also defined the limits of reformed religion within his diocese. For instance, although some supporters of the new religion wanted to eliminate the blessing of all earthly things as superstitious, he continued to approve some practices, including giving holy water or holy bread to the laity. However, he prescribed the specific words to be used during those distributions. For instance, when giving holy water the priest was to say:

> Remember, your promise in Baptism,
> Christ, his mercy and blood-shedding,
> By whose most holy sprinkling
> Of all your sins you have free pardoning.[42]

None the less, in his visitation injunctions of 1537 Latimer also stipulated a number of reforms which went beyond the official religious policy of the

---

[40] *L&P*, vol. XIII, part II, no. 710; Latimer, *Sermons*, vol. II, pp. 407–8; *VAI*, vol. II, pp. 38, 48.

[41] Brigden, *London*, pp. 281–2. Cf. F. Heal, *Of Prelates and Princes: a Study of the Economic and Social Position of the Tudor Episcopate* (Cambridge, 1980), pp. 165–6.

[42] Latimer, *Sermons*, vol. I, p. 294.

Crown. For instance, two years before the suppression of the larger monasteries, he declared that the clergy were to 'suffer no religious persons, friars, or other, to have any services' in their churches. Furthermore, while royal proclamations issued the year before had required every parish church to obtain a Bible in English and encourage parishioners to read it, Latimer went further in his insistence that lay people learn the basic tenets of their faith in English. The clergy of the diocese were not to admit 'any young man or woman to receive the sacrament of the altar, until that he or she openly in the church, after mass or evensong, upon the holiday, do recite in English the *Pater*'.[43]

The efforts of Latimer and his preachers affected members of the laity both positively and negatively. Some, like the half-brothers Thomas Bell, junior, and Thomas Bell, senior, of Gloucester, tried to curtail the reformers' activities. Thomas Bell, junior, was sheriff of the city of Gloucester in 1535, while Thomas, senior, was mayor the following year. They joined forces with Dr John Bell (the archdeacon of Gloucester and Latimer's successor as Bishop of Worcester but apparently no relation to the Thomas Bells) in an attempt to convince the Crown and the ecclesiastical hierarchy that the 'disorderly and colorable preaching' of the bishop and his preachers was bringing 'disquiet' to the Christian people of Gloucestershire. Dr John Bell even went so far as to call Latimer a 'horesone heretycke' on one occasion.[44] A number of gentry came forward in support of one faction or the other in the dispute. Sir Nicholas Arnold and Arthur Porter (who were brothers-in-law) wrote to Cromwell and described one of the Thomas Bells as 'ungodly', while Sir William Kingston, Constable of the Tower and future beneficiary of the dissolution of the monasteries, seems to have sided with the Bells.[45] Kingston was a powerful, well-connected ally, who in his role as Constable of the Tower was intimately involved in enforcing royal policy in the mid-1530s. He served as a conduit from the shire to the king for information concerning nonconformity in Gloucestershire. He also had custody of Cardinal Wolsey at the time of the latter's death, and of Bishop John Fisher, Sir Thomas More and Anne Boleyn at the time of their executions. (He informed Cromwell of the queen's utterances while she was imprisoned.) Additionally, Kingston, along with his son, Anthony, Sir John Bridges, and Sir Nicholas Arnold were among those chosen to attend the christening of Prince Edward.[46] However, even with politically prominent

[43] Latimer, *Sermons*, vol. I, pp. 242–4, 294.
[44] *L&P*, vol. X, no. 1099; vol. XII, part I, no. 308; S. R. Wabuda, 'The Provision of Preaching', pp. 109–12; 'History of Gloucester', p. 21.
[45] *L&P*, vol. XII, part I, nos. 308, 831; W. C. Hearne, 'Flaxley Grange', *TBGAS* 6 (1881), p. 285; J. M. Hall, 'Haresfield: Manors and Church', *TBGAS* 19 (1894), p. 303.
[46] *L&P*, vol. VI, no. 864; vol. VIII, nos. 886, 919, 974; vol. X, nos. 790, 793, 797, 798, 876, 890, 910; vol. XII, part II, no. 911 (ii); *A&M*, vol. IV, p. 616; vol. V, pp. 505–6.

supporters such as Kingston, those trying to bring Latimer down were unsuccessful. As long as Cromwell stayed in power Latimer would remain bishop and his preachers would continue on their circuits.

A number of others (both clergy and laity) expressed their displeasure with the break with Rome, as well as with evangelical theology, rather than specifically targeting their reforming bishop. In 1533, an individual in South Cerney uttered treasonous statements against the royal supremacy, as did a servant of Sir John Huddleston some four years later. (Huddleston was constable of Sudeley and Gloucester castles and a noted patron of Hailes Abbey. His wife was a granddaughter of Sir Thomas de la Pole and a patron of Hailes Abbey in her own right.) Then, in 1535, Richard Clyve of Winchcombe Abbey was accused of 'railing against the King and Queen Anne, and upholding Queen Catharine and the authority of the Pope'. He was alleged to have asserted that 'it was as lawful to appeal to the weathercock as to the Chancery in accordance with the Act [of Supremacy]'.[47] Over the following several years other similar incidents occurred. In 1536, a priest 'of little reputation and less discretion, of no promotion or learning' criticised the king while frequenting an ale house in Tewkesbury; and, in 1540, parish priests in Cowley, Painswick, Stroud and Avening were all accused of heresy for persisting in the old religion in violation of royal proclamations. One of those, Thomas Trowell, parson of Avening, was accused of having a mass book with Thomas Becket's name written in it 'and not rased'.[48]

In 1536, the prominent and powerful Lady Anne Berkeley, widow of Thomas, Lord Berkeley, also defied official religious policy, as John Barlo, dean of Westbury in the diocese of Worcester, reported to Cromwell: 'On Michaelmas day, as I was riding to quarter sessions at Gloucester, I found at the church house of the parish of Yate, Gloucester, where the Lady Anne Barkley dwelleth, fourteen evil-disposed persons playing at the unlawful game of tennis during morning service.' Barlo had intended to prosecute them at the quarter session, but the jury included too many of Lady Berkeley's servants, so he postponed bringing charges against them until the assizes, a move which resulted in Barlo and a number of his friends being charged by Lady Berkeley's servants with numerous instances of trespassing on her lands. She was clearly a formidable foe, and while it is not clear whether her actions and those of her servants were motivated by a lack of acceptance of the new religion in this case, other actions on her part would tend to support such a judgment. Some of the accusations of trespass dated

[47] *L&P*, vol. IX, no. 52.
[48] *L&P*, vol. VI, no. 477; vol. IX, no. 52; vol. X, no. 693; vol. XII, part II, no. 815; vol. XV, nos. 183, 406–9; C. R. Hudleston, 'Sir John Huddleston, Constable of Sudeley', *TBGAS* 48 (1926), pp. 117, 120; GCL, Hockaday Abstracts, vol. CCXXVIII, 1519 (unpaginated).

from a year earlier, when Barlo and Sir Nicholas Poyntz had tried to seize William Norton, a priest who kept 'books not reformed of the bishop of Rome's name, and a book of bishop Fisher's in defence of the bishop of Rome's authority', and had accused Lady Berkeley of shielding him.[49] Lady Berkeley's strategies in support of traditional religion (and in opposition to the current official policy) differed from those of her male counterparts among the county's elite. Given societal conventions which usually pre-cluded female participation in the hierarchies of the shire and diocese, she chose to use the considerable power she held over her manor, her private domain, to further her public cause by having her male servants act in her stead in quarter sessions.

Of course, not everyone rued the day Hugh Latimer arrived in the diocese. One who probably welcomed both Latimer's episcopate and the new religion was the scholar William Latymer (no relation to the bishop), who was rector of Saintbury in Gloucestershire. As a prominent humanist and sometime chaplain to Anne Boleyn, he had demonstrated his Protestant leanings by making trips to the continent to buy forbidden ('heretical') books by Tyndale and others, and then smuggling them into England for the queen. He was just returning from his last trip in that capacity when his patron was arrested and imprisoned in the Tower. Latymer was appre-hended at Sandwich and chose to cooperate with the authorities. As a consequence, a number of the books he was carrying were forwarded to Anne's silkwoman, Joan Wilkinson, who was from Kings Stanley in Gloucestershire.[50] Perhaps the instinct which led him to cooperate in that instance was also responsible for his remaining out of the spotlight during the volatile 1530s in his Gloucestershire parish, or he may have been non-resident as a result of his other duties. In any case, his particular influence within the diocese remains a matter of speculation, although his tenure at Saintbury may explain the presence in that parish of a literate shepherd who possessed a copy of Polydore Vergil's *De Inventoribus Rerum* in 1546.[51]

Meanwhile, in the Forest of Dean others who were less prominently placed were encouraged by Bishop Latimer's policies and activities to articulate openly their acceptance of the new religion and their repudiation of the old, sometimes demonstrating a preference for a version of Protes-tantism which went beyond Latimer's. In Easter Week 1539, one William

[49] *L&P*, vol. XI, no. 1041; H. S. Kennedy-Skipton, 'The Berkeleys at Yate', *TBGAS* 21 (1896), p. 28.
[50] *L&P*, vol. X, no. 827; M. Dowling, 'Introduction' in 'William Latymer's Cronickille of Anne Boleyn', in Camden Miscellany (Camden 4th ser., vol. XXXIX, London, 1990), p. 28; PRO PROB 11/42B, fos. 233–5. Cf. T. S. Freeman, 'Research, Rumour and Propaganda: Anne Boleyn in Foxe's "Book of Martyrs"', *HJ* 38 (1995), pp. 802–4.
[51] D. Hay, *Polydore Vergil: Renaissance Historian and Man of Letters* (Oxford, 1952), p. 69.

Clerke of Hartpury was heard to describe the Eucharist as 'but a vayne glorye' and to assert that he 'dyd never beleve in the vij sacramentes of the church, nor never wold'.[52] In that same year, during harvest time, a group of people, including Clerke, met in a mill near Upleadon where James and Elizabeth Knolles lived. They had gathered to talk 'abowte the blessed sacramente of thalter togethers', and while they were there Matthew Price of Staunton 'openly saide that the sacramente of thalter was not the bodye of Christ, but that it was bredde and wyne, and not made by God, but by mannes hande, for Christ toke his owne body with hym up in to heven, and left it not behynde hym'. Furthermore, while visiting a shop in Upleadon, the same Price declared, 'that hit was as goode to confesse hym to a tree, as to a prest, and . . . [that he] dispised . . . hole bred, matence [matins], evensonge and buryinge'. At about the same time, Price also appeared at evensong in Upleadon parish church with William Baker, another parishioner of Staunton,

and in the presence of dyverse of the parisheners there . . . Price tooke in his hande tholy water dassell sayinge to . . . Baker, remember thy baptysm, and thean and there the saide Baker in contempte of the saide holywater turned his ars towardes the saide Matthew, and the same Matthew . . . spryncled and cast holy water upon the saide William Baker's ars.[53]

The words 'remember thy baptysm' echo the first phrase from the words Bishop Latimer had directed his clergy to use when administering holy water to their parishioners. Thus, by this action Price and Baker appear to have flaunted their bishop's authority, while simultaneously demonstrating their impatience with the pace of reform under his leadership.[54] The gathering in the Upleadon mill was not the only private discussion of the Eucharist held in the Forest of Dean in the late 1530s: a similar discussion involving a number of people was held in Newent at the house of one Barbor, where a child is reported to have asserted that 'the verey fleshe and [blood]' were not present in the sacraments of the altar, 'for hytt ys no [obliterated] passyon of christ'.[55] Moreover, earlier in the sixteenth century, prior to the introduction of Protestant ideas, a number of individuals had been presented in the church courts for relatively minor offences such as being absent from divine services on Sundays, and one person was accused of heresy. In addition, in 1517 or 1518, one Johanna Howells of Newent not only ate meat on a certain Wednesday and Friday, but also refused to make an offering on the day of the purification of the Blessed Virgin Mary, saying that she would rather offer a candle to a mountain. Perhaps

[52] HWRO 802 BA 2764, p. 107.   [53] HWRO 802 BA 2764, pp. 109–10, 115, 172.
[54] Latimer, *Sermons*, vol. I, p. 294.
[55] GCL Hockaday Collection 18(12)–18(35), 18(39), 1479–1530, 1537–9 (unpaginated).

remaining vestiges of Lollardy, combined with the Forest's inhabitants' general resistance to outside authority, created a climate that encouraged a greater concentration of radical responses to the advent of Protestantism than was evident elsewhere in the county. However, there was only one recorded instance of iconoclasm in either the county or the Forest before 1540, and that occurred in 1528 when Roger Wrytte, priest of Littledean, removed an image from the church of St John the Baptist in nearby Lydney. Even in the Forest of Dean other traditional religious imagery remained intact. A number of churches were robbed by a group of men, but their primary motivation seems to have been financial, with lack of reverence for religious images and objects being possible mitigating factors, rather than the other way around. The iconoclasm which destroyed the rood screens at Rickmansworth and Dovercourt in 1522 and 1532, respectively, and which manifested itself in image-breaking in London in 1533, is almost completely missing from the extant records of Gloucestershire in the 1520s and 1530s.[56]

Followers of the new religion in other areas of the county in the late 1530s appear to have been just as firm in their beliefs and as articulate in stating them as the inhabitants of the Forest had been; however, they were spread more thinly among the populace, and they were certainly less ribald than Price and Baker. On Sunday, 18 April 1540, Humfrey Grynshill, a weaver from Stonehouse,

was redynge the byble in englyshe in Cryste Church in Gloucester . . . and immediately aftre he had redde . . . [he] dyd affirme and saye [that] . . . hit can not be proved nether founde in any part of the hole scriptur, that there is any moo places wherin christen soules departed may be, but only hell and heven, and therfore he sayde that he wolde have no prayers sayde for his sowle when so ever he shall dye, nor any other suffragies of the churche [because they would not help his soul].[57]

Others uttered similar beliefs. John Dydson of Coaley disparaged prayers and dirges for the souls of the departed, while John Androwes, curate of Wotton-under-Edge, chose to disagree with the policies of his bishop, as had Matthew Price. He declared that 'for as much as he dyd preceyve that certeyne people doth put certeyne confidence and trust of salvacion in the ceremonyes of the churche as is holy bred holy water and such other therefore to reprove suche abuse', and invoked the fourth chapter of St Paul's Epistle to the Galatians, which described such ceremonies as 'weke and begerly'. Furthermore, he refuted most auricular confession, asserting

[56] *L&P*, vol. VIII, no. 584; Haigh, *Reformations*, pp. 69–70; M. Aston, 'Iconoclasm at Rickmansworth 1522', *JEH* 40 (1989), pp. 524–52; MacCulloch, *Suffolk*, p. 155; Brigden, *London*, pp. 288–93.
[57] HWRO 802 BA 2764, p. 137.

that a synner beynge mynded to be confessed of his syne and cummynge to his goostly father to confesse the same is not bounde to declare and nowmbre his synes in specie but that hit is sufficient for hym to confesse hym self generally that he is a synner except hit be any greate thynge that grudgeth his conscience wherin he wolde have counsell.[58]

Such utterances were not confined to the countryside and market towns: the city of Gloucester had its share of clergy promoting the new religion as well. John Erley and Hugh Rawlyns had disrupted the city with their preaching. In addition, Harry Costen proclaimed from the pulpit of All Saints, Gloucester, 'that [neither] the masse nor suffrages of the same wyll helppe nether proffyt the solles departyd'. Thus, a number of the inhabitants of the southern vale, the Forest and the city of Gloucester (clergy and laity) very openly expressed their aversion to traditional beliefs and practices and their preference for the new religion during Latimer's episcopate.

Likewise, some testators during this period revealed non-traditional sentiments less publicly in the preambles to their wills, especially in wills written as the decade was drawing to a close. This paralleled the pattern of declarations of faith in Kent at that time.[59] Thomas Dyar of Stow and Thomas Collett of nearby Upper Slaughter each bequeathed his soul 'to almythe God to be saved by the merytes and sufferyng of hys sonne Jhesus which oneli hath pacyfyed the wrathe of hys father for my trespasses and fawtes'.[60] Others, such as John Davys of Stroud, were less equivocal. Davys declared in 1538:

I bequethe my soule to allmyty god trystyng that be the merytys off crystes passyon I shall have eternall lyffe, havynge no confydense in the werkys that I have done or doo, wyche ar butt fruttes of faythe, but all my conffydence ys to be savyd by the blod schedyng of my savyor Jhesus Crysyte.[61]

A similarly clear statement of Protestantism, which even employed some of the same language, can be found in the testament of John Dennys of Cirencester, who declared in 1538:

I bequeth my sowle to Jesu Cryst my savyour and redemer, strustyng faygthfully to have remyssyon of my synnys by hys deth and to be purgyd frome my synfulnes thrugth the shedyng of hys bloud, throwgth whome and by whome all that beleve are savyd, so that I will trust yn no other thynges as concernyng my redemtyon salvatyon and remyssyon of my synnys, neverthelesse all my good dedes the which I have done I take them as fruttes of my fayth to shewe to the world my ynward fayth, takyng Jesu Cryst for a full and a hole savyour nedyng no other helpe of man, not denyyng the decent and cumly ordre taken by man and so alowyd.[62]

---

[58] HWRO 802 BA 2764, p. 131.
[59] Clark, *Society*, p. 59. See Appendix A for a discussion of the methodology employed in the analysis of the religious content of early-modern English wills.
[60] HWRO Wills, 1538/111, 1538/119.   [61] HWRO Wills, 1538/265.
[62] HWRO Wills, 1538 and 1539/289.

Later that same year, Thomas Benett of Stow committed his soul to Almighty God 'to be saved by the merytes and passyon of hys sone Jhesus and by no other which Jhesus onely hath redemed me and pasyfyed the wrathe of his father for my fawtes'. Thus both Dennys and Benett anticipated the use of the phrase 'and by no other means', which would become a more common way of explicitly rejecting traditional means of grace in the 1570s.[63] William Furdes's will, dated 1539, contains even more assertively Protestant language, and his statement was further buttressed by scriptural references, possibly provided by his scribe, John Dydson, the vicar of Coaley, who had spoken so vehemently against purgatory. Furdes's will committed his soul

to God Allmyghty accordyng to the ensample of Christe .Luc. cap. xxiij. and my body to be buryed yn the churche yerde of Coalleye trustyng withowt any dowte or mystruste that throught hys grace and mercye and the merettes of Christes passyon and vertu of hys resurrettion I have and shall have remyssyon of all my synnys. Isaii.53. Matth .26. John .1. Rom. 3. 4. 5. Ephe. 1. Coll. 1. 2. 1. Pet. 2. 1. Joh. 1. Revel. 1. Resurrecction of body and soule. Job. cap. xjx. Joh. cap. 5. 6. 11. Corrinth. 25. and everlastynge lyfe with God. Joh. cap. 3. 5. 6. 10. 11. accordyng to the artycles of owre fayth and Godes promesse Mar: cap. ulti., wych canott lye. Tit. cap. 1.[64]

Hence, several Gloucestershire testators from the southern vale and the Cotswolds chose to include in their wills religious preambles which asserted their adherence to the new religion, as had William Tracy of the northern vale, while inhabitants of the Forest and the city of Gloucester who favoured Protestantism expressed their preferences through more public actions and declarations. (William and Richard Tracy provide the only extant evidence of support for the new religion among the laity in the northern vale during the decade.)

None the less, whether they were expressing their beliefs publicly or privately, the presence of articulate and in some cases irreverent Protestants in Gloucestershire in the late 1530s should not be allowed to distort the general picture of lay religion in the county at that time. In fact, the number of such individuals was quite small: only seventy-seven Gloucestershire wills survive from the period prior to 1541, when the diocese of Gloucester was founded (and these include the wills of both elite and ordinary testators). Of these, half contained traditional soul bequests, as did the will of John Cooke of Bledington, in which he bequeathed his soul 'to

[63] HWRO Wills, 1538/263. The reference to Jesus Christ pacifying the wrath of his father for the sake of the testator appears in several of the wills from this period and was probably inspired by William Marshall's radically Protestant *Prymer in Englyshe*, published by John Biddell in 1534 (STC 15986). HWRO Wills, 1538/18, 1538/28, 1538/47, 1528/260, 1538/261, 1538/262.

[64] GRO Gloucestershire Dispersed Wills, Bundle III/83A.

allmygthtye God to our blessed lady and to all the holy company of seyntes in hevyn'.[65] Another 40 per cent made ambiguous declarations (typically just bequeathing their soul to Almighty God), while just 10 per cent declared their Protestantism. Furthermore, while they provided interesting and sometimes colourful stories of pre-Reformation lay piety in Gloucestershire, only a few people were presented for behaviour or beliefs which were at variance with established policy. Most people (both elite and non-elite) still held traditional views. Moreover, with the passage in June 1539 of the Act of Six Articles, which reasserted key traditional beliefs, Bishop Latimer was forced to resign. He was succeeded by his detractor, Dr John Bell, who moved immediately to discover and punish all those who held beliefs which conflicted with his more conservative theology.[66] Thus, the swing back toward a more traditional official religious policy, which may have been perceived as gradual in some parts of England, was quite abrupt and definitive in Gloucestershire on the eve of the creation of the new diocese.

The responses of the county's elite reveal the embryonic emergence of affinity groups, centred in part on religious preference but also reflecting and building on existing kinship networks and long-standing disputes. (An example of the latter was the dispute among the Berkeleys in Gloucestershire and between the Berkeleys and the Lisles of Warwickshire for control of the Berkeley estates.[67]) Thus, Sir Christopher Baynham (Sir Alexander's brother), Sir William Kingston, Sir Edmund Tame, Sir Edward Greville, Sir John Huddleston and Lady Anne Berkeley devoted their energies and considerable wealth to preserving and enriching traditional religion and resisting the introduction of Protestantism. Meanwhile, William Tracy, Sir John Walsh, Sir Anthony Poyntz (Walsh's brother-in-law), Sir Richard Tracy, Sir Maurice Berkeley, Sir Giles Poole, Sir Nicholas Arnold and Arthur Porter all supported and promoted the spread of the new religion within the county.[68] Other issues would emerge which would both strengthen and modify these alliances, but the division would persist. It remains to be seen, however, what if any effect such an alignment among the elite would have on the religion of the ordinary laity of Gloucestershire.

[65] HWRO Wills, 1538 and 1539/35. Using the same methodology and categorisation scheme as was used for the post-1540 Gloucestershire wills, only 6 per cent of the wills from the 1530s were clearly Protestant, while 26 per cent were traditional and 68 per cent were ambiguous.

[66] S. R. Wabuda, 'The Provision of Preaching', pp. 112–14; HWRO 802 BA 2764, pp. 107–82, *passim*.

[67] See chapter 7.

[68] The Berkeley family was divided between those who inherited the honour and those who did not. H. S. Kennedy, 'The Berkeleys at Yate', *TBGAS* 21 (1896–7), pp. 25–31.

3

The new diocese of Gloucester
(1540–1546)

Wherefore, considering that the Scite of the said late Monastery of St Peter of Gloucester, in which many famous Monuments of our renowned Ancestors, Kings of England, are erected, is a very fit and proper Place for erecting, instituting, and establishing an Episcopal See . . . We have decreed, and by these Presents We do decree the Scite of the said Monastery to be an Episcopal See, and to be created, erected, and established a Cathedral Church . . . And We also Will and Ordain . . . that our whole Town of Gloucester be from henceforth and for ever a City . . . And We do by these Presents make and ordain the said City and County [of Gloucester] to be the Diocese of Gloucester.[1]

By the time the new diocese of Gloucester was created, official religious policy, so definitively Protestant in the county in the late 1530s, had begun to move toward a modified form of traditional doctrine. The last monastery had been dissolved in March 1540, and Thomas Cromwell, a leading force for the Protestantisation of England in the 1530s, had been beheaded in July of that same year.[2] Furthermore, 'The Act of Six Articles' had been approved by Parliament in June 1539.[3] All of this signified a swing back toward the old religion. However, the conservative trend was not unequivocal, as was demonstrated by the continued attempts to enforce 'The Act for the Abrogation of Certain Holy Days', and the injunctions and proclamations which ordered every parish church to obtain a vernacular Bible. The efforts to place English Bibles in every parish church began in 1536, with slightly modified orders being issued in 1538 and 1541. Further changes were made in the list of approved and abrogated saints' days in a proclamation dated 22 July 1541, which reinstated the feasts of St Luke, St Mark and St Mary Magdalen, and abrogated the feasts of St Elyn and of

---

[1] R. Atkins, ed. and trans., 'The Charter of the Diocese of Gloucester', in *Glostershire*, pt. I, pp. 44–5.
[2] Dickens, *Reformation*, p. 143; G. R. Elton, *Reform and Reformation: England, 1509–1558* (Cambridge, MA, 1977), p. 292.
[3] 31 Henry VIII, c.14.

the Exultation of the Cross. It further ordered the suspension of all 'super-stitious and childish observations' of the feasts of St Nicholas, St Catherine, St Clement and the Holy Innocents.[4] 'The King's Book', published in May 1543, reaffirmed and clarified some aspects of the increasingly traditional official religion of the realm. For instance, caution was now urged in weighing the value of images as opposed to their abuse, in contrast to the Injunctions of 1538, which had implied that most images were probably being abused and urged their removal.[5] How did the religious views of the king, council and Parliament which prompted the change in policy affect the religion of the laity in Gloucestershire during the waning years of the reign of Henry VIII and the first years of the new diocese? Did the county or ecclesiastical elite play a particular role in mediating or facilitating the reception of the shifting official policy of those years?

John Wakeman, the last abbot of Tewkesbury and first Bishop of Gloucester, seems to have been given the bishopric as something of a 'retirement package'. He may have been trying to position himself for favourable treatment when, in February 1533, he had agreed to give Thomas Cromwell the farm of the manor of Stanway, although he had stipulated at that time that whoever actually became the farmer had to be resident and agreeable to the monastery. (The monastery had previously refused to rent that manor to the Protestant pamphleteer Richard Tracy, their 'neighbour', presumably because the latter was deemed to hold unacceptable religious views. Ultimately, however, Tracy obtained the manor by grant from Cromwell, thus thwarting the wishes of Wakeman and the monks of Tewkesbury.) Wakeman re-paid the king for appointing him to the see by dutifully conforming to the changing official religious policies of Henry's last years, and reliably visiting his diocese on a regular basis.[6] None the less, Wakeman's episcopate contrasted with those of his predecessors in the diocese of Worcester, Hugh Latimer and John Bell, especially when compared with Latimer's vigorous preaching programme and Bell's equally energetic promotion of his traditional beliefs at the expense of ardent Protestants. Bishop Wakeman did conduct the requisite visitations, but there is no evidence of the vigorous promotion of any doctrinal position such as characterised the episcopates of both Latimer

---

[4] The 'Act of the Abrogation of Certain Holydays' was passed by Convocation in 1536. A. Wilkins, *Concilia*, pp. 823–4; 'The First Royal Injunctions of Henry VIII', in *VAI*, vol. II, p. 9; 'The Second Royal Injunctions of Henry VIII', in *VAI*, vol. II, pp. 35–6; 'Ordering Great Bible to be Placed in every Church', in *TRP*, p. 297; 'Altering Feast Days', in *TRP*, vol. I, pp. 301–2.

[5] 'The Second Royal Injunctions of Henry VIII', in *VAI*, vol. II, p. 38; M. Aston, *England's Iconoclasts*, pp. 226–40.

[6] *L&P*, 6, no. 161; J. Strype, *Ecclesiastical Memorials, Relating Chiefly to Religion and the Reformation of It* (Oxford, 1822), vol. II, part II, p. 291.

and Bell. Wakeman appears merely to have presented the image of a conscientious bishop without actually doing very much. The parishes and lay people of Gloucestershire seem to have had little or no contact with him during the early years of the diocese beyond two pro-forma visitations (in 1542 and 1545).[7] Official policies concerning the keeping of parish registers (1538), and the placing of Bibles in English in every parish church (1536) may have been promoted, but there is no evidence that they were systematically enforced in the new diocese.

During these last years of Henry's reign, especially between 1542 and 1545, religious conservatives were in the ascendancy at Court, and the incidence of both actions and publicly uttered words motivated by Protestantism diminished substantially all across the realm. While inhabitants of Gloucestershire may have just been responding in concert with the rest of the kingdom and acquiescing to the return to a more traditional official religion, the nearly complete absence of evidence of nonconformity in the county may be due to additional mitigating circumstances. The records may have been lost, or perhaps the people of Gloucestershire passively accepted the modified version of English Christianity then being promulgated. It seems highly unlikely, though, that adherents to the new religion would have quietly returned to conformity of their own volition. A far more probable explanation lies in Wakeman's execution of his office.

Wakeman may have been less vigorous than his predecessors in enforcing the Crown's religious policy, perhaps as a result of the apparent ambiguity of that policy during that portion of Henry's reign; or he may have been a 'time-server', merely occupying the office of bishop to fund his retirement. However, the evidence or lack thereof could be read in another way. Wakeman was the first bishop of a new and very poor diocese, and it may have taken some time to establish the ecclesiastical structure he would have needed to administer the see effectively. Certainly that was the case in the diocese of Peterborough, which was also newly established and poor.[8] In 1541, Bishop Bell of Worcester had informed the Court of Augmentations that the chancels in numerous Gloucestershire parishes in the king's possession were 'in such great decay as to need immediate repair'.[9] Wakeman's visitation of the diocese in 1542 revealed a similar level of decay in church buildings, especially chancels, throughout the diocese, and in his visitation of the cathedral in 1542 he found things in disarray. Two sub-canons' positions were vacant; some of the daily offices were not being sung canonically; they lacked some of 'the books . . . necessary to divine worship'; the building needed to be repaired; the dean had not made a

[7] Wakeman conducted episcopal visitations in 1542, 1545, 1547 and 1548. GRO GDR vol. II, pp. 2–5, 8, 11–43; vol. IV, *passim*.
[8] W. J. Sheils, *Puritans*, p. 5. [9] *L&P*, vol. XVI, no. 648.

proper account of cathedral affairs; and the stipendiary clergy did not 'perform their duty in a proper way . . . [or] go into the choir with a modest demeanour'. Rather 'they come in too wanton and dissolute a dress . . . with daggers, even long ones, quarrelling and chiding with one another'.[10] Thus, the challenge which confronted the new bishop, his chancellors and the rest of the clergy and lay leaders of the diocese in those early years may have been too great for the mechanisms in place at the time. Early in the reign of Edward VI, Wakeman would conduct a much more thorough visitation, which would not only highlight decaying church properties, but also identify parishioners who were not conforming. The difference in thoroughness and vigour with which the later visitation was executed may have been due to the increased clarity of policy under Protector Somerset. On the other hand, the difference may have been a result of the establishment over the previous seven years of an effective diocesan administrative structure.

In any case, the possible explanations of deficiencies at the diocesan level only address a portion of the puzzle. What about the secular state records, especially those from the courts of chancery, requests and Star Chamber? These records are nearly silent on the subject of religion in Gloucestershire late in Henry's reign. What state records do reveal, though, is a marked preoccupation with first the threat, and then the reality of war with both Scotland and France during the period under discussion. The Crown was primarily concerned with finances, and the county elite, who usually served as justices of the peace and were often involved in enforcing religious conformity, were devoting their time, energy and wealth to raising money and men to support the king in battle. Religious policy had definitely been set aside; preparation for and execution of war were the primary concerns. John Arnold, Sir Anthony Kingston and Sir Nicholas Poyntz were members of the commission to collect the benevolence for the campaign against France. At approximately the same time, Sir Nicholas Arnold and Sir Anthony Kingston were members of the Chantries Commission for the county, another potential source of funds even though its title implies a religious purpose. This commission was initially responsible for assessing the value of every chantry in the diocese and passing that information to the Crown.[11] Furthermore, everyone would have been affected by dearth and bad weather, which descended upon England in 1545, simultaneously with the threat of a French invasion. Among those responsible for

---

[10] GRO GDR vol. II, 2–5, pp. 11–43; translated in GCL Hockaday Collections 6(4), 1542 (unpaginated).
[11] *L&P*, vol. XVII, no. 882 (M.2); vol. XIX, part I, no. 273, p. 154, no. 274, p. 163, nos. 275, 276; vol. XX, part I, no. 623, p. 325; vol. XXI, part I, no. 302 (30); vol. XXI, part II, no. 436.

implementing religious policy the demands of those events and threats may have overshadowed the awareness of demonstrations and declarations of religious beliefs, and the enforcement of conformity. There is no evidence that the Gloucestershire elite focused on issues relating to religion or consolidated alliances based on religious preferences, as did the elite in Kent.[12] Thus, distractions and disorganisation, plus the lack of a clearly articulated religious policy within the diocese, may well have combined to minimise the extent to which nonconformity was either detected or punished in the diocese of Gloucester during Henry's last years on the throne.

The surrender of the abbeys and priories at the end of 1539 had also contributed to the challenges inherent in administering the new diocese, bringing both physical changes, such as the destruction and transfer of monastic property, and a massive transfer of parish patronage within the diocese from the larger monasteries to the Crown. Just two houses had been suppressed in 1536: Flaxley Abbey and St Oswald's Priory, Gloucester. Eight more were dissolved following the act of 1539: Deerhurst Priory, Kingswood Abbey, Winchcombe Abbey, Hailes Abbey, Cirencester Abbey, Llanthony Priory and St Peter's Abbey, Gloucester, and Tewkesbury Abbey.[13] This probably had an even greater impact locally than the elimination of pilgrimages which had occurred during Latimer's episcopate, because of the extensive monastic holdings in the county. The Crown granted some parish advowsons to prominent local gentry, but a substantial proportion (101 of the total of approximately 270 benefices) were given to individuals residing outside the diocese or to new or neighbouring cathedrals. (At the time of Hooper's visitation in 1551, Worcester Cathedral held four, Bristol Cathedral held five, Oxford Cathedral held six, and Hereford Cathedral held seven. No non-resident individual held more than four, except the king who held ninety.) Among the local elite, most held only one or two. As of 1551, only Henry Clifford, Sir John Bridges and Sir Richard Leigh held three, and Sir Anthony Kingston held four.[14] The concentration of livings in the hands of individuals and institutions outside the diocese may have negatively impacted on local religious life by decreasing the level of accountability for proper maintenance of the chancels, rectories and vicarages. This seems to have been the case for parishes still in the king's gift in 1542. On the other hand, the king could have used his patronage to

[12] Clark, *Society*, p. 65; D. MacCulloch, *Thomas Cranmer, a Life* (New Haven, CT, and London, 1996), pp. 297–332, *passim*; Glyn Redworth, *In Defence of the Church Catholic: The Life of Stephen Gardiner* (Oxford, 1990), pp. 177–98, *passim*; M. L. Zell, 'The Prebendaries' Plot of 1543: a Reconsideration', *JEH* 27 (1976), pp. 241–53.

[13] G. Baskerville, 'The Dispossessed Religious of Gloucestershire', in *Gloucestershire Studies*, ed. H. P. R. Finberg (Leicester, 1957), pp. 130–44.

[14] 'Visitation Booke', pp. 17–77.

place clergy sympathetic to official policy in vacant parishes. As was the case in the diocese of Lincoln, no individual other than the king held enough advowsons to influence local religion, but the king did not take advantage of his opportunity in either instance.[15]

Secular property previously held by religious houses also changed hands in vast quantities as a result of the dissolutions, placing a set of lay landlords in control of large numbers of tenements and lands throughout the diocese. In Tewkesbury, Giles Geast, a mercer, was able to purchase the house he lived in, along with a number of others, improving his condition to the extent that at his death in 1557 he would be able to endow a charity for the benefit of the poor, funded from the rents of the properties he had thus acquired.[16] Similarly in Gloucester, Sir Thomas Bell, sometime mayor and manufacturer of caps, as well as one of Latimer's leading adversaries, purchased property previously held by the Blackfriars, and at his death some twenty-five years later would establish an almshouse in one of the buildings, and endow it with the rents from several of the other tenements acquired after the dissolution.[17] Others among the Gloucestershire elite who profited handsomely included both Kingstons, Sir William and Sir Anthony, and Sir Thomas Throckmorton.

The suppression of monasteries in Gloucestershire may have been more significant for Tewkesbury than for other congregations in the diocese, since the parish had traditionally worshipped in the nave of the Abbey church. When John Wakeman as abbot surrendered the Abbey on 9 January 1540, the Crown intended to demolish the church, as well as the cloister, refectory and other monastic buildings.[18] In June 1543, however, 'the bailiffs, burgesses and commonalty of the borough and town of Tewkesbury' raised £483 and purchased 'the said abbey church with the bells etc. and the churchyard etc.' from the king 'to be used for ever there after by the bailiffs, burgesses and commonalty and other parishioners as their parish church and churchyard'. The survival of the 'whole fabric' of the church at Tewkesbury was particularly remarkable. There were only a few other cases where a large abbey church survived intact and became a parish church, although there were a number of smaller abbeys which were transferred. The large abbeys of Christchurch in Devon and Wymondham in Norfolk had a similar fate to their counterpart in Tewkesbury, while at Bolton, Pershore and Malmesbury parishioners or patrons also purchased abbey churches for use by their parishes. However, in each of the last three

---

[15] M. Bowker, *The Henrician Reformation: the Diocese of Lincoln under John Longland 1521–1547* (Cambridge, 1981), p. 171.

[16] PRO PROB 11/40, fos. 284v–7v. The records of the charity are deposited in GRO D2688, 'Giles Geaste's Charity Accounts'.

[17] GRO Wills 1566/150.   [18] *L&P*, vol. XV, no. 139 (iv).

cases the 'monastic portion had been shorn off', whereas at Tewkesbury, Christchurch and Wymondham it remained. Smaller abbey churches which survived included Leonard Stanley and Deerhurst in Gloucestershire. These remarkable survivals were contrary to the instructions given to the commissioners responsible for the dissolution, who were to pull down all such churches, as well as other monastic structures.[19] The purchase of Tewkesbury Abbey was financed by a combination of small donations from a large number of parishioners, and a substantial bequest from Alexander Pyrry, who gave £150 'toward the redempcion of the late abbey churche of Tewkesbury', and £84 for 'the leddes and belles of the same of the Kinges magestie for a parishe church', a funding pattern similar to that adopted at nearby Winchcombe some years earlier, when the parishioners had built the nave of their new parish church with the aid of Lord Sudeley.[20]

The purchase of the Abbey church by the parishioners of Tewkesbury was obviously an unusual action, incurring extraordinary expenses which required the use of uncommon resources. The regular expenses needed to operate Gloucestershire parishes in the 1540s were typically met by a combination of pew rents, small, ritualistic bequests of just a few pence each from testators, rental income from tenements, and lands held by the parish, 'knelys of ther frendes that departyd owte of the said parische', and special gifts designated for particular uses such as purchasing or refurbishing the paschal candle at Easter. Tewkesbury and St Michael's used such sources to support the ongoing life of their parishes.[21] The greatest expenses facing Gloucestershire churchwardens during these years were those associated with worship and with the maintenance of the fabric of the parish, and these expenditures provide additional evidence of continuity with the old in parish religious practices. The shrines may have gone, the pilgrimages have stopped, and English Bibles have been required, but there is little evidence in the surviving churchwardens' accounts to indicate that changes in official policy were noticeably affecting local corporate liturgical practices.

Parishes still had to maintain their buildings, and still chose to provide for traditional forms of worship. For example, 36 per cent of St Michael's expenses were for upkeep: the clock and chimes were 'kept', ornaments washed, the eagle and candlesticks scoured, bell ropes and baldrics replaced, and the walls and roof of the church repaired. However, St Michael's also spent an equivalent amount in support of parish worship:

---

[19] GRO TBR B2/1, fo. 1; D. Knowles, *The Religious Orders of England*, vol. III, *The Tudor Age* (Cambridge, 1959), pp. 384–6.
[20] PRO PROB 11/30, fo. 335. See chapter 2 for a discussion of Winchcombe's building project.
[21] See chapter 2.

washing, making and mending surplices and albs, mending the pyx, service books and the organ, purchasing wax and tapers, 'candles at Christmas', and oil and 'coles at Estur', and setting up and watching the Easter sepulchre. The latter item was closely tied to traditional lay piety and would soon disappear with the swing to Protestantism following Edward VI's accession. Pre-Reformation parishes were required to provide the sepulchre in some form and it served as a focus for worship during Holy Week, encompassing both Christ's death and passion and his resurrection. Some were elaborate, permanent structures as at Long Melford in Suffolk where a benefactor's tomb was also the sepulchre. Others, such as those at St Michael's, Gloucester, and St Mary Redcliffe in Bristol, were wooden frames, although even those might be elaborately decorated with gilded images, as was that at St Mary Redcliffe. Once the sepulchre had been erected it became the object of a watch or vigil from Good Friday to Easter Sunday morning with a great number of candles blazing the whole time.[22] By providing for the proper maintenance of both the church properties and the accoutrements of worship, parishes such as St Michael's were able to present an image of a stable, healthy, vital institution, dedicated to Christian worship, even in a time of religious upheaval.

One of the expenses of traditional religion was lights, an important aspect of pre-Reformation and Henrician worship in Gloucestershire as elsewhere; however, they were not funded exclusively, or even primarily, by the parish chest. Individual parishioners and parish guilds generally assumed that responsibility as a traditional expression of lay piety. In particular, from 1541 to 1546 approximately 15 per cent of all Gloucester-shire wills included a small bequest for lights before one or more of the parish altars, the rood or the reserved sacrament, and these continued through the end of 1546. During the last year of the reign, in fact, over 50 per cent of the wills included such bequests.[23] In addition, most parishes had at least one guild which assumed the responsibility for providing lights for at least one parish altar. At Chipping Sodbury a guild was responsible for the lights at the altar of St Mary, while Tewkesbury had guilds associated with the altars of St Mary the Virgin, St Thomas, and St John, and at St Michael's the Fraternity of Weavers was responsible for St Anne's chapel.[24] The continuation of these bequests and of guild activities to keep the lights burning right through to Henry's death provide further testimony of adherence to the old religion, and in Gloucestershire the surviving

---

[22] GRO P154/14 CW 1/1, 1/2; Duffy, *Stripping*, pp. 31–2.
[23] This is based on the analysis of the systematic sample of 393 Gloucestershire wills written from 1541 to 1546.
[24] 'Chantry Certificates', pp. 255, 277, 281.

evidence from parishes and wills supports the perception of continuity, rather than change.

During the last years of Henry's reign, parish worship in general was largely unchanged from its pre-Reformation form in Gloucestershire. Some holy days were no longer celebrated (though that restriction seems to have been slow to take effect), pilgrimages had been eliminated, and some churches had probably procured the requisite large Bible in English. However, the basic liturgical practices and visual symbols of parish worship appear to have remained in their unaltered pre-Reformation forms. Images and lights remained in use in Gloucestershire until nearly the middle of Edward's reign.[25]

None the less, a few cases of nonconformity are included in the rather sparse extant records from the period. In one such case, John Weldon indicated his aversion to images by asserting that visual representations of Christ and the Virgin Mary were of no value, an unacceptably radical opinion given the relative conservatism of the early 1540s. These same records also disclose that parishioners from North Cerney complained in 1542 that their rector did not celebrate divine service at the proper time, and that William Moore was presented for violating the king's injunctions (although the records do not give the specific nature of his transgression).[26]

One of the few other cases of contentious behaviour in a parish involved a dispute over the order of procession, rather than any act or statement in defiance of official religious policy. In Ashelworth, as Guy Webbe, aged eighty-seven, stated,

he dothe knowe that sithen the tyme of his mariage which was about lx yeres now past he never dyd know the contrary but that the custome of the parishe of Ashelworthe was alweys duryng all his tyme and longe before as he haithe harde hys elders tell that every man and woman of what state or degre so ever they were which dyd contynually dwell and abyde within the parishe of Ashelworthe aforsaid shulde have their place in going in processyon accordyng unto the tyme of theyre mariage in as moche as the yonger brother haithe alweys and yet dothe goe before his elder brother in procession if so be that the yonger brother be first maryed.

Shortly after Webbe had married, he and another parishioner had exchanged blows in a similar dispute over their relative positions in the parish procession. Now it was alleged that John and Alice Smyth 'dyd now of late about ester last past wilfully goe out the place where they have goyn yn the space of this ix [years] quietly unto a nother place before . . . thirtene of

[25] GRO GDR, vol II, *passim.*

[26] Weldon's parish is not given; however, he resided in the deanery of Cirencester. The case appears to have come to the attention of the authorities during the diocesan visitation to the deanery in June 1542. GRO GDR, vol. II, p. 21.

couples of their neybours'. For this disorderly act they had been brought before the diocesan consistory court.[27]

The gentry's experience with the enforcement of religious policy paralleled that of their more humble neighbours. Only one individual was punished for his religion: Sir Richard Tracy, son of the early Protestant testator and the man who had confiscated the Blood of Hailes with Bishop Latimer, had written a number of pamphlets promoting the new religion. These included *The Profe and Declaration of thys Proposition: Faythe only Justifieth*, and *A Supplycacion to our Moste Soveraigne Lorde Kynge Henry the Eight*.[28] In 1546, the king issued a royal proclamation deploring 'that under pretense of expounding and declaring the truth of God's Scripture, divers lewd and evil-disposed persons have taken occasion to utter and sow abroad . . . sundry pernicious and detestable errors and heresies'. It continued by describing as 'corrupt and pestilent' the teachings contained in certain books, and then proceeded to ban a number of books and pamphlets, including New Testaments translated by William Tyndale and Miles Coverdale, and all the works of Frith, Tyndale, Wycliff, Coverdale and Tracy, among others.[29] Thus, Richard Tracy found himself in illustrious company, and this would not be the last time he was called to account for his religious beliefs.

The continued and even increased strength of traditional beliefs and practices reflected in parish accounts and diocesan court records from the last years of Henry's reign is also evident in the wills of ordinary Gloucestershire lay people, illustrating the ongoing acceptance and support of pre-Reformation practices. Traditional soul bequests, which had suffered a decrease in popularity in the late 1530s and were present in just 35 per cent of the wills in 1541, were the choice of an increasing proportion of the laity through the first half of the decade, before their popularity levelled off at just over 50 per cent in 1546.[30]

---

[27] GRO GDR, vol. I, pp. 39–40. This was just the sort of 'contention and strife' Edward's and Elizabeth's royal injunctions would seek to eliminate in 1547 and 1559, respectively. *TRP*, vol. I, 399; vol. II, p. 122. Cf. Duffy, *Stripping*, pp. 451–2.

[28] R. Tracy, *The Profe and Declaration of thys Proposition: Faythe only Justifieth* (London, 1543?), STC 24164; R. Tracy, *A Supplycacion to our moste Soveraigne Lorde Kynge Henry the Eight* (London, 1544), STC 24165.5. (Another edition of the latter was also published in Antwerp in 1544: STC 24165.)

[29] 'Prohibited Heretical Books', in *TRP*, vol. I, pp. 373–6.

[30] See Figure 3.1 and Appendix A. This is based on the analysis of a sample of 393 Gloucestershire lay wills proved in the consistory court of the diocese, including 148 women's wills, and 245 men's wills, numbers which are too small to support an analysis based on gender. In total, there are 182 traditional soul bequests, 209 broadly categorised as ambiguous, and 2 clearly Protestant. The sample was drawn from a total of 1,023 extant wills proved in the diocese of Gloucester from 1541 to 1546. Thus, assuming the highest possible variability of the sample from the population, the results of the analysis of this sample will be within 2.49 per cent of that for the entire population at a confidence level of

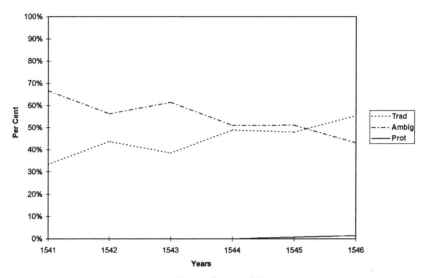

Figure 3.1   Non-elite will preambles (1541–1546)

During the same period, however, the variety of preamble formulas employed expanded significantly.[31] Between 1541 and 1543 just seven categories of soul bequests were used, including both the most standard of all ambiguous statements bequeathing the soul to 'Almighty God', and the most popular traditional bequest to 'Almighty God, our Blessed Virgin Mary and all the whole company of heaven', the two most popular formulas by a wide margin. However, they also included preambles such as those of Thomas Atkins, who bequeathed his soul to 'God my maker only', and Jacob Smythe, who left his soul 'to Jhesu Chryst thorowe the merites of whose pastion my hoope fayth and trust ys to be savid', both of which were written in 1542 and both of which were theologically equivocal.[32] In the same year William Robyns expressed a similar belief in the saving grace of Christ's passion, but also reaffirmed his faith in the traditional intercessory powers of the Blessed Virgin Mary and the saints when he bequeathed his soul

to the grett mercy of my lord God and fathfully trustyng to be savyd by the merytes

---

95 per cent. R. S. Schofield, 'Sampling in Historical Research', in *Nineteenth-Century Society: Essays in the Use of Quantitative Methods for the Study of Social Data*, ed. E. A. Wrigley (Cambridge, 1972), pp. 154–8.

[31] This is based on the analysis of two sets of Henrician wills from the systematic sample. Those from 1541 to 1543, totalling 143 wills, and those from 1545, totalling 131.

[32] GRO Wills 1543/64, 1542/18.

of his blessyd passyon and blood desyeryng the most gloryous virgyn our lady Seynt Marye and all the celestyall companye of heven to pray for me.[33]

While these testators and many others like them had chosen or been given soul bequests which went beyond the basic declarations of the most popular ambiguous and traditional preambles, most were still not making Protestant statements of faith. For the most part they were merely articulating their beliefs in more detail than others. Statements describing God as 'my maker only' or declaring one's faith in salvation through Christ's passion were entirely consistent with the teachings of the pre-Reformation church, and there was nothing odd or contradictory in expressing such a belief and then proceeding to ask for the prayers of St Mary and all the saints.

Within only three years the number of preamble types had doubled. In 1545, in addition to those forms already described, some testators now chose to bequeath their souls to 'almighty God only, and to be associatt wyth owre blessyd ladye and all the holye company in hevyn', as did Elizabeth Weley of St Nicholas, Gloucester.[34] The same year, in Old Sodbury, Thomas Sergeant left his soul to God's mercy, 'desiring and trusting that hit may have the fruition of his glorie with our blessed lady Saynt Marye and all the holy company in heven'.[35] Testators and scribes had found still more ways of expressing traditional beliefs concerning the salvation of their souls. In addition, a few testators opted for the ambiguous middle ground, leaving their souls to God's mercy, or invoking the Trinity, as did Joan Awall of Arlingham when she gave her soul 'to allmyghty God the holy trinite of whom I axe marcy of all my sinnes'.[36] Additionally, one testator expressed blessed assurance in his salvation when he gave his soul to Almighty God, 'trustyng undubtyly to be savyd be the merittes of Christ my saver only', a clearly Protestant preamble.[37] But the overwhelming continuation of traditional piety in the diocese is underscored by the five wills from the random sample which were written in 1546 and included provisions for 'Diriges' and masses. Such arrangements had disappeared from wills ten years earlier in the north Nottingham market town of Retford.[38]

An examination of the wills of the county's elite reveals a similar pattern, although only thirty-four of these wills survive for the period. Of these, two testators declared their Protestant faith (one each in 1544 and 1545), while the remaining thirty-two wills are split evenly between traditional and

33 GRO Wills 1542/46.   34 GRO Wills 1545/42.
35 GRO Wills 1545/331.   36 GRO Wills 1545/184.
37 GRO Wills 1545/9, 1545/48, 1545/405, 1545/239.
38 GRO Wills 1546/31, 1546/102, 1546/217, 1546/234, 1546/240; D. Marcombe, *English Small Town Life: Retford 1520–1642* (Oxford, 1993), p. 221.

ambiguous preambles. These wills also generally match the more ordinary inhabitants' wills in that there is a clear increase in traditional statements of faith through the years from 1541 to 1546. There is also some expansion and increased specificity in the preamble language employed, although the difference is not as pronounced as in the wills from the lower levels of society. Notably, there is no intrepid testator among the elite who left wills in this period; no one included a distinctive, radically Protestant preamble. Rather, this set of wills is marked by its reliance on standard forms, which generally express either traditional beliefs or opt for ambiguity. One characteristic which does set this group of wills apart, however, is that it signals the passing of a number of members of the last pre-Reformation generation, including Gloucester aldermen William Hassarde, Robert Pole, John Fawkner and David Lewys, prominent Gloucester widows Dame Joan Cooke and Anne Poole, and county gentry such as John Arnold, Sir George Baynham, Sir John Huddleston, Sir William Kingston, John Poyntz, Sir Edmund and Dame Elizabeth Tame, Sir John Walsh, Thomas Whittington and Robert Wye.

Through these early years, at all levels of society, there seems to have been an increasing need or desire to express one's faith in wills using specific rather than general terms. Perhaps this trend was driven by the embryonic expansion of scribes' preamble repertoires, or possibly the reverse was true and the variety of options was expanding at the behest of testators. In either case, neither the increasing assortments of preamble types, nor the presence of a few wills espousing the faith of the new religion can obscure the fact that conservative or traditional expressions of faith were the choice of most testators and scribes between 1541 and 1546, and this development cannot be explained by diocesan administrative problems, wars or lost records. The lack of Protestant wills from the last years of Henry's reign was probably the result of the swing toward a more traditional official religion in the early 1540s, when Gloucestershire was still in the diocese of Worcester. The move away from reform had its local manifestation in the ascendance of John Bell to the bishopric in the diocese of Worcester. Bell had given Gloucestershire a brief taste of 'the wave of repression' of reformed practices and beliefs similar to that which would begin in London two years later.[39] There was a key difference, however: the creation of the diocese of Gloucester just one year into Bell's episcopate diminished the impact of his campaign to punish Protestants. Even so, Bell's actions may have turned the tide and discouraged further development of Protestantism (or at least its public manifestations) in the region for the time being.

---

[39] 'Bishop Bell's Visitation Book, 1540', *passim*; Brigden, *London*, p. 339.

Charitable bequests contained in the wills from the last years of the reign of Henry VIII further enhance the picture of traditional lay piety seen in preambles. Over half those testators left distinctive, though not necessarily large, traditional gifts to their parishes. William Vynar of Churchdown left wheat to the high altar and a cow to Our Lady Service, while John Brayne, gentleman, of Longney left wheat to the high altar and a mass book to the parish, and Margaret Edun, widow, bequeathed 6d and her best table cloth to the high altar.[40] Furthermore, gifts for construction and maintenance projects, so common before the break with Rome, had not yet completely disappeared. John Bubbe of Whitcombe gave 12s to the new chapel in his parish, and Thomas Typper gave 6s 8d to the maintenance of Fairford church.[41]

In contrast with gifts to parishes, bequests to the poor occur more frequently in elite wills than in the wills of ordinary inhabitants, with approximately 40 per cent of the gentry leaving something to the poor, while less than 10 per cent of the wills from the lower levels of society mention their less fortunate neighbours. A number of the gentry made significant bequests, as did John Fawkener, parishioner of St Michael's, alderman and former mayor, who left £40 to endow a loan fund for poor tradesmen, in addition to providing £20 for general distribution to the poor.[42] Others also left something to paupers. Margery Hallydaye, widow of Stonehouse, gave £10 to be distributed at her burial, and £6 8s 8d to be given away each month for the first year and annually in subsequent years.[43] Jone Morste, a single woman of Harnhill, after providing for diriges and masses, directed that the residue of her goods were to be sold and the proceeds distributed to the poor on her burial day, her month's mind, monthly for the remainder of the first year and yearly thereafter, as long as the money lasted.[44] Alexander Pyrry, the generous Tewkesbury donor, directed that 100s be distributed to the poor at his burial and again one month later, that 12 black gowns be given to men of 'age and debylitie', and 12 white gowns be given to women, and that the residue of his estate be used for works and deeds of charity 'for the wealth' of his soul. John Nevill of South Cerney left £20 to be distributed to the poor at his burial and then every year after that, while both Thomas and Elizabeth Twesell designated one-third of the residue of each of their estates for the poor. Anne Poole, widow of Gloucester, left 40s to the poor of her parish, and also directed that white gowns and kerchiefs be given to 12 poor women. However, the most substantial bequest to the poor was that of Dame Joan Cooke, widow of the Gloucester alderman and sometime mayor, John

[40] GRO Wills 1543/76, 1544/53, 1545/221.   [41] GRO Wills 1545/97, 1545/352.
[42] PRO PROB 11/30, fo. 283.   [43] GRO Wills 1544/66.
[44] GRO Wills 1546/102.

Cooke, a gift she made in both her name and that of her deceased husband. He had left her a substantial sum, which she was to use during her lifetime. She was to use part of it to endow a free grammar school, which she did in cooperation with the mayor and alderman of the city. Christ's School was founded in 1539, six years before her death. However, her munificence was not limited to education. At her death she also left 10s to St Bartholomew's Hospital and 5s to each of the other hospitals for the poor in Gloucester, Magdalen and St Margaret's. In addition, she directed that £20 be distributed to the poor at her burial, £10 each at her month's and year's mind, and 12d each in monthly alms to the poor of the hospital of Magdalen. Not all renowned benefactors bequeathed substantial sums to the poor, however. For example, Sir Edmund Tame, who had finished the rebuilding of Fairford Church begun by his father, rebuilt Rendcomb Church and contributed substantially to the rebuilding of St John Baptist in Cirencester, left a ritualistic gift of 20s to the poor.[45]

Those records that do survive for the last years of the reign of Henry VIII indicate that local lay piety in the diocese of Gloucester adjusted to the shifts in official religious policy fairly promptly. Bishop Bell of Worcester may have provided the initial impetus. Then, following a period of ambiguity and administrative confusion after the new diocese was created, the Gloucestershire laity seem to have followed the lead of the Crown and Bishop Wakeman, and moved back toward traditional religious beliefs and practices. This is evident from the surviving wills, and there are hints of it in the parish records of St Michael's in Gloucester. Soon official religion would change again, and there would be a new set of policies to assimilate or resist, but through the end of the reign of Henry VIII the Gloucestershire laity appear to have settled quietly into a modified version of the old religion.

[45] PRO PROB 11/29, fo. 143v; PROB 11/30, fos. 183, 220v, 335; PROB 11/31, fos. 31v, 75v; *L&P*, vol. XIII, part I, nos. 1115 (17), 1179; vol. XIV, part II, no. 264 (6); R. Austin, 'John and Joan Cooke's Gift to Gloucester', *TBGAS* 65 (1944), pp. 199–219.

4

The advent of Edwardian Protestantism (1547–1553)

After years of religious ambivalence, the reign of Edward VI unequivocally ushered in English Protestantism, beginning with a Royal Visitation in 1547. Through a series of such visitations, royal proclamations and parliamentary acts, both the language and the imagery of worship were changed. During the first few years the swing to the new religion was fairly gradual, but there followed an abrupt shift to a much more vigorous enforcement of Protestantism. Bishop Wakeman presided over the diocese during the gradual phase, while Bishop Hooper was a key figure during the later, more active phase. Over the course of the reign, many churches whitewashed their walls and other painted surfaces to cover forbidden images, removed their rood lofts, lights and images, and began using the new Prayer Book, the Homilies and the English Bible. How quickly did these changes take place in Gloucestershire, and how widespread were they? Finally, how did the laity respond?

As official policy changed, so did that of John Wakeman, whose episcopate continued through the first two years of Edward's reign. Continuing to conform but approaching the enforcement of the new policies of Edwardian Protestantism with increased vigour, Wakeman conducted a visitation in 1548, in which he sought to abolish 'superstitious abuse' of religious ceremonies, 'all images shrynes and the lyke thynges mysse used in tymes past', all invocations to saints, and the use of lights before images. He also required every church to have 'an honest pulpit sett in some conveniente place'.[1] Beyond those stipulations, all of which were based on the Royal Injunctions of the previous year, Wakeman made the normal enquiries concerning the physical condition of parish buildings.

In the parish of Tudenham several of these concerns converged when the vicar, Sir William Lyvynge, was presented for having 'broken the glasse wyndowes in the bodie of the church, and by that means [they] are gretly in decaye'. He and a parishioner had also 'cast downe a stone cross in the

---

[1] GRO GDR vol. IV, pp. 7–10.

churchyard', and he was accused of no longer saying mass.[2] Other parishes also reported their worship disrupted by their priests' refusal to say mass or by the omission of certain aspects of the liturgy such as saying the Ave Maria, which had not yet been abrogated. With their desire to maintain traditional worship, these parishioners demonstrated greater attachment to the old ways than did their clergy.[3] With the exception of these few cases, however, those expressing displeasure or irreverence for the established ceremonies were lay people, rather than clergy. William Bowre and the teen-aged William Cloterboke of Slimbridge were accused of disturbing the people by reading 'openly in the churche', of calling the mass 'a stynkyng idol', and of describing holy oil as only fit 'to greyce sheepe and bootes'.[4] Not far away, in Oldbury, John Clement described the Eucharist similarly as 'baggage', a characterisation he claimed to have heard from licensed preachers. When he appeared in court, he claimed to be unlearned and to have just repeated what he had heard, going on to recant that belief and recognise 'the veritie accordynge to goddes word of the said blessed sacrament'.[5] In addition to visitation presentments, a few cases even came to the attention of the Privy Council. John Stevens of Bourton-on-the-Hill was accused of heresy, and a singing man at the cathedral was labelled 'a rebel', possibly as a result of the type of unruly behaviour previously attributed to the sub-canons during services in Gloucester Cathedral. Both were ordered to appear before the Council.[6] In each of these cases the individual presented was anxious for more, rather than less, Protestant innovation. In fact, several of the individuals mentioned may have been among those whose actions had prompted the passage of the 'Act against Revilers of the Sacrament', which was intended to stop just such disrespectful behaviour toward divine services.[7] However, the total number of incidents was still quite small, and in the cases of the priests who were presented, their parishioners seem to have wanted to keep the traditional ways undisturbed. Thus, we have evidence of a few of the hotter sort of Protestants (both clergy and laity) being reported by others who either wanted little or no change or accepted official policy. Meanwhile, most people seem to have conformed, been members of parishes composed of like-minded individuals who saw no need to present anyone for nonconformity, or at least 'kept their heads down' in the face of changing liturgical requirements.

Similarly, only a few parishes were reported for either nonconformity or neglect of parish buildings during Wakeman's Visitation in 1548, further

[2] GRO GDR vol. IV, p. 55.
[3] These included the curates of Dymock and Wollaston. GRO GDR vol. IV, pp. 43, 54.
[4] GRO GDR vol. IV, p. 34.   [5] GRO GDR vol. IV, p. 37.   [6] APC, pp. 162, 318.
[7] 1 Edward VI, c. 1.

underlining the conforming trend in Gloucestershire early in Edward's reign. Leaders of seven parishes acknowledged that they did not have an English Bible, while nine lacked the *Paraphrases*, two volumes which were supposed to be purchased jointly by the rector and people in each parish.[8] Other aspects of the maintenance and operation of parishes were the exclusive responsibility of either the parishioners or their rectors. The laity of seven parishes were found to have allowed either the church nave, that is, the body of the church, or their churchyard to fall into disrepair, while the rectors or proprietors of twenty-one parishes had 'ruinous' chancels, rectories or vicarages. Three other parishes reported broken windows, which may have been additional results either of iconoclasm or of neglect.[9] Most parishes, however, either met the requirements of the visitation articles and injunctions or simply kept quiet about their faults. The continued reiteration of the requirement for an English Bible in successive sets of Royal Injunctions dating from 1536 implies that parishes had been slow to conform to that particular requirement, and other directives (both royal and episcopal) may have suffered the same fate.

Some of the standards were also sufficiently vague as to leave room for local interpretation. For instance, what constituted 'superstitious abuse' of ceremonies, or misuse of images? Clues are perhaps provided by those ceremonial practices and accoutrements which were still in use in 1547, but not in 1548. Fourteen parishes reported having forbidden lights before images in 1547, including the parish of Haselton with 'a light afore the rode of 13 tapurs and in the quyer a lights of 20 tapurs'. No similar lights were mentioned by any parish during Wakeman's visitation the following year. Similarly, in 1547, the royal visitors discovered an image of St Blase at Frampton-upon-Severn, and the former priest of St Owen's in Gloucester was presented for keeping 'certayne jewells *viz* . . . 2 payres of beades gawded withe silver withe a brouche and a rynge' (presumably jewels which had adorned the image of a saint).[10] Again, no comparable present-ments were made to Wakeman a year later. Meanwhile, at St Michael's in Gloucester, parishioners' gifts for the Easter taper and for lights and 'knelys' in memory of individuals who had died continued through both 1547 and 1548. Likewise, the churchwardens continued to purchase holy

---

[8] Wakeman does not specifically mention the *Paraphrases* in his visitation articles; however, the presentments included reports that they were missing from certain parishes, possibly in response to the Royal Injunctions of the previous year. *TRP*, vol. I, p. 395.

[9] In five of those cases the king is described as the rector, and in two others the Bishop of Gloucester was responsible. Furthermore, one of the naves needing repair was that of Tudenham, where the glass had been deliberately smashed by the rector. GRO GDR vol. IV, pp. 21–146. The number of churches and chancels needing repairs would increase significantly by the early years of Elizabeth's reign. (See chapter 6.)

[10] GRO Furney MS B/1, pp. 101–9.

oil to anoint the sick and the newly baptised through 1548. However, although they still celebrated obits and erected and watched the Easter sepulchre in 1547, both disappeared in 1548. Similarly, they purchased coals to heat the incense in 1547, but not in 1548.

While the financial demands of traditional ceremonies were beginning to wane, they were being replaced by new requirements associated with Protestant worship, which unfortunately coincided with financial demands prompted by the Crown's continued involvement in military conflict with Scotland. Parishes were supposed to purchase the *Order of Communion* and the *Book of Homilies*.[11] The revenues at St Michael's easily covered the increased expenditures resulting from these demands, but this was not true everywhere. A number of other Gloucestershire parishes resorted to the sale of church plate to finance their obligations, often giving precedence to military demands over those associated with liturgy. The parish of Newnham, for instance, used such sales to equip soldiers 'goyng furthe towardes the kynges warres and upon other charitable uses'; while Long-hope sold 'one chalice, one pixe and one litull crosse of silver parcell gilte' to equip soldiers to fight in Scotland 'or in to some other place to the kynges majesties use', and also to repair the highway between the parish and Huntley. Focusing on the care of their property, rather than on other demands, the churchwardens of Tudenham, Newland, Staunton and English Bicknor sold comparable goods to finance needed church maintenance. Tudenham sold a 'sencer', a pyx and a small crucifix to repair their church tower. Newland sold plate worth £20 to pay for tiling an aisle, and painting, whitewashing and pointing the church and steeple. Using proceeds from similar sales, Staunton carried out general maintenance, and English Bicknor repaired their parish house.[12]

Just when liturgical costs and the demands for military support were weighing most heavily on Gloucestershire parishes, the Crown moved to take away a key (if indirect) source of parish support, and in the process disrupted lay piety even more, through the Chantries Act of 1547. Chantries had become a very popular form of charitable bequest among the elite of both the county and the towns, as well as among religious guilds. Individuals and groups established endowments to pay priests to intercede and say masses for the benefactors, their deceased family members and friends (or in the case of the guilds, for members and kin who had died). Chantry priests' roles extended beyond the confines of the chantry chapel, however; they often also played key roles in the life of the parishes with which their chantries were affiliated. In addition, substantial wealth was tied up in chantry endowments. This last characteristic had prompted

---

[11] *TRP*, vol. I, pp. 417–18, 432–3.   [12] GRO GDR vol. IV, pp. 47, 48–9, 55–8.

Henry VIII to have Parliament pass an act in 1545 which gave him the right to confiscate chantry endowments in order to finance his wars with Scotland and France.[13] This act had resulted in a survey of chantry lands and properties in 1546 to determine their value. In Gloucestershire, the commissioners who conducted the survey had included Sir Nicholas Arnold, Sir Anthony Kingston and Richard Pates (recorder and member of parliament for the city of Gloucester).[14] A new act was needed in 1547 because there was a new king, but the second act differed from its predecessor in its emphasis. Rather than citing the finance burden of defending the realm as had the earlier law, the later act began by declaring

that a greate parte of superstition and errors in Christian religion hath byn brought into the myndes and estimacion of men . . . by the abuse of trentalles chauntries, and other provisions made for the contynuance of the saide blyndness and ignoraunce.

It went on to assert that a far better use of the funds contained in chantry endowments would be the establishment of schools, and that the king was the best person to see to that conversion.[15]

The actual confiscation was achieved through local Chantry Commissions, which were, like their predecessors, composed of representatives of the local elite. In Gloucestershire, Richard Pates served again and was joined by Arthur Porter, Richard Tracy and Sir Thomas Throckmorton.[16] An examination of the composition of the Edwardian commission, combined with clues from the 1530s, provides additional fragmentary evidence of a possible alignment of the country gentry based in part on religious preference. There can be no doubt about the Protestantism of Richard Tracy, while Arthur Porter had been a supporter of Bishop Latimer's chaplain, Hugh Rawlyns, and had been mentioned as a possible member of a commission to investigate Thomas Bell following the latter's attack on Latimer. Sir Thomas Throckmorton was related to Richard Tracy by marriage and was also affiliated with Somerset. One of Sir Thomas's daughters was married to Tracy's great-nephew, Sir John Tracy, and another was the second wife of Sir John Thynne, secretary to the Duke of Somerset and manager of the latter's estates. Sir Thomas was also Sir Giles Poole's brother-in-law, while the latter was already associated with Tracy and Porter by 1539. Thus, these key members of the second Chantry Commission were probably all supporters of the new religion, and the publicly declared motivation for the confiscation may have gained additional validity, given the presence of known Protestants on the Commission in Gloucestershire.

[13] 37 Henry VIII, c. 4. [14] *L&P*, vol. XXI, part I, no. 302 (30).
[15] 1 Edward VI, c. 14. [16] 'Chantry Certificates', vol. VIII, p. 232.

The dissolution of the chantries did not produce the revenues anticipated by the Crown. In fact, the cumulative effect of the dissolution of Gloucestershire chantries through the end of Edward's reign was a huge deficit of over £967. The Crown sold most of the lands rather quickly, but had a continuing obligation to pay former chantry priests' wages and pensions. The short-term gain was much too small to cover those continuing expenditures, much less fund any other projects.[17] Meanwhile, the impact on parishes and the laity was three-fold. First, it substantially reduced the number of clergy serving parishes. This created particularly acute problems for large parishes such as Cirencester with 1,825 communicants and Tewkesbury with 1,600, each of which had just one priest once the chantries were dissolved. This led the commissioners in Gloucestershire to recommend that each be granted at least one additional priest. Second, schools were established in Tewkesbury, Newent and Cirencester.[18] The third effect was more profound: the dissolution removed a key component from the structure of the single religiously traditional community of the living and the dead, with its reliance on the existence of purgatory and the efficacy of prayers for the dead. It was still possible to provide for intercessions, masses and the like in one's will, and many testators did, but the mechanism by which such provisions had previously been implemented had been eliminated. The government's true reasons for the dissolution may have been secular and financial, but a notable result was the unmistakable signal it sent of repudiating such beliefs and intercessions. Once again, as when pilgrimages were eliminated, lay pious practices had been curtailed by official religious policy.

By 1549, additional change could be detected in parish worship as a result of the introduction of the first *Book of Common Prayer*, which was in general use by Whitsunday (June 9); in other respects, however, the life of the parish community continued as before.[19] In addition to the oft-noted impact of a liturgy which was totally in English, the Prayer Book contained rubrics promoting a new level of lay involvement in the Eucharist, which replaced traditional aspects of lay devotion associated with the mass, including gazing upon the consecrated host and kissing the pax. A rubric forbade the priest to show the elements of the Eucharist to the people, and

---

[17] For the kingdom as a whole the deficit exceeded £12,000 by the end of 1553. P. Cunich, 'The dissolution of the chantries' in *The Reformation in English Towns*, ed. P. Collinson and J. Craig (Basingstoke, 1998). I would like to thank Dr Cunich for allowing me to read his forthcoming essay, and for providing the detailed financial statistics for the diocese of Gloucester.

[18] GCL, Hockaday Abstracts, vol. XXXI, 1548 (unpaginated).

[19] G. J. Cuming, *A History of Anglican Liturgy* (2nd edn, London, 1982), p. 47; GRO P154/ 14 CW 1/3–1/4; R. Hutton, 'The Local Impact of the Tudor Reformation', in *The English Reformation Revised*, ed. C. Haigh (Cambridge, 1987), p. 125.

directed him to exhort them regularly to come to communion. These provisions reflect Cranmer's aversion to the way people ran 'from their seats to the altar, and from altar to altar . . . peeping, tooting and gazing at that thing which the priest held up in his hands'.[20] Furthermore, traditional practices associated with prayers for the dead, such as 'bidding the beads', that is, reading the roll of those in whose memory gifts had been made to the parish, were now omitted.[21] In addition, at least in the conforming parish of St Michael's, coals, incense and the taper were no longer used at Easter. None the less, this parish continued to provide for worship with the same conscientiousness as in the past, carrying out both new and old responsibilities, such as washing ornaments, mending surplices, and purchasing a new psalter.

Meanwhile, in the parish of Standish, near the city of Gloucester, more traditional practices persisted. For instance, the distribution of holy bread continued unabated, at least through November 1550. Each parishioner 'offered to the priestes handes ij^{d}in money every Sonneday and there was brought to the churche every Sonneday ij^d in bredd' for the 'holy loffe', as well, unless a parishioner 'did geve the holy loffe twise together . . . by reason wherof the first day he bryngethe but iij loffes to the churche, and the later day . . . [he] doith bryng iiij loffes to churche, because the iiijth loffe remayneth'.[22] Further, there is no indication that anyone in Standish saw anything wrong with this practice, although the Royal Injunctions promulgated three years earlier had sought to discourage it by directing the parish clergy to teach that anyone 'bearing about him holy bread' did so 'to the great peril and danger of his soul's health'. In addition, the Prayer Book of 1549 included a rubric ordering that 'in recompense [for the charges incurred in providing bread and wine for the communion] the Parishioners of every Parishe shall offer every Sonday . . . the juste valour and price of the holy lofe . . . to the use of theyr Pastours'. None the less, Bishop Wakeman did not include any enquiry concerning this prohibition in his visitation articles in 1548. Hence, at Standish and perhaps elsewhere the custom continued. The dispute which finally brought this practice to the attention of the authorities involved an individual shirking his responsibility, rather than any sense of local disapproval of the practice. In general, Bishop Wakeman seems to have turned a blind eye to those practices which were to be discouraged as harmful, but had not been expressly forbidden. His conformity led him to enforce the explicit prohibitions, but he saw no

---

[20] *Prayer Books*, p. 223; Duffy, *Stripping*, pp. 95–102, 125; T. Cranmer, *The Remains of Thomas Cranmer*, ed. H. Jenkyns (Oxford, 1833), p. 442. Cf. V. Reinburg, 'Liturgy and the Laity in Late Medieval and Reformation France', *SCJ* 23 (1992), pp. 526–47.

[21] *Prayer Books*, pp. 212–30; Duffy, *Stripping*, pp. 124–5.

[22] GRO GDR vol. VIII, p. 33.

need to go beyond that. Other traditional practices could therefore continue.[23] This may also explain some of the apparent differences in worship and imagery between 1547 and 1548. The royal visitors may have been more vigorous in detecting offending behaviour and images in 1547 than Bishop Wakeman would be a year later.

Meanwhile, most parishes continued conscientiously to perform the regular maintenance of their buildings and other possessions, including laying new tiles, and repairing church pews, bells and the clock.[24] Of course, there were exceptions, but most of the Gloucestershire laity still cared about their parishes, and tried, despite increased liturgical costs, resulting from purchasing books and modifying worship spaces, to keep their buildings and furnishings in good repair. The worship experience had changed, but the quality of the experience and lay commitment to the parish remained constant.

Not all regions of England, however, were as peaceful as Gloucestershire in 1549. Demanding a return to the old religion and complaining of excessive taxation and dearth, people in Devon and Cornwall rose up against the government. As Sir William Kingston had supported the Crown in 1536 at the time of the Pilgrimage of Grace, so now in 1549 his son, Sir Anthony Kingston, rode in support of Somerset. At first it appeared that Sir Anthony was just a zealous supporter of Protestantism anxious to restore order and Somerset's authority, and indeed he may have been; he did have John Reynolds, a Protestant priest in his service, preach to the royal troops involved in putting down the revolt. However, Sir Anthony soon gained a reputation for ruthlessness and cruelty, and his behaviour apparently did not change when he returned to the county. Two years later John Hooper, then Bishop of Gloucester, would have occasion to rebuke him for his immorality and 'wonton severity'. In response, Sir Anthony reportedly gave the bishop 'a blow on the cheek before all the people, and loaded him with abuse', for which he was ultimately fined £500 and required to do penance.[25] He may have wanted to appear to be a loyal supporter of the Crown and religion, but he had been corrupted by power.

Meanwhile, the king and Council were giving renewed precedence to the spread of Protestantism, and both Sir Anthony's actions and the Western Rising are evidence of the degree to which people in the localities recognised this. In both instances, actions were rhetorically linked with Protestantism; in one case in support of it, and in the other in opposition to

[23] *TRP*, vol. I, p. 400; GRO GDR vol. IV, pp. 7–10; *Prayer Books*, p. 230.
[24] At St Michael's in 1550 most of the parish expenditures were for such maintenance. GRO P154/14 CW 1/4.
[25] *L&P*, vol. XI, no. 580; Hooper, *Later Writings*, p. xxi; John ab Ulmis to Henry Bullinger, from Oxford, 4 December 1551, in *Original Letters*, p. 442.

it. The discourse of John Hiche, the schoolmaster in Tewkesbury, uttered in 1550 in defence of his actions, similarly underscores the point. He had been accused of mistreating his servant, Mabel, and found himself opposed by some of the most powerful people in the county, including Sir John Bridges, Sir Edmund Bridges, Sir Giles Poole, Sir Anthony Hungerford, Richard Pauncefoote, Hugh Westwood, Arthur Porter, William Reed and William Bridges. Reed had rescued Mabel after she had allegedly been severely beaten about the arms and shoulders. Hiche responded by filing a complaint of his own in the Court of Requests charging that Reed, along with William Bridges and several others, had attacked him as he walked to evensong. He did not, however, cast the incident as merely a case of assault; rather, he claimed that it was his Protestantism which had led to the attack. He began:

> Firste for Roberte Erean curate of the said Tewkesbury and a preachor auctorysed and your said orator have to theuttermost of theire powre, witt and discrecion, favored, maintayned and dyvulged the kinges grace procedynges and of long tyme reproved, abuses, frequented and used in the Church befor thextirpacyon of the detestable and most abhominable popysshe masse and papisticall ceremonyes, whear by they mirrored the implacable hatred and indygnacyon of the said gentlemen, in soo mooche that the said William Bridges dyvers and sundrye tymes laid wayte for the said curate and him twyse with his naked swoord chaced and drawe into his chambre / And also dyd beate ij other prestes for the lyke cause, which served under the said curate.

Hiche then went on to recount the attack he had suffered and his rescue by three men of Tewkesbury.[26] Thus, in his defence of his own actions he painted the entire affair as motivated by religious difference, presumably even the initial accusation that he had beaten his maidservant. Clearly, Hiche believed that he could improve his chances in court by presenting himself as a defender of reform and victim of religious persecution.

Despite evidence of the inculcation of the new religion, the progress of reform was still rather slow in Gloucestershire until the arrival of the radically Zwinglian John Hooper as Bishop in 1551; thereafter, it accelerated dramatically. There had been a long hiatus between John Wakeman's death on 6 December 1549 and Hooper's consecration on 8 March 1551, owing primarily to Hooper's refusal either to take the prescribed oath of obedience or to wear the requisite vestments. Hooper had previously described the Ordinal as promoting 'the kingdom of antichrist, especially in the form of the oath', since the latter required 'swearing by God, the saints, and the holy apostles'. This aspect of the disagreement was resolved quite promptly, and he was allowed to swear by God (only). However, the dispute over vestments could not be settled so easily, and it escalated into a

---

[26] PRO Req. 2/19/17.

struggle for control of the Reformation in England, involving Archbishop Cranmer, Bishop Nicholas Ridley of London, the king and the Council. Ultimately, the conflict was resolved, but not until Hooper had spent three weeks as a prisoner in the Fleet. Even then he would only agree to be consecrated in the requisite vestments with the proviso that he could still dispense with them on other, less ceremonial occasions.[27]

Following his long-awaited arrival in the diocese, however, Hooper wasted no time in beginning to reform the people and clergy. In a letter to Bullinger, written on 5 February 1550, he had lamented that the people, 'that many-headed monster, is still wincing [owing to the distress caused by reform]; partly through ignorance, and partly fascinated by the unveiglements of the bishops, and the malice and impiety of the mass-priests'.[28] Now he, as one of the bishops, could do something about both the 'mass-priests' and the 'many-headed monster', by preaching the word of God, and administering his diocese with the goal of vigorously promoting Protestantism among both the clergy and the laity. Hooper preached frequently, but, more importantly, he conducted an exhaustive visitation of his diocese and turned the diocesan consistory court into a virtual court of audience, presiding over nearly every session himself.

In the summer of 1551, in what may have been the most detailed set of visitation articles, injunctions and inquiries issued during the sixteenth century, Bishop Hooper addressed issues ranging from diligent preaching and teaching based exclusively on scripture, to the removal of altars and the need to avoid certain language in the religious preambles of wills.[29] Items promoted justification by faith alone, and the efficacy of praying directly to the Godhead, rather than through the saints, and Hooper urged the clergy 'faithfully and diligently [to] teach and instruct the people committed unto their charge' in these matters.[30] Other articles addressed aspects of public worship, as did that which declared that 'the sacraments are instituted by Christ to be used, and not to be gazed upon', and so, 'as many as be present ought to communicate, or to depart in the time of the Administration'.[31] Adoration of the sacrament had been discouraged in both editions of the Prayer Book, but was now explicitly prohibited in the diocese of Gloucester. Furthermore, the scriptures were always to be read in such a way 'that all the people may understand the treasures, and unspeakable riches of Gods lawes and promises', and, to that end, if the

---

[27] Lambeth Registrum Cranmer, fos. 105, 332–3; GCL Hockaday Abstracts, vol. XXXI, 1549; vol. XXXIII, 1551 (unpaginated); John Hooper to Henry Bullinger, from London, 27 March 1550, in *Original Letters*, vol. I, pp. 81, 81n; Hooper, *Early Writings*, p. 479; Primus, *Vestments*, pp. 61–4; G. Burnet, *The History of the Reformation*, vol. II, p. 286.

[28] Hooper to Bullinger, from London, 5 February 1550, in *Original Letters*, vol. I, p. 76.

[29] 'Visitation Booke', pp. 1–16.   [30] 'Visitation Booke', p. 2.

[31] 'Visitation Booke', pp. 3–4.

church was constructed so that the minister could not be heard in the nave, or if he had 'so small and soft a brest or voice that he cannot be heard', then he was to move into the body of the church for the readings of scripture and the psalms.[32] The interiors of churches were also to be altered: parishioners were to

take downe and remove out of their churches and chapells . . . tabernacles, tombes, sepulchres, tables, footstooles, rood-lofts, and such other monuments, signs, tokens, reliques, leavings, and remembrances where such superstition, idolls, images, or other provocation of idolatry have been used . . . And to take downe all the chappells, closetts, partitions, and separations within . . . [their] churches, whereas any masse hath been said, or any idoll, image or relique used to be honoured.[33]

In addition, when any glass needed to be replaced, Hooper directed that the new glass was to be clear, rather than painted, unless it was painted with flowers or foliage.[34] Most significantly for parish worship, he exhorted the people 'to erect and set up the Lords board, after the forme of an honest table, decently covered in such place as shall be thought most meete, so that the ministers and communicants may be seene heard and understood of all the people there being present'. Furthermore, his instructions specified that parishioners were not only to 'take down and abolish all the altars' in the church, but also to remove any stairs that went to any altar and the corresponding elevated area where the altar had stood. St Michael's churchwardens had the earth removed from their church in response to this directive. This was arguably Hooper's most radical article. Nicholas Ridley, first as Bishop of Rochester and then as Bishop of London, had issued a similar directive regarding the replacement of altars with common tables. In fact, the language used in his London Injunctions in 1550 is almost identical to that used by Hooper in Gloucester in 1551; however, Hooper was alone in his insistence that the stairs leading to any altar, and therefore the elevated area, be removed as well.[35]

Nor were parish liturgical practices the only aspects of lay piety to be placed under Bishop Hooper's microscope; he was concerned with all facets of lay religion, both public and private. Thus, mid-wives were not to utter invocations to saints or use any 'superstitious meanes' while assisting in childbirth; parishioners were not only to learn the Ten Commandments, they were to be 'diligent willing and glad' to do so; men and women were

---

[32] 'Visitation Booke', p. 7.   [33] 'Visitation Booke', p. 9.

[34] Perhaps this directive helps explain the survival of the stained glass at Fairford. There was no requirement in these visitation articles and injunctions that glass containing images be removed. The only prohibition pertained to new glass and images painted on walls; the latter were to be defaced. 'Visitation Booke', p. 11. See also chapter 2.

[35] 'Visitation Booke', pp. 6, 9; Hooper to Bullinger, from London, 27 March 1550, in *Original Letters*, vol. I, p. 79; 'Ridley's Injunctions for London Diocese, 1550', in *VAI*, vol. II, pp. 243–4.

not to be permitted to keep 'any Latin Primers, beades, images, reliques or any other monuments of superstition', even in their own houses; people were not to criticise the current order of divine service, while lauding the old way; and no one was to use the will preamble 'with this stile, I commend my soule unto God, to our blessed Lady and the Saints of heaven, which is injurious to God, and perilous as well for the salvation of the dead, as dangerous unto the maker'.[36]

Bishop Hooper had a clear sense of the religious beliefs and practices he found acceptable. His most fervent desire was that Gloucestershire, and ultimately all of England, would come to know and accept what he believed to be the true religion of God. Hooper's theology had been influenced primarily by Zwingli. After probably being educated at Oxford and serving for a short time as a Cistercian monk, he had fled England in 1539 because his beliefs were too radically Protestant for the times. He had lived on the continent for the next ten years, spending at least the period from 1547 to 1549 in Zurich, where his theology continued to develop under the tutelage of Heinrich Bullinger, Zwingli's successor. When Hooper returned to England, he quickly became an outspoken opponent of the moderate Protestantism then being introduced.[37] In an effort to promote the true religion as he understood it, Hooper moved beyond his inquiries into lay practices, aspects of parish worship, and the actions of the clergy. In addition, he surveyed the clergy to determine their fitness for the preaching ministry, which was so essential to the spread and sustenance of the Protestant faith. He ordered all diocesan priests to demonstrate that they could recite and provide the scriptural basis for the Lord's Prayer, the Ten Commandments and the Articles of Faith (or Apostles Creed), as well as identifying the author of the Lord's Prayer.[38] The results revealed that of the 312 priests examined, just under 20 per cent (65 priests) were judged to be learned, with 4 of those serving more than one parish each. The knowledgeable pluralists were Hugh Whittington, rector of St John Baptist, Gloucester and Wollaston, John Williams, vicar of Holy Trinity, Gloucester, and Painswick, rector of Beverstone with Kingscote, and chancellor of the diocese, Laurence Gase, rector of the neighbouring parishes of Colne St Denis and Colne Rogers, and William Ramsey, vicar of Chipping Sodbury

---

[36] 'Visitation Booke', pp. 9, 12, 16.
[37] Hooper to Bullinger, from Strasbourg, 27 January [1546], *Original Letters*, pp. 33–5; C. Nevinson, 'Biographical Notices', in Hooper, *Later Writings*, pp. vii–xii; D. G. Newcombe, 'The Life and Theological Thought of John Hooper, Bishop of Gloucester and Worcester, 1551–1553' (University of Cambridge, PhD, 1990), pp. 54–6. Primus seems to have dated Hooper's flight from England after the latter's conversion to Zwinglianism; however, according to his letter to Bullinger, Hooper was introduced to that set of theological beliefs after he reached Strasbourg. Primus, *Vestments*, pp. 3–5.
[38] 'Visitation Booke', p. 17.

and Old Sodbury (also neighbouring parishes).[39] The few parishes with learned clergy were widely dispersed throughout the diocese and varied greatly in size, from Tewkesbury with 1,600 communicants to Welford with 44.[40] Another 5 parishes, ranging in size from 40 to 1,000 communicants each, had two resident priests, who were qualified to preach and teach the basic precepts of Protestant Christianity.[41]

The majority of the parishes in the diocese, however, were less fortunate. The most common reply to Hooper's interrogatories, given by over a third of the respondents, indicated adequate knowledge of the Lord's Prayer, combined with knowing that there were Ten Commandments and that they could be found in Exodus 20. However, the typical respondent was not able to recite them, and, while he could demonstrate a knowledge of the Apostles Creed, he was unable to prove it in scripture. Others knew only a little more: some were able to recite the Apostles Creed, but could not prove it in scripture, and others were able to recite it only imperfectly, but knew where to find the supporting passages in the Bible. Some historians have pointed out how appalling it is that so many priests knew even less. Fifty-five per cent (172) could not name the author of the Lord's Prayer or were not able to repeat the Ten Commandments.[42] More importantly, however, these so-called 'religious leaders' did not have as much knowledge as their parishioners were supposed to demonstrate before taking communion. Additionally, these clergy certainly lacked the knowledge needed to expound on scripture.[43] Bishop Hooper had a difficult road ahead of him.

Though Hooper's over-arching objective was the Protestantisation of the laity, he justifiably saw the parish clergy as important agents in that process; hence the survey. But he also provided for further study by the

---

[39] This analysis is based on 'Visitation Booke', pp. 17–77; and GCL Hockaday Abstracts, vol. XXXIII, 1551 (unpaginated). Cf. J. Gairdner, 'Bishop Hooper's Visitation of Gloucester', *EHR* 19 (1904), pp. 98–121. Every historian who has analysed the results of this clergy survey has produced slightly different numbers for most categories of response, which is not surprising given the organisation of the returns, and especially the difficulty in accurately identifying all pluralists. Newcombe, 'Life and Theological Thought of John Hooper', pp. 268–77; Gairdner, 'Bishop Hooper's Visitation of Gloucester', pp. 98–100; Hooper, *Later Writings*, p. 151.

[40] 'Visitation Booke', pp. 18, 28, 49, 50, 62, 73; 'Chantry Certificates', p. 281; BL Harleian MS 594, fo. 232v.

[41] 'Visitation Booke', pp. 46, 52, 61, 69, 70.

[42] Twenty-nine priests (9 per cent) did not know who first uttered the Lord's Prayer, and twenty-seven of those also could not recite the Ten Commandments. Newcombe counted thirty-eight who did not know the author of the Lord's Prayer, while Gairdner and Nevinson each tallied thirty-one. Newcombe, 'Life and Theological Thought of John Hooper', p. 272; Gairdner, 'Bishop Hooper's Visitation of Gloucester', p. 98; Hooper, *Later Writings*, p. 151.

[43] 'Visitation Booke', p. 8. Phillipa Tudor makes a similar point with regard to catechising the young. P. Tudor, 'Religious Instruction for Children and Adolescents in the Early English Reformation', *JEH* 35 (1984), p. 410.

clergy even before he knew the results of his examination of their knowledge. The Visitation Injunctions which called for the survey also commanded the clergy to study specific portions of the Bible, and called for quarterly meetings of all the clergy with the bishop or his representative 'for the determination of such questions, and doubtful matters in religion, as may happen to stand and be in controversie betweene men learned and them'.[44] Thus, a scheme of continuing education for diocesan priests was already in place when, through his exceptionally thorough visitation, Bishop Hooper gained substantial information about their level of religious training and knowledge.

The visitation also revealed priests who were still promoting the old religion, and in characteristic fashion Hooper moved quickly to correct the detected errors. Thus, in the space of six weeks, he warned nineteen priests to cease all superstitious practices, and to teach the contrary to their parishioners. Except for the fact that three priests judged very learned were among those ordered to reform their superstitious ways, this group proportionally represents the various levels of learning revealed by the clergy survey. Those clinging to the old religion included priests from all levels of learning and knowledge found within the diocese.[45] Robert Hodges, the curate of Sandhurst, received special attention. He was ordered to declare publicly the need to abolish superstition in his parish. Meanwhile, Roger Wynter, rector of Staunton and Wollaston in the Forest of Dean, was ordered 'from hensefurthe [not to] preache nor teache any transubstantiation or any reall or corporall presens of Christ to be in the sacrament', and, further, to speak out in his parish against pilgrims, relics and all sorts of superstitions.[46] In some cases Hooper went further still, depriving John Hyckes of Cromhall, Robert Sperrie of Charfield and William Horsam of Erlingham as a result of similar, but more serious, deficiencies.[47] Three others were accused of violating unspecified portions of the Royal Injunctions, two of whom, the rector of Hampnet and the vicar of Turkdean, were deprived.[48] Others previously accused of superstition, like Henry Dawkes, rector of Aston Somerville, and Simon Sowtharne, rector of Hinton, however, were spared when they re-appeared and certified the requisite corrections, and had their cases dismissed. In

[44] The clergy were to study Romans the first quarter, Deuteronomy the second, the Gospel of St Matthew the third, and Genesis the fourth. 'Visitation Booke', p. 8.

[45] GRO GDR vol. VI, pp. 45–8, 81–3, 107–8, 112, 152, 166; 'Visitation Booke', pp. 38, 45, 49.

[46] GRO GDR vol. VI, pp. 6, 50, 96.

[47] Hyckes refused to accept the doctrine of justification by faith, Sparrie refused to read the Bible aloud, and Horsam could not recite the Apostles Creed or the Ten Commandments. GRO GDR vol. VI, pp. 88–9, 92.

[48] GRO GDR vol. VI, p. 102; 'Visitation Booke', pp. 48, 52.

response to earlier mandates, they had seen to the destruction of their parish altars and had performed other stipulated reforming acts. Similarly, Walter Turbot of Yanworth appeared and certified that all superstitious things had been removed from his church as ordered by the bishop.[49] A few lay people who preferred the old religion were called to account for their behaviour as well. John Tailour of Iron Acton was accused of possessing unspecified church goods and jewels previously belonging to his parish church; John Boxe had allegedly shown contempt for the king's authority; and a number of individuals were accused of superstitious practices.[50]

Just as his visitation was characterised by vigour and thoroughness, so too was Hooper's involvement with the diocesan consistory court, where he confronted an entrenched, complacent hierarchy, presided over by John Williams, rector of one parish, vicar of two, and the first and only chancellor the diocese had ever known. Thus, Hooper's decision to preside was both a response to the presence of the less zealous and less godly Williams and a result of his own desire for vigorous reform. He heard all manner of cases, ranging from sexual incontinence and defamation, to sorcery and lack of knowledge of the Ten Commandments.[51]

Hooper placed great emphasis on the Ten Commandments, and not just as a test of clerical knowledge or worthiness to receive communion. Writing from exile in 1548, he had exhorted his readers to 'diligently' learn and 'religiously observe' the Ten Commandments, which 'teach abundantly and sufficiently in few words, how to know God, to follow virtue, and to come to eternal life'. Everyone was 'to know as perfectly these commandments as he knoweth his owne name', for 'without the knowledge and obedience of this law no person in the world can justly and conveniently serve in his vocation or condition of life, of what degre soever he be'.[52] Here Hooper was articulating one of the central tenets of Zwinglian Protestantism. The Ten Commandments were at the heart of the reformers' concept of sin and Christian ethics, and they were a regular feature of public worship and a key element in the catechising process.[53] Therefore, in his visitation injunctions, Hooper instructed the clergy of the diocese to require all potential communicants to recite the Ten Commandments, along with the creed, before receiving communion, and he directed the laity 'to make open confession of the Ten Commandments, the Articles of the Faith, and the *Pater Noster* in English' every Christmas Day, Easter Day,

---

[49] GRO GDR vol. VI, pp. 45, 103, 109; 'Visitation Booke', p. 40.
[50] Hockaday Abstracts, vols. XXXIV–VI, 1551 (unpaginated).
[51] F. D. Price, 'The Administration of the Diocese of Gloucester', pp. 78–99.
[52] J. Hooper, 'A Declaration of the Ten Holy Commandments of Almighty God', in Hooper, *Early Writings*, pp. 255–82.
[53] J. Bossy, *Christianity in the West, 1400–1700* (Oxford and New York, 1985), pp. 129–30; E. Cameron, *The European Reformation* (Oxford, 1991), pp. 115, 397–8.

Whitsunday, and the first Sunday in September, 'so that . . . the people may come to the knowledge of God in Christ, of the which if they be ignorant [out] of negligence or contempt they cannot be saved'.[54]

Matters considered by the consistory court, as well as punishments rendered, shed further light on local manifestations of the primacy Hooper gave to the Ten Commandments. On 10 August 1551, John Trigg of Dursley was ordered 'upon Sonneday next cummynge . . . [to] bee in his sherte onelye standyng upon a fourme and there . . . openly saye that I suffer this penance by cawse I can not say oon of the cammaundementes of allmyghtie God but I am more like an ethnick than a christen man'.[55] Lack of such knowledge could also cause significant distress and generate conflict, as had occurred a month earlier at Hardwick when John Jenyns, priest, was teaching some children the catechism. '[John] Hollboroughe beyng present than and there a litull girle than recityng the catechisme the saide curate praysed the girle and so did this Hollboroughe.' After that, Jenyns asked Hollboroughe 'whather he could declare the x commaundementes, and the articles of the fayth with the lordes prayer'? Hollboroughe answered: '"What hast thow to doo [with me?]" And upon this occasion than and there revyled the said curate.'[56] The Ten Commandments could also be used in punishing individuals, and Hooper often employed such penance. Three men from a parish in Winchcombe Deanery were accused in August 1551 of disturbing divine services, and as punishment they were to learn and recite in public the Ten Commandments and the Apostles Creed. Two of them were dismissed when they returned to court and recited the Ten Commandments reasonably well, though not perfectly; the third disappeared from the records.[57] In October of the same year, the churchwardens of Wollaston were ordered to commit the Ten Commandments to memory and to destroy the images remaining in their church, the presence of the offending images apparently having been the reason for their penance.[58]

Although Hooper could certainly not be faulted for the thoroughness and vigour which characterised his administration, coercion was not an efficacious means of achieving true conversion to the new religion. That would come with the acceptance of the beliefs of Edwardian Protestantism through knowledge and education. Hooper could force outward conformity, but he needed the help of the Gloucestershire clergy to achieve his ultimate goal, and they lacked the requisite knowledge to do their part. Therefore, while Hooper's episcopate was characterised by vigorous en-

---

[54] 'Visitation Booke', p. 8.   [55] GRO GDR vol. VI, p. 53.
[56] GRO GDR vol. VI, p. 41.   [57] GRO GDR vol. VI, pp. 64, 91.
[58] GRO GDR vol. VI, p. 96.

forcement of Protestant faith and practice, the results fell well short of creating the godly diocese for which he had striven.

The beliefs of lay people revealed in their wills show that while individuals may have backed away from overt expressions of traditional faith during Hooper's episcopate, they did not move to embrace Protestantism. In her will, written in February 1551, Elizabeth Lane, a widow of Sandhurst, bequeathed her soul 'to Almyghty God to our Lady and to all the hoole Company of Heaven'. One of her witnesses was Robert Hodges, her vicar and 'ghostly father', and she included a bequest of 4d to the 'Mother Church'.[59] Although the traditional pre-Reformation bequests to the Mother Church (i.e. the cathedral) and references to 'my ghostly father' continued through the remainder of Edward's reign, this may have been the last Edwardian will in Gloucestershire to include that most traditional of all soul bequests. Here, then, we can see the direct effect of Hooper's explicit prohibition of that particular will preamble. Just six months after Elizabeth Lane's will, in September 1551, the will of Jone Davis of Nimpsfield began:

I commytt me unto God and to hys mercye trustyng without eny dowett or mysstrust in his grace and the meryttes of Jhesus Chryst and bye the virtue off hys passyon and off hys resurrexyon off boddye and soll: For I belev thatt my redemer lyveyth and yn the last daye I shall ryse owett off the yearth and yn my flesshe shall see my savyowre thys my hope ys laid up yn my bosom.[60]

This was an exact copy of the opening paragraph of William Tracy's will of 1531, which had been printed in four editions (one each in 1535 and 1546, and two in 1548).[61] A few other wills similarly espoused the new religion, either by adapting Tracy's will to their purposes or by choosing or creating other distinctly Protestant statements.[62] However, the juxtaposition of these two wills is misleading. Forbidding the use of a traditional form did not ensure either its replacement with Protestant statements or the concomitant acceptance of Hooper's 'true religion' even though a few testators were again making notably Protestant declarations of faith for the first time since 1539.

---

[59] GRO Wills 1551/16.   [60] GRO Wills 1551/62.

[61] *The Testament of Master Wylliam Tracie*, STC 24167; 'The Testament of W. Tracie Expounded by W. Tindall', in *Wyclyffes Wycket: Whyche he Made in King Rycards Days the Second in the Yere of our Lorde God M.CCC.XLV* (London, 1546), STC 25590; 'The Testament of W. Tracie Expounded by W. Tindall and J. Frythe', in *Uvicklieffes Wicket. Faythfully over Seene and Corrected* (London, 1548), STC 25591; *The Union of the Two Noble and Illustrate Famelies of Lancastre and Yorke* (London, 1548), STC 12721, fos. 211–11v. William Tracy's will included the first explicitly Protestant formula to be used as a guide by other English testators. Cf. 'Wills as Propaganda', pp. 425–31, *passim*.

[62] Cf. GRO Wills 1547/98, 1551/62, 1552/9, 1552/10, 1552/13, 1552/30, 1552/43.

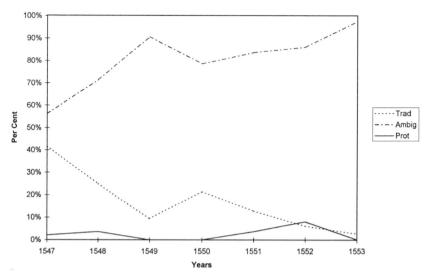

Figure 4.1   Non-elite will preambles (1547–1553)

An overwhelming preference for ambiguous statements dominated Edward's reign in Gloucestershire under both Wakeman and Hooper. Even elite testators preferred ambiguous declarations of faith in their wills, although by a smaller margin. From 1544 to 1546 testators' expressions of faith, no matter what their position in society, had been approximately equally divided between traditional and ambiguous religious preambles. This pattern began to change immediately after Edward's accession, with more and more people choosing ambiguous formulas in preference to the more traditional statement, and Hooper's appointment to the bishopric in 1551 may have actually accelerated the trend.[63] However, among the gentry more people proclaimed their adherence to the new faith than did those among their more humble neighbours, with approximately 23 per cent of the elite Edwardian testators including Protestant statements in contrast to just 6 per cent of the non-elite wills.[64] A few people below the

[63] See Figure 4.1 and Appendix A. This is based on the analysis of a sample of 280 wills, 138 from women and 142 from men, with 47 traditional preambles, 225 ambiguous and 8 distinctly Protestant, drawn from approximately 1,035 extant wills written between 1547 and July 1553 and proved in the diocese of Gloucester. Thus, assuming the highest possible variability of the sample from the population, the results of the analysis will be within 3.07 per cent of that for the entire population at the 95 per cent confidence level. Schofield, 'Sampling in Historical Research', pp. 154–61.

[64] See Figure 4.2 and Appendix A. A total of just thirty-five wills survive from Edward's reign, too small a number for statistical significance, However, when all elite and non-elite wills from the period from 1541 to 1580 are analysed, the greater proportion of gentry espousing Protestantism is significant with a chi-square value of 15.79 with 4 degrees of freedom.

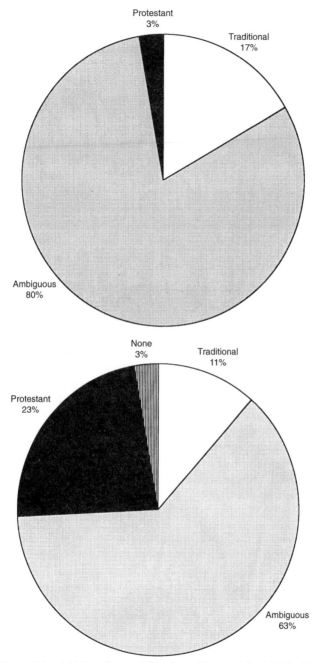

Figure 4.2   (a) Non-elite and (b) elite will preambles (1547–1553)

level of the gentry were also making Protestant declarations, as had Jone Davis, but their numbers are not significant among the lower levels of society, while there are too few extant elite wills from Edward's reign to make any generalisations concerning the county gentry.[65] More people were choosing to state their faith in terms similar to those employed by Thomas Bower of Berkeley in 1547 and Agnes Walwyn of Bourton-on-the Water in 1553, both of whom had employed the most ambiguous soul bequest of all: 'I bequeth my soull unto almyghty God'.[66] Others, such as William Whitfield and Alice Pycher of Thornbury, bequeathed their soul 'unto allmyghty God trustyng by the meryttes off crystes passyon to inherrytte the kyngdum of hevyne'. This statement was still equivocal, but more elaborate than that used by Bower, Walwyn and many others.[67]

The more detailed, but still ambiguous, soul bequests employed by Whitfield and Pycher are but one example among many of the veritable explosion of different and more complex preamble formulas employed during the ascendancy of Edwardian Protestantism. The trend which had begun slowly during the last years of Henry's reign was gaining momentum, and not just among those opting for ambiguous statements of faith, but among testators expressing a wide range of beliefs. Most of the Protestant will preambles used in Edwardian Gloucestershire were unique or at least somewhat idiosyncratic. This probably reflected the value Protestants gave to the intellectual side of their faith, over and above the ritualistic side. A scripturally based faith used reason and discernment as means of conversion, and articulation of that faith was a key part of the process. William Tracy's testament provided the pattern for one other will in Gloucestershire during this time, that of Jone Tymmes of Sutton-under-Brailes.[68] Others espousing the new religion may have used phrases from Tracy's testament, but some either found other guides or they or their scribes created original statements. In 1547, Margerie Bedyll of Dorsington committed her soul 'into the mercyfull handes of Allmyghty God trustyng withowt any dowght or mistrust that by the merites of Christis passion that I have and shall

---

[65] Only 3 per cent (8 wills in the sample of 280 from Edward's reign) specifically rejected traditional salvation theology or expressed unequivocally Protestant beliefs.

[66] GRO Wills 1547/163, 1553/3.

[67] The wills of William Whitfield and Alice Pycher were written in 1547 and 1551, respectively, and their identical and slightly distinctive language indicates the possibility of a common scribe, although in neither case is he identified in the document. (Such identification was not common in Gloucestershire prior to the mid-1550s.) GRO Wills 1547/169, 1551/5. A number of wills of testators residing in the Vale of Berkeley employed this same formula, however, providing further evidence for the presence of another scribe with his own distinctive preamble formula, like those in Tewkesbury and Cirencester. See Appendix A.

[68] The two 'Tracy' wills were written at opposite ends of the county, one in the south and the other in the north-east corner. GRO Wills 1551/66, 1552/43.

[have] for gyvenest of my sinnes'. Five years later, Hugh Hulles of Upper Slaughter declared:

I comyt my soulle as farr forthe as in me lygth into the handes of the lyvinge God whom I beseche of his infinyt mercye to accept and receve into thandes of hys mercey, my bodye . . . I beleve shalbe reysyde up from the yerth. at the last day of judgment, and unityd to my soll and so to be with God everlastingly in the kingdome of heven, and that by the only meryts and deservinge of our only redemer Jesus Christ offerid upon the crose, and not by any worke or works of myne or of any other for me, savyng the only worke of Christ aforsayd.[69]

In the wills of both Margerie Bedyll and Hugh Hulles we hear echoes of William Tracy, as Margerie Bedyll had no 'dowght or mistrust', and Hugh Hulles included Job 19:26 and declared that his salvation would not be 'by any work or works' of his or anyone else's. However, neither Protestants nor those opting for ambiguous statements had a monopoly on variety in will preambles. Isabel Dunnynges of Lydney employed a formula in 1548 that was quickly gaining favour among those who clung to the old religion, when she bequeathed her soul 'to Almyghty God, and ower Lady and all the sayntes in hevyn to pray for me'. Using another new formula a year later, Katharine Frere of Erlingham gave her soul to almighty God, 'to be sociate withe the celestial companye in heaven'. [70] In all, the number of distinctly different preamble formulas increased by over 40 per cent between 1547 and 1552.[71]

Charitable bequests in wills in Edwardian Gloucestershire changed even more than religious statements, as old reasons for such provisions were forbidden and old objects of devotion were removed. Testators may still have hoped that their gifts would result in prayers for their souls, as had traditionally been the case, but belief in purgatory had been declared to be contrary to officially condoned religious doctrine. Before the Reformation the poor who became the beneficiaries of a testator's largesse were explicitly obligated to pray for the soul of their benefactor, and it is quite possible that, by employing the same language as before but merely omitting the clause requesting prayers, some testators still hoped that their wish for intercessions would be recognised without being explicitly stated. In any event, those leaving wills reflected official policy by seldom articulating the desire for prayer for their souls and the souls of their loved

---

[69] GRO Wills 1547/98, 1552/30; *Prayer Books*, p. 269.
[70] GRO Wills 1548/35, 1549/126.
[71] This analysis employs the methodology described in Appendix A and is based on the wills written from 1547 to 1549 and 1551 to 1552, which are included in the systematic sample of lay wills proved in the diocese of Gloucester. The sample includes 118 wills from 1547 to 1549, 62 written by women and 56 by men, and 109 wills from 1551 to 1552, 52 by women and 57 by men.

ones during Edward's reign.[72] Just 5 per cent requested that a priest or priests sing for their souls or that the poor who received their gifts pray for them.

None the less, bequests to the poor, especially small, ritualistic gifts of money, bread or drink, increased substantially during this period in the wills of ordinary people, jumping from the Henrician level of just under 7 per cent to an average of over 25 per cent through Edward's reign. (Meanwhile, over 40 per cent of the gentry wills contained some provision for the poor.) This was consistent with the pattern of giving to the poor seen in the wills of testators in the diocese of Lincoln at that time. In the archdeaconries of both Lincoln and Huntingdon bequests to the poor jumped from 6 and 2 per cent respectively, to 30 per cent between 1545 and 1550. This increased giving may well have been due to the fact that bequests to the poor were the only pre-Reformation act of charity to continue to be condoned by Protestants, as Eamon Duffy has suggested. In the absence of other options, at least this act was still available to those holding on to traditional beliefs, and thus they consolidated their charitable bequests, with the poor being the beneficiaries. Additionally, such gifts were not the exclusive purview of the old religion, but were also promoted by Protestants. Such giving was even encouraged with renewed energy, and facilitated by the presence in each parish church of the statutory poor box.[73] Other small ritualistic bequests, namely, those designated for civic or municipal uses and those intended for the use of the parish, appeared much less frequently in wills written during this period than they had in those written under Henry. Gifts, such as those for roads and bridges, dropped slightly from just under 15 per cent to an average of approximately 10 per cent between 1547 and 1553. Parish bequests, on the other hand, dropped substantially over the same period, as only 15 per cent of all testators left anything to their parish church, compared with nearly 65 per cent during the previous 6 years. The prohibitions on lights, side altars and 'bidding the beads', as well as the campaign to remove all imagery, clearly had an effect on individual testators' final gifts, as they turned their attention elsewhere when making their wills, at least for the time being.

Parishes undoubtedly felt the financial impact of the reduction in bequests; however, the main reason parishes were having difficulty meeting their expenses at this time was the increase in the cost of worship rather than the decrease in gifts from the dead. Following Bishop Hooper's visitation, churches were to eliminate all decoration and any furniture

---

[72] See Appendix B.
[73] Duffy, *Stripping*, p. 505; Bowker, *The Henrician Reformation*, p. 177; K. Wrightson and D. Levine, 'Death in Wickham', in *Famine, Disease and the Social Order in Early Modern Society*, ed. J. Walter and R. Schofield (Cambridge, 1989), pp. 164–5.

which evoked now-forbidden beliefs, and were to eliminate them in an orderly fashion, that is, by paying for their removal. Furthermore, in addition to the requisite books and Bible essential for godly worship, each parish was to have an appropriate stand for the Bible, a communion table in place of the altar, and if there was not one already, a well-placed pulpit for preaching the gospel. Each of these requirements had an associated cost. Thus, in a conscientious parish such as St Michael's an increasing proportion of parish expenses went to satisfy changing liturgical needs. The removal of earth from the chancel in preparation for the communion table was but the most dramatic of a long list of similarly motivated expenditures made in response to the directives in 'Bishop Hooper's Visitation Booke'. The communion table had to be built, the church whitewashed, the rood loft removed, and a new Bible and the *Paraphrases* purchased. Fortunately for those parishes willing to part with the vestiges of the old religion who had not depleted their inventory earlier, there was an additional, one-time-only, source of revenue: the sale of church goods. Now, faced with an immediate need for more money, St Michael's divested itself of items worth over £27, by selling church goods which a conforming parish no longer needed to prominent parishioners.[74] Through such actions, St Michael's and other similarly inclined parishes would have been able to meet the mounting expenses which resulted from the advent of Edwardian Protestantism overlaid with Bishop Hooper's particular additional demands, and provide a suitable setting for the exercise of Hooper's 'true religion'. This strategy also enabled parishes to thwart the planned confiscation of such items by the Crown and keep the proceeds from their sale in local hands.[75]

Edward's reign, and with it Edwardian Protestantism, came to an abrupt end with the king's death on 6 July 1553, but in the brief span of six-and-a-half years much had changed. Religion in England had moved from being a mix of the old and the new, with the emphasis on the old, to a form of Protestantism which gave even Bishop Hooper reason to hope for 'true reform' in England. The reign had begun with a gradual but definite shift toward the new religion in official religious policy, epitomised by the Chantries Act of 1547, the *Order of Communion* of 1548, and the *Book of Common Prayer* of 1549. In Gloucestershire during those early years, Bishop Wakeman's episcopal style had been appropriate for the archbishop's strategy of gradual reform. The second half of the reign, on the other hand, was characterised by a much more forceful and uncompromising brand of Protestantism, and John Hooper, then Bishop

---

[74] Items sold included a silver spoon, 'the lentyne clothe', several copes, the timber from the rood loft and from St Anne's Chapel, another complete chapel, and the old pulpit. GRO P154/14 CW 1/5.

[75] Dickens, *Reformation*, p. 283.

of Gloucester, was well-suited to promote these additional steps toward 'true religion'. The parishes and people, meanwhile, had not been so quick to switch to Protestantism. True, some parishes revamped their interiors, as did St Michael's, and some individuals residing in widely scattered parts of the county included strong and clear assertions of the new faith in their wills. However, other parishes seem to have done as little as possible to conform to the liturgical and iconoclastic requirements of the day, and a majority of the lay people making wills opted for the safe middle ground of ambiguous preambles. Furthermore, the Gloucestershire gentry did not exert leadership with respect to religion, either traditional or reformed. Although they may have publicly eschewed declarations or actions in support of the old religion, the gentry, like their less illustrious neighbours, chose religious ambiguity in most instances. Even Sir Anthony Kingston's response to the Western Rising in 1549 seems to have been motivated more by his lust for power than by his religious beliefs. The majority of the lay people of the diocese of Gloucester, whatever their social position, resisted the new religion. Some resisted for deeply held theological reasons, but more resisted because they preferred the familiar over the new. Thus, following the king's death in 1553, most would have welcomed the return to the public practices and private devotions of the old religion. In spite of a vigorous, activist bishop, the new religion had a long road ahead before full acceptance.

5

A return to the old religion
(1553–1558)

Our king has been removed from us by reason of our sins, to the very great peril of our church. His sister Mary has succeeded, whom I pray God always to aid by his Holy Spirit, that she may reign and govern in all respects to the glory of his name. The altars are again set up throughout the kingdom; private masses are frequently celebrated in many quarters; the true worship of God, true invocation, the right use of the sacraments, are all done away with; divine things are trodden under foot, and human things have the pre-eminence. May God be present with his church, for the sake of his only Son Jesus Christ! . . . In haste, from prison, at London. Sept. 3, 1553.[1]

Mary's succession to the throne following Edward VI's death on 6 July 1553 may not have been either automatic or immediate; however, she had claimed the Crown by 19 July.[2] Bishop Hooper, who had supported her despite the future religious implications of her rule, was arrested and committed to the Fleet on 1 September 1553.[3] Two days later he wrote to Henry Bullinger in Zurich to express his fears and prayers for religion in England. Much was changing very quickly, as Mary and her advisors moved to annul the Protestant innovations of the previous twenty years, remove its leading advocates, and restore Catholicism.

Thus, during the first years of Mary's reign there was an abrupt and dramatic swing in official policy from the most reformed version of Protestantism ever embodied in official English religion to a form of Catholicism which would include full restoration of the mass and obedience to the Pope. This fundamental change affected the episcopate, the parishes and ultimately the people of Gloucestershire. The radical Protestant John Hooper was replaced as bishop by the ardent Catholic James Brookes and parishes replaced or retrieved vestments, church plate and

---

[1] John Hooper to Henry Bullinger, from prison, 3 September 1553, in *Original Letters*, vol. I, pp. 100–1.

[2] Twenty-four men from the city of Gloucester were among those who supported Mary's efforts to gain the throne. GRO GBR 2/1, fo. 234.

[3] *Original Letters*, vol. I, p. 100n.

service books. Meanwhile, lay people either welcomed the return to the old religion, adamantly asserted the truth and correctness of the new in the face of possible death or exile, or dutifully conformed to yet another series of changes. However, most welcomed the restoration of Catholicism.

Bishop John Hooper had not only been one of the hottest of the Edwardian Protestants, but also an effective administrator. Most parishes and many individuals had felt the impact of his episcopate. Within two months of Edward's death, he was gone, to be replaced by the learned, articulate and religiously conservative master of Balliol College, Oxford, James Brookes. Hooper had opted not to flee, choosing instead a martyr's death; however, he would spend a significant amount of time in prison before his execution. He was held for three months in 'close prison' in the Fleet, and then, apparently through the good offices of Joan Wilkinson, a widow and gentlewoman of Gloucestershire and London, he was allowed to leave his room for meals. He was deprived of his see on 15 March 1554, and sentenced on 29 January 1555. His return to Gloucester to be executed was marked by a reunion with key individuals he had known while serving as bishop. He stayed in the home of Robert and Agnes Ingram and was officially received by the sheriffs of Gloucester, one of whom was the Protestant former mayor William Bond. Bond's warm welcome was particularly heartening to Hooper. The commissioners charged with carrying out Hooper's execution included Sir John Lord Chandos (Lieutenant of the Tower), his son, Sir Edmund Bridges, and Sir Anthony Kingston. Kingston, whom Hooper had chastised several years earlier for his 'wonton cruelty', visited Hooper the night before the execution and tried to persuade him to abjure and save his life, asserting that 'life is sweet, and death is bitter'. Hooper responded by thanking him for his 'friendly counsel, although it be not so friendly as I could have wished', and then went on to reaffirm his willingness to suffer and die for God's truth.[4] He was burned just outside the gates of Gloucester Cathedral eight days after his sentencing. Among the commissioners, Kingston was the only Protestant, albeit only nominally so. The Bridges (father and son) had welcomed the return of Catholicism, and their involvement in Hooper's burning was just one of many ways in which they supported the queen. (Sir John had been named Lord Chandos in May 1554 as a reward for his service to the Crown.[5])

[4] F. D. Price, 'The Administration of the Diocese of Gloucester', p. 100; GCL Hockaday Abstracts, vol. XXXVIII, 1555 (unpaginated); *A&M* vol. VI, pp. 647–59; *APC*, vol. IV, p. 422. The city of Gloucester expended a fairly large sum in conjunction with Hooper's burning, giving 40s 'in reward to the kynge and Quenes servauntes at the bryngyng down of maister Hooper', spending an additional 49s 4d on food and drink for 'the lord Chandos and other gentilmen at the maister maires howse', and for 'maister Kyngeston and other' at the house of Agnes Ingram. GRO GBR F4/3, fos. 49v–50.
[5] R. F. Butler, 'Brimpsfield Church History', *TBGAS* 81 (1962), p. 79.

Kingston's relationship with the Crown, on the other hand, was not good. He may have gained membership on this commission through the good offices of his brother-in-law, Henry Jerningham, one of Mary's earliest supporters, a member of her Privy Council, beginning in July 1553, and then vice-chamberlain of her household.[6]

England officially returned to Catholicism very shortly after Mary's accession, and soon Cardinal Reginald Pole, as Archbishop of Canterbury, would join with Mary to mount a campaign to re-establish the old religion in all its richness and complexity throughout the realm.[7] On the continent the Council of Trent was in recess, having just concluded the first portion of its work; the nature and scope of much of what would become known as the Counter- (or Catholic) Reformation were being held in abeyance pending the re-convening of that assembly. In England, the queen and her archbishop faced several rather daunting challenges inherited from the previous reigns. Their vision was of a church consisting of able, dedicated clergy, re-established monasteries, and visually rich Catholic ceremony in parishes and cathedrals. The most serious impediments to achieving that set of goals were the long history of pluralism, non-residency and impropriation of rectories which had plagued parishes for years, and the lack of financial resources necessary to rectify the situation, provide for monasteries and fund the requisite acquisitions and changes for Catholic worship. The drain on the church's financial resources which had resulted from the dissolutions of the monasteries and chantries, as well as the sale and confiscation of church goods, had been devastating. Previous regimes had been forced to deal with the problems which hindered effective parish ministry, and future ecclesiastical leaders would experience similar frustrations and difficulties. The deprivation for marriage of a significant number of highly qualified clergy exacerbated the problem. However, although the ongoing challenge of obtaining adequate numbers of qualified clergy was intractable, it was the financial difficulties which would create serious divisions within the realm and prove the greatest hindrance to the prompt and complete restoration of Catholicism.[8]

Wrapped up and entangled with ecclesiastical finances was the issue of

---

[6] D. MacCulloch, ed. and trans., 'The *Vita Mariae Angliae Reginae* of Robert Wingfield of Brantham', in *Camden Miscellany*, vol. XXVIII (Camden Society, 4th ser., vol. XXIX, London, 1984), pp. 189, 258–9; R. Tittler, *The Reign of Mary* (London and New York, 1983), pp. 12, 75.

[7] Haigh, *Reformations*, p. 208.

[8] R. H. Pogson, 'The Legacy of Schism: Confusion, Continuity and Change in the Marian Clergy', in *The Mid-Tudor Polity c. 1540–1560*, ed. J. Loach and R Tittler (Basingstoke, 1980), pp. 116–36, *passim*; R. H. Pogson, 'Revival and Reform in Mary Tudor's Church', in *Reformation Revised*, ed. C. Haigh (Cambridge, 1987), pp. 139–56, *passim*; Duffy, *Stripping*, pp. 525–36, *passim*; Haigh, *Reformations*, pp. 209–17, *passim*; Garrett, *Marian Exiles*, pp. 4–6.

individual wealth and status gained through the dissolution and re-distribution of church properties and possessions. Catholicism could not be fully established without monasteries, and the cost of the restoration of Catholicism to parishes would be overwhelming without the recovery of items needed for traditional worship, including vestments, books, chalices and roods. However, the laity who had benefited from the dissolutions and divestments of ecclesiastical holdings and goods were loath to give up their new acquisitions.

With tensions mounting and divisions deepening, the announcement of the planned marriage between Mary and Phillip II of Spain aggravated an already volatile situation. This combination of issues culminated in the summer of 1555 in some heated, threatening and even possibly treasonous rhetoric in Parliament. The following November a conspiracy to remove Mary as queen and install her Protestant half-sister, Elizabeth, on the throne in her place was conceived, based largely in the western counties. The leader of the opposition to the Crown in Parliament was Sir Anthony Kingston, who at one point obtained the keys to the House of Commons and refused to let anyone leave until they had defeated the Crown's attempt to weaken their property rights (a move seen as the first step in a campaign to regain control of church lands).[9] He was committed to the Tower for two weeks for his efforts, but was then released, in all likelihood benefiting again from his connection to Jerningham.

Sir Anthony was soon back in the thick of the plot, along with a number of other Gloucestershire gentry, including Sir Nicholas Arnold, Sir Arthur Dennys and Sir Nicholas Poyntz (father of a Protestant exile). They were joined by a number of others, including Lord Bray (father-in-law of Sir Edmund Bridges), as well as two members of the Throckmortons of Worcestershire, John and Sir Nicholas. The scheme was complex, involving people in both England and France, but ultimately the conspirators were identified and the principals taken into custody. Sir Nicholas Arnold had previously declared that he could not in good conscience serve 'the Spanishe Kynge' and that 'next to the Quenes Majestie he would serve' the Lady Elizabeth, utterances which undoubtedly did not help his cause.[10] He was committed to the Tower of London sometime before 18 January 1556, transferred to the Fleet Prison the following September, released in December, and allowed to return to Gloucestershire in February 1557.[11] Sir Anthony Kingston was less fortunate, and this time not even Jerningham could help him. He was apprehended in Gloucestershire in 1556, but died at Cirencester (possibly as a result of suicide) while being escorted back to

[9] *APC*, vol. V, pp. 207, 208; PRO SP 11/7/24, 11/7/25, 11/7/48, 11/8/2, 11/8/3, 11/8/49.
[10] PRO SP 11/3/13.   [11] *APC*, vol. V, pp. 90, 283, 359; vol. VI, pp. 47–8.

London and the Tower by Sir John Bridges. While this plot had obvious religious overtones, the main motivations appear to have been financial and political. Those involved were split religiously between those who favoured Protestantism and those who welcomed the restoration of Catholicism. However, they did have two things in common: they were all politically powerful, and they had all benefited substantially from the dissolution of both the monasteries and the chantries.[12]

Among the gentry of Gloucestershire the only overt resistance to the return to Catholicism based solely on theological grounds came from a familiar source: Richard Tracy, Protestant pamphleteer and son of the Protestant testator. He appeared before the Privy Council on 9 June 1555 and 'shewed a verie earnest desire to be a conformable man from hensfurthe' concerning religion. However, just three months later, in September 1555, he was back before the Council, accused of having 'hitherto . . . behaved himselfe verye stubbornely towardes . . . the bisshopp of Gloucestre'. He was ordered 'to repayre home into the countrey, and to declare to the said bishop his conformitie in matters of religion, whiche he himself bothe offred and promised to do'.[13]

James Brookes, the bishop who had to contend with Tracy, had been consecrated on 1 April 1554, just two weeks after Hooper's deprivation. Born in 1512 and educated at Corpus Christi College, Oxford, Brookes had been master of Balliol since 1546.[14] Once consecrated as bishop, he distinguished himself more by his activities outside the diocese than within it during his episcopate. His dealings with Tracy, therefore, may have been an exception to the normal focus of his interests and responsibilities. He assisted in Hooper's trial, was one of those commissioned to examine Nicholas Ridley and Hugh Latimer before their executions, and represented the Pope in the examination of Cranmer.[15] In his diocese, except for his representation of Cardinal Pole in the metropolitical visitation in 1556, he seems to have relied primarily on his chancellor, John Williams, for the implementation and enforcement of the Marian Restoration of Catholicism and the execution of unrepentant Protestant heretics.[16]

In fact, only five Protestants, including Hooper, are known to have been

---

[12] For further discussion of the conspiracy to remove Mary from the throne see D. M. Loades, *Two Tudor Conspiracies* (Cambridge, 1965), pp. 151–238, *passim*.

[13] *APC*, vol. V, pp. 145, 181.

[14] A. A. Wood, *Athenae Oxonienses: an Exact History of all the Writers and Bishops who Have Had their Education in the University of Oxford* (London, 1813), vol. I, cols. 314–15.

[15] J. Strype, *Ecclesiastical Memorials*, vol. III, pt. I, p. 286; *A&M*, vol. VIII, pp. 45–9, 59–62; Latimer, *Sermons*, vol. I, p. 283.

[16] Wilkins, *Concilia*, vol. IV, p. 145; 'Brooks' Injunctions for Gloucester Diocese. 1556', in *VAI*, vol. II, p. 401.

burned in Gloucestershire, and Williams supervised at least three of these executions, including Hooper's. He also presided over the burnings of Thomas Drowry, a blind boy, and Thomas Croker, a bricklayer, both of the city of Gloucester, after serving as judge at their trials.[17] According to John Louth, Williams's successor as chancellor, Williams admonished Drowry to 'do as I have done . . . , [recant] and escape burning'. The boy refused, and after reminding the chancellor that he had learned his heretical beliefs from Williams's sermons in the cathedral, exclaimed, 'Godes wyll be fulfylled!', and was condemned to die.[18] Two other Gloucestershire Protestants, Edward Horne of Newent and Isabel Denye of Wotton-under-Edge, appear to have suffered the same fate just weeks before the end of Mary's reign.[19] The short list of Protestant martyrs in Gloucestershire stands in sharp contrast to the much larger numbers who died in the south-east, in East Anglia and London, but in the west of England only the city of Bristol, with nine, saw more burnings.[20]

Not everyone who held Protestant beliefs, however, was condemned to die. Most of the consistory court records from Brookes's episcopate have been lost, but among those that survive are accounts from 1555 and 1556 of a number of individuals who were accused of heretical views, but chose to abjure and do penance rather than burn for their faith.[21] Elizabeth Marshall, of Tewkesbury, was accused of rejecting the Real Presence of Christ in the Sacrament of the Altar, and ordered to recant publicly.[22] Henry Hickes, John Grene and his wife, and Agnes Greene were all accused of holding unacceptable beliefs and, similarly, chose to abjure.[23] Hugh Dorington of St Michael's, Gloucester who, according to some of his fellow-parishioners, had refused to show proper reverence for either the consecrated host or the altar light, was required 'upon Sondaye nexte [to] stande under the pulpitte in the tyme of the priestes beinge at the beades and there . . . [speak] certen wordes to be written unto him'.[24] Undoubtedly, there were also others who chose to conform rather than burn.

Still others opted for exile, in preference to either acceptance of Catholicism or death as martyrs. These included a number of clergy: John

[17] *A&M*, vol. VIII, pp. 144–5; Powell, 'Beginnings', p. 154; GRO GDR vol. XI, p. 207.

[18] J. Louth, 'The Reminiscences of John Louth, Archdeacon of Nottingham, Written in the Year 1579', in *Narratives*, pp. 18–20. Drowry first appeared in court on 28 March 1556.

[19] Powell, 'Beginnings', p. 154; *A&M*, vol. VIII, p. 251; J. Deighton, 'Martyrdom of Edward Horne at Newent in 1558', in *Narratives*, pp. 69–70.

[20] Dickens, *Reformation*, pp. 290, 295; Whiting, *Blind Devotion*, p. 164.

[21] The responses of these individuals fit Andrew Pettegree's description of Marian 'Nicodemites' in 'Nicodemism and the English Reformation', in *Marian Protestantism: Six Studies*, ed. A. Pettegree (St Andrews Studies in Reformation History, Aldershot, Hants., and Brookfield, VT, 1996), pp. 86–117, *passim*.

[22] GRO GDR vol. XI, p. 36.   [23] GRO GDR vol. XI, pp. 201–2, 233.

[24] GRO GDR vol. XI, p. 205.

Parkhurst, rector of Bishop's Cleve in Gloucestershire and future bishop of Norwich; Guy Eaton, archdeacon of Gloucester and chaplain to Bishop Hooper; John Reynolds, who had been in the service of Sir Anthony Kingston; and William Walton, possibly a former Dominican friar from Gloucester.[25] They also included a future dean of Gloucester cathedral, Lawrence Humphrey, and a future prebend, Arthur Saule.[26] Members of the laity from Gloucestershire also fled to the continent, including Edward Oldesworth, brother-in-law of Arthur and Sir Thomas Porter, and probably brother of Nicholas, the rector of St Michael's, Gloucester, who had been deprived for marriage. John Poyntz, son of Sir Nicholas Poyntz of Iron Acton, and John Sanford, a merchant from Stonehouse and a friend of John Hooper were also among the exiles. Sanford died in Frankfurt, probably in 1557. In his will he left £5 each to the English congregations at Frankfurt and Geneva. His overseers included Thomas Semys, future alderman and mayor of Gloucester, and Dr Richard Cox, whom he had met in Frankfurt and who would become the Elizabethan Bishop of Ely. Sanford's son, Toby, was to be raised and educated with knowledge of 'true christianitie' by John Rastall, Sr, Sanford's father-in-law and an alderman of Gloucester, of whom John Hooper had thought quite highly.[27]

Joan Wilkinson of King's Stanley in Gloucestershire, who had interceded for Hooper during his imprisonment, also went into exile.[28] She was the widow of a mercer and a sister of Lord North of Cambridgeshire, and had been a silkwoman in Anne Boleyn's household in the mid-1530s, and met Anne's chaplain, William Latimer. While there she had also had the opportunity to read and discuss the Scriptures and prohibited Protestant books. In that capacity she had received a shipment of Protestant books just after Anne's arrest in 1536, which had been sent from the continent by

[25] Garrett, *Marian Exiles*, pp. 181, 244, 270–1, 320; *A Brieff Discours off the Troubles Begonne at Franckford in Germany Anno Domino 1554* (Heidelberg, 1574), STC 25442, p. 16; Rodolph Gualter to Lord Francis Russell, from Zurich, 16 January 1559, in *Zurich Letters*, vol. II, p. 10; Christopher Goodman to Peter Martyr, from Geneva, 20 August 1558, in *Original Letters*, vol. II, p. 771.

[26] Garrett, *Marian Exiles*, pp. 193–4, 284–5; I. M. Kirby, comp., *Diocese of Gloucester, a Catalogue of the Records of the Bishop and Archdeacons* (Gloucester, 1968), p. 134; GRO GDR vol. IIa, p. 141; *DNB*, vol. XXVIII, pp. 238–9; vol. L, p. 313. See chapters 6 and 7 for a discussion of the involvement of Humphrey and Saule in the implementation of Elizabethan Protestantism.

[27] Garrett, *Marian Exiles*, pp. 260–1, 278; J. Maclean, 'Manor of Tockington, Co, Gloucester and the Roman Villa', *TBGAS* 12 (1887), p. 152. Sir Nicholas Poyntz had hosted Henry VIII and Anne Boleyn on their progress through the county in 1535. GRO GBR B2/1, fos. 117v–19; *L&P*, vol. VIII, no. 989; PRO PROB 11/43, fos. 304–5; SP 10/13/24; GRO GBR B2/1, fos. 27, 29. Thomas Oldesworth, who was probably Edward's brother, also went into exile, while Nicholas apparently did not. Garrett, *Marian Exiles*, pp. 187, 242; GRO GDR vol. Ib, p. 13.

[28] PRO PROB 11/42B, fo. 233v. Susan Brigden discusses aspects of Joan Wilkinson's involvement with the Protestant cause in Brigden, *London*, pp. 221, 418–19, 562, 604.

Latimer.[29] During the first half of Mary's reign, Mrs Wilkinson had ministered to imprisoned Protestant divines who were soon to be martyred for their faith, providing them with gifts of food and clothing. In addition to John Hooper, this grateful and illustrious group included John Bradford, Miles Coverdale, John Harley, Hugh Latimer, Nicholas Ridley and Thomas Cranmer.[30] In fact, Cranmer had written to Mrs Wilkinson urging her to flee from England in order to preserve herself 'to truly and rightly serve God', rather than be martyred, and so she had.[31] However, her closest connection and friendship seems to have been with Hooper. She died in Frankfurt in 1556, and in her will she bequeathed 'all those my bokes which Mr Hooper hadde the use of during his lif . . . to the proufett of Cristes Churche'. Additionally, she left £20 for the education of Hooper's son, Daniel, who was living in Frankfurt under the guardianship of Edward Oldesworth and Valerand Pullain, a leader of the French exile congregation in Frankfurt and a relative of Hooper's wife, Anne.[32]

Thus, a number of individuals held fast to the Protestant faith. Some of the most ardent, probably those who were wealthier, had gone into exile, while a few, whose faith was just as strong as that of the exiles, had chosen martyrdom. On the other hand, there were a few prominently placed individuals, including some of those involved in the conspiracy to remove Mary from the throne, whose opposition to the Crown may have been motivated more by financial and political concerns, embodied in the re-possession of former monastic lands and the Spanish marriage, than by their religious beliefs, although they preferred the new religion over the old as well. Most of the Gloucestershire laity, however, simply went on with their lives. Some continued to profess Protestant beliefs after Mary's accession, even to the extent of being presented and having to recant and do penance. However, the great majority seem to have chosen one of three responses: they held on quietly and secretly to their Protestant faith, gave it

---

[29] *L&P*, vol. X, no. 827; M. Dowling, 'Anne Boleyn and Reform', *JEH* 35 (1984), pp. 33, 43; 'William Latymer's Cronickille of Anne Bulleyne', pp. 50–1, 62. Cf. T. Freeman, 'Research, Rumour and Propaganda', pp. 797–819.

[30] *The Writings of John Bradford*, ed. A. Townsend (Cambridge, 1853), vol. II, p. 39n; John Hooper to Mrs Wilkinson, from prison, n.d., in Hooper, *Later Writings*, pp. 601–2; John Bradford to Mrs. Wilkinson, from Prison, n.d., in *The Writings of John Bradford*, pp. 39–40, 45–6, 51, 121, 182–3; Nicholas Ridley to John Bradford, from prison, n.d., in *The Writings of John Bradford*, pp. 84, 95; Hugh Latimer to Mrs Wilkinson, from prison, n.d., in Latimer, *Sermons*, vol. II, p. 444; Ridley to Bradford, from prison, n.d., in *The Works of Nicholas Ridley*, ed. H. Christmas (Cambridge, 1841), p. 360; Ridley to Augustine Berneher, from prison, n.d., in *The Works of Nicholas Ridley*, p. 382.

[31] Thomas Cranmer to Mrs Wilkinson, from prison, n.d., in *Miscellaneous Writings and Letters of Thomas Cranmer*, ed. J. E. Cox (Cambridge, 1846), pp. 444–5.

[32] PRO PROB 11/42B, fo. 233v; *The Troubles Begonne at Franckford*, p. 5. Hooper's wife, Anne, had preceded her son to the continent by six months.

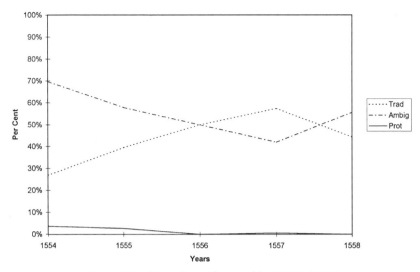

Figure 5.1   Non-elite will preambles (1554–1558)

up quickly with the change in official policy, or turned away from nominal conformity under Edward to welcome the return to Catholicism.

As Mary's reign unfolded and she and Cardinal Pole began to restore the old religion, testators increasingly chose to employ traditional preambles and provide traditional bequests. The percentage of non-elite testators choosing traditional will preambles in Gloucestershire increased steadily from 1553 to reach over 57 per cent by 1557. Furthermore, while Protestant soul bequests vanished, the most significant difference from Edward's reign was the move away from ambiguous statements.[33] Under Mary, individuals who had clung to the old religion were free once again to proclaim their beliefs publicly, and over half the Gloucestershire testators took advantage of that opportunity. The proportion of wills containing traditional preambles was even higher under Mary than it had been during the last years of the reign of her father, and the pronounced swing in this direction after Edward's death lends credence to the assertion that the choice of ambiguous statements when Protestantism held sway was, in fact,

[33] See Figure 5.1 and Appendix B. This is based on the analysis of a sample of 514 Gloucestershire lay wills from Mary's reign, including 263 women's wills and 251 men's wills. There were a total of 241 traditional soul bequests, 269 ambiguous statements, and 4 Protestant formulas. The sample was drawn from a total of 1,545 extant wills proved in the diocese of Gloucester from 1554 to 1558. Thus, assuming the highest possible variability of the sample from the population, the results of the analysis of this sample will be within 1.62 per cent of that for the entire population at a confidence level of 95 per cent. R. S. Schofield, 'Sampling in Historical Research', pp. 154–61.

a means of safely concealing one's true Catholic faith.[34] Also, in contrast to Edward's reign (and to the reign of Henry as well), the wills of Marian testators represent a fairly broad cross-section of the county's inhabitants. Wills are usually a 'lagging indicator' of beliefs, because they are ordinarily written by the old and the affluent, those least likely to accept change. However, the massive influenza outbreaks in 1557 and 1558 brought not only a sharp increase in the death rate, but also a widening of the socio-economic and age ranges of testators; younger people and individuals with fewer possessions and less wealth were making wills. Thus, in Mary's reign testators' declarations of faith and choices for charitable giving may have been more representative of the general populace than in previous reigns.[35] In addition, a new pattern had been established: in the future those writing wills would be more socially and economically diverse.

Some historians have asserted that the preference among Marian testators for traditional faith statements was a result of official coercion rather than genuine belief. However, while it is certainly true that such changes reflect the influence of official policy, the response in this case appears to have been to welcome the return to the old religion, especially when considered in conjunction with provisions for worship which were being made at the same time. Furthermore, pressure from the ecclesiastical hierarchy and the Crown may very well have dissuaded most testators from employing explicitly Protestant formulas; but ambiguous preambles would still have been an acceptable alternative, as they had been under Edward. Such statements served multiple purposes. In cases where the testator was too sick to express a preference or, more rarely, dictate the contents of a statement of faith, or where such a statement was not important to the testator, an ambiguous preamble would have provided the obvious solution. However, such declarations could also be used to conceal one's true beliefs, and that, in fact, is probably what those with traditional beliefs had done during Edward's reign. Now the wills of those who had clung to the old religion during the previous reign included traditional soul bequests.

None the less, the renewed preference for traditional preambles did not mean that Marian testators and their scribes had settled back into the same limited set of faith statements used by their Henrician predecessors. Simple soul bequests were still common; however, the variety of specific formulas in wills of both the gentry and their more humble neighbours had multiplied under Edward, and the Marian Restoration did not stop that trend. Preambles may have returned to expressions of traditional beliefs, but they

---

[34] See chapters 3 and 4, and Appendix B.
[35] This phenomenon can also be seen in the extant wills from the North Nottingham market town of Retford. D. Marcombe, *English Small Town Life*, p. 227.

did not necessarily return to traditional forms. Emphasis on the Christological aspects of faith had begun to grow in importance before the introduction of Protestantism, and that trend continued.[36] There was also an increasing desire to express one's personal faith more fully in the preamble than had previously been the case. Both testators and scribes appear to have perceived the need for more complete and complex descriptions of salvation theology than had been deemed necessary before the introduction of Protestantism. Thus, when Jone Holder, widow of Charlton Kings, wrote her will in 1556, she was expressing traditional beliefs in bequeathing her soul

unto Almightye God my creator and redemer unto whose mercye I commytt my selfe unto, trusting by the merytes of hys passion to inheryt the kingdome of heavin, and also desiring owre blessid Ladye with all the whole companye off heavin to preye for me.[37]

Similarly, a year later, John Dyston of Winchcombe committed his soul

to Almighty God and to Jhesus Christ his only son and to all the hole blessyd company of heaven most stedfastly beleving that the thing that is commyttyd to their charge can not perysshe but be preservyd and in better wyse be restoryd at the latter day.[38]

Explicitly articulated faith in salvation through Christ's death and passion, combined with either requests for intercessions of behalf of the testator by the Blessed Virgin Mary and all the saints or invocations to the saints, was a common feature of Marian wills.

The pattern of gentry preambles is similar to that of the ordinary testators in Marian Gloucestershire, although with only seventy-four wills the analysis of elite wills can not be as reliable as that of the 514 ordinary testaments. Traditional preambles, which had disappeared from elite wills by 1549, reappeared in 1554 and constituted approximately 50 per cent of testators' religious statements by the following year. They then maintained that level through the remainder of Mary's reign, with ambiguous declarations appearing in most of the other extant wills. Only one or two wills each year employed Protestant preambles, and while the proportion of such wills was higher than among those of non-elite testators, their incidence was still not significant. No testament was sufficiently radical to be refused probate. One of those was, none the less, quite distinctive. John Pynnock of Longbarrow wrote his will in January 1555, and included a clear and substantial assertion of his faith:

---

[36] I discovered this characteristic in Marian wills when doing the research for my PhD, while Eamon Duffy's important book *The Stripping of the Altars* was in press, and I would like to thank Dr Duffy for discussing my findings with me at that time.

[37] GRO Wills 1556/64.   [38] GRO Wills 1557/224.

I commit my soule unto almighty God who is my maker and redemer my cumforthe my joye and hope / My salve and my medicine for by his worde I larne that he did cum into the world to save sinners / Amonge whome I accompte my self one / Therefore I most humbly beseche the that the swete sacrafice of his body and blode may now make the attonment betwix the wroth of God which I have deservyd and me / O Lord lett all the meryttes of thy passion be my salvacion for in theym I trust and not in any workes that I have done. All the good dedes that I have done are my dewtye and farre under that which of dewtie I am bounde to do / Geave me grace O Lord that this faith and trust which I have in the and thy meryttes never decey in me but waxe stronger and stronger so long as I live / So that both lyving and dying I being repentante for my synnes may suerly beleve wythout distrust that thy blode haith pergett me from my synnes and brought me into Godes favor haith delyvred me out of the develled bondage and made inheritor of thy kyngdome in heaven / In this faith O Lord I professe I have lyved and in this faith I purposse fully by thy grace and helpe to dy and rest / Therefore I besech the mercifull saviour to graunt that when death shall shutte uppe my bodyly eyes I may behold the with thy eyes of my soule / And when the use of my tong is takyn from me / That my harte yett may saye unto the O Lord I commend my soule into thy handes Lord Jesu receyve my sprete.[39]

The length and eloquence of this preamble notwithstanding, most testators (both elite and ordinary) included not Protestant but either traditional or ambiguous declarations of faith in their wills, yet still ventured beyond the simple short forms employed by their Henrician and Edwardian predecessors.

The effects of Protestantism can also be seen in the nature of charitable bequests contained in wills from this period. Small, ritualistic gifts to parishes had nearly vanished under Edward, and although they did return under Mary, the percentage of wills containing such bequests never reached the late Henrician level of over 60 per cent. Similarly, provisions for prayers for the dead had disappeared by the early 1550s, and while a few wills included such requests between 1554 and 1558, the annual percentage never exceeded 4 per cent, whereas under Henry in the mid-1540s approximately 18 per cent of the wills had made that provision. The reverse, however, was true for gifts to the poor, which had increased markedly under Edward. Following Mary's accession, the proportion dipped from an annual average of approximately 25 per cent to 15 per cent, not as low as in Henry's reign but a definite break in the upward trend established under Edward.[40] The additional opportunities for charitable giving introduced by the restoration may have diminished support for the poor. However, patterns of charitable giving generally still showed the

---

[39] PRO PROB 11/39, fos. 78v–9.

[40] See Appendix B for statistics on provisions for prayers for the dead, and gifts to parishes and the poor.

effects of Edwardian Protestantism, as they never returned to the proportionate levels seen under Henry.

As in other periods, the numbers of distinctive legacies to parishes and the poor contained in extant wills from 1541 to 1580 is too small for rigorous analysis; none the less, they had virtually disappeared under Edward and returned following Mary's accession to approximately the same level as during the mid-1540s. Some testators left the poor unrestricted gifts of money to be distributed at their burial, as did John Falkener of Tewkesbury in 1555, and Thomas Blysse of Painswick and William Adys of Oxenhall in 1558.[41] Others, such as John Dyston, whose complex but traditional preamble was quoted earlier, directed that part of their gift of money be distributed at their burial and the remainder at their month's mind, an unarticulated indication of the expectation that the recipients would pray for the soul of their benefactor. Pre-Reformation practices had included prayers for the health of the souls of the departed one month after death, and yearly thereafter. Thus, an instruction which specified distribution to the poor on one or both of those anniversaries may well have been intended to include an implied request that such prayers be offered by the recipients of the testator's generosity.[42] Still others made more complex bequests, but with no apparent expectation of prayers in return. James Kempe directed that 6s 8d, a fairly small amount, be distributed to the poor of his parish, Beckford, while an additional £6 10s was to be given to his poorest kinsfolk.[43] Joane Hale, a widow from Oddington, left £5 to the poor of each of two towns, to be distributed by her brother-in-law at his discretion. As with John Dyston, she may have hoped for prayers for her soul, for, although her preamble was in the simplest ambiguous formula, she used the traditional reference of the 'mother church' in designating her gift of 2d to the cathedral and left 12d to the 'high altar', another term which had faded during the ascendancy of Protestantism.[44] John Hickes of Tewkesbury, whose will was written in 1557, left the residue of his goods to be distributed among the poor.[45] While none was large enough to have a sustained effect over time, each of these bequests would have had a significant, immediate impact on the lives of the recipients.

On the other hand, in Tewkesbury in 1557, one bequest was substantial enough to have a long-term impact on the community, and complex

---

[41] Falkener left £20, while Blysse and Adys each left £5. GRO Wills 1556/114, 1558/506, 1559/360.

[42] GRO Wills 1557/224.

[43] His will includes the simplest form of an ambiguous soul bequest and a ritualistic gift of 12d to his parish church, in addition to his bequest to the poor. GRO Wills 1558/194.

[44] GRO Wills 1561/82.   [45] GRO Wills 1557/135.

enough to require special provisions for its management. Giles Geast was a mercer, clothier and long-time resident of the town. His name appears on the muster list for 1539, and at the time of the dissolution he was living in one of the houses which belonged to the Abbey. He had been appointed bailiff and collector of the lands of Tredington in 1545, and was given similar responsibilities for Washbourne Manor and Ashchurch a year later. Sometime early in Mary's reign he had purchased the tenement in which he lived, along with a number of others that had once been held by the Abbey. He wrote his will on 20 August 1557.[46] It begins with a unique preamble:

I doo give and bequeathe my soule to Almightie God prainge hym throughe his infallyble promyse, his most mercyfull forgivenes of my synnes for the meryttes and deservinge of the passyon of our Saviour Jesus Criste my redeamer whereby onely I truste to be saved.

The will goes on to make provision for the establishment of a major charity to aid the poor, funded by the rents from numerous lands and tenements within the town of Tewkesbury, including the house that Geast and his wife had lived in, once his wife had died. The fund was to be independent of the parish and the town, administered by co-feoffees who were to report to the bailiffs of the town annually.[47] This will is significant, not only because of its generous bequest to the poor, but also because of its soul bequest. Not only is the latter unique, but, written as it was at the height of the acceptance of Marian Catholicism, it is noteworthy that this is not a traditional preamble. Rather, it was a distinctive if slightly ambiguous statement of beliefs, which leans toward Protestantism. As noted above, Geast refers to God's 'infallyble promyse' to forgive his sins, and goes on to assert his faith in Christ's saving passion, 'whereby onely I truste to be saved'. These words could have been written by a Marian Catholic; but why would he use them? This is the type of preamble one might expect to see from an Elizabethan Catholic when equivocation was the order of the day, but not under Mary. The preamble is unique among the Gloucestershire wills from the forty-year period of this study. Geast had clearly created his own form, and, given the contemporaneous religious climate, he could have chosen much more traditional language without difficulty. Rather, it appears that he was trying to conceal his Protestant beliefs behind a somewhat ambiguous form, much as followers of the old religion had done under Edward.[48] He does not appear to have been motivated in his largesse by a desire for prayers for his soul either. Instead, he seems to

[46] GRO D837, p. 1; GRO P329 MI/1, fo. 5v; *L&P*, vol. XX, pt. I, no. 620(8); vol. XXI, pt. I, no. 1538(164); pt. II, no. 774(228); GCL Hockaday Abstracts, vol. CCCLXIX, 1545 (unpaginated).
[47] PRO PROB 11/40, fos. 284v–7v.   [48] See chapter 4.

represent a new type of benefactor, that of the prominent resident of the town who sets examples for others of both generosity and good steward-ship of God's bounty in the writing of his will. Such gifts and endowments would become more common during Elizabeth's reign. The particular provisions of this act of charity may have been a result of the spread of Christian humanism, which placed a high priority on eliminating poverty, preferred secular to ecclesiastical administration of funds, and saw indis-criminate giving to the needy as poor stewardship. Giles Geast's bequest instructed that the money was to be 'distributed amongst the poore people inhabitinge within the saied Burrough of Tewkesbury foresaied by the discrecion of the saide Bayliffes and . . . ffeoffes yerely'. Thus, he carefully defined the geographic origin of the recipients and directed that a group of secular officials were to exercise discretion in the distribution of funds.[49]

Other elite testators specified similarly restrictive, if less ambitious, provisions for the distribution of bequests to the poor. Thus, Joane Hale of Oddington left specific small sums to a number of named individuals; John Cooke of Westbury left 40s each to the poor of his parish and to the nearby parish of Painswick; and Richard Colymor of Chipping Campden gave 12d to each of his servants without ploughlands, 3s 4d to each of his weavers, and 12d to each poor householder in the town.[50]

Moreover, the poor were not the only recipients of generous and creative gifts from testators in Marian Gloucestershire. Parishes in this western diocese, like churches all over England, also benefited from the restoration of the accoutrements and practices of traditional Catholic worship, which provided both the motivation and the objects of such gifts.[51] Money, tablecloths or sheets, barley, wheat and livestock, sometimes in generous quantities, were given to various parish altars, lights and chapels. Alice Byglyn, widow of Bishop's Cleve, left barley to the high altar and the rood light, while Annes Kyte, widow of Pebworth, gave a sheep to the parish and a linen sheet to the parish altars. Agnes Reve of Dumbelton bequeathed her best tablecloth to the high altar, and Annes Lyttull of Maisemore gave money to the high altar and the church bells.[52] William Kerke, hus-bandman of Charlton Kings, left 2s per year for 12 years for the maintenance of Our Lady's service in his parish church.[53] However, the most generous gift to a parish at this time came from a priest, rather than a lay person. John Assum, priest of Tewkesbury, wrote his will in April 1557,

[49] PRO PROB 11/40, fo. 286v. For a discussion of the effects of humanist thought on charitable giving in aid of the poor, see M. Todd, *Christian Humanism and the Puritan Social Order* (Cambridge, 1987), pp. 133–8, *passim*.
[50] PRO PROB 11/39, fos. 101v–2v, 11/41, fos. 89v–90, 140v–41.
[51] Duffy, *Stripping*, p. 551.   [52] GRO Wills 1556/3, 1556/7, 1558/30, 1558/40.
[53] GRO Wills 1559/338.

bequeathing his soul 'to Allmyghty God' and 20s to the poor. Those were its ordinary aspects; he also went on to leave vestments of blue and yellow silk, albs, amices, stoles and a velvet chasuble to the parish, and a red and green cloth with fringes, a second altar cloth and a cross with a relic to the high altar. In addition, he gave the parish a black velvet funeral pall, and directed that it was for the use of both the rich and the poor.[54] The cathedral also benefited from giving in support of the restored Catholic liturgy. In his will written in August 1557, John ap Richards of Gloucester gave 20s to the high altar of the cathedral to be used 'for its furnishing', 'if the said aulter be made all parfitt and readie before Whitsuntide next'. He also provided for the adorning of two other altars with altar cloths or 'palles thone of greene tapheta with images and gold, thother is sattyn . . . red and greene with a crucifixe uppon it'.[55] The cathedral's high altar was apparently not yet being used or at least had been neglected to some degree. The deadline included in Richards's will for its 'perfection' was five years into Mary's reign, and just six months before the reign would come to an abrupt end. Apparently, the cathedral was having trouble completing the changes required by the Marian Restoration. John ap Richards's gift must have been most welcome.

The return to Catholicism placed a financial strain on parishes, as well as on the cathedral. On 4 March 1554, in a move which was consistent with Cardinal Pole's vision and goal for the restored church, Mary issued a set of religious injunctions, which were sent with a covering letter to all bishops and directed that 'the laudable and honest ceremonies which were wont to be used, frequented and observed in the Church, be hereafter frequented, used and observed'.[56] A survey of the extant churchwardens' accounts from throughout the realm reveals that all the parishes represented had rebuilt or re-installed their altars and obtained a significant percentage of the requisite items of Catholic worship by the end of 1554.[57] This directive carried with it a high price for many parishes, as they had either disposed of the books, vestments, lights, roods and altars needed to perform such ceremonies in an orderly fashion, or else the items had been stolen. For instance, there is no record of any Gloucestershire parish having the foresight of Cratfield in Suffolk, where 'the table that is at the altar' had been stored in the vicarage barn and merely had to be retrieved and set up in the chancel following Mary's accession.[58] However, one Richard Thorne of Thornbury was accused in 1556 of having 'a crosse stolen out of the

---

[54] GRO Wills 1557/163.   [55] PRO PROB 11/41, fo. 141v.
[56] 'Queen Mary's Articles', in *VAI*, vol. II, pp. 322–9.
[57] R. Hutton, 'Local Impact', p. 129.
[58] Suffolk Record Office, Ipswich, FC62/A6/23. I would like to thank Dr Botelho for this reference.

parishe church', and Henry Tame of Burton-on-the-Water had 6- and 8-ounce chalices, which had belonged, respectively, to his parish and to a neighbouring parish.[59] The return to Catholic worship was clearly facilitated at Tewkesbury by Assum's gift, but that parish may well have been favourably positioned for the restoration, having in all probability held on to its chalices, candlesticks, altars and images. On the other hand, conforming parishes like St Michael's, Gloucester, which had done so much under the previous regime to meet Bishop Hooper's requirements for godly, Protestant worship, were now in a particularly difficult financial position, one which had been aggravated by the sale of church goods in 1551 and the dissolution of the chantries three years earlier.[60]

At St Michael's, the churchwardens immediately moved to rectify at least some of their parish's liturgical deficiencies. They constructed a temporary altar from three boards and a long plank, and then had it painted; they also purchased tapers and coals for Easter, and constructed the sepulchre, as did parishes in other parts of England.[61] William Bond, parishioner, alderman and sometime mayor, sold the parish 'a vestement of redde velvett', 'a patente of a chales of sylver and gilte', and a bell, possibly a sacring bell, all of which he had probably purchased in 1551, when the parish had divested itself of all such items.[62] The churchwardens bought a cross, a cloth for the pyx, and an 'olde rope of sylke' from other parishioners. They also acquired the material needed for albs and had them made, and purchased a sencer, cruet and pyx. Later in that tumultuous year, work began on a permanent altar. The churchwardens purchased stones, and, just three years after they had paid to have dirt removed from the chancel area of the church, paid a hauler for eight loads of earth to provide a raised platform for the new altar. Still, the acquisitions (and the drain on the parish chest) continued with the addition of 'a crosse staff of copper and gilte', a 'tresyll for the sacramente', and service books worth over £6.[63] Two years later, Humphrey Walkeley, parishioner and father of two future churchwardens, gave the parish a processional and sold it two other books, and John Webley, a churchwarden just two years earlier, gave it a torch. That same year, 1555, the parish again erected the Easter sepulchre and paid to have it watched.

---

[59] GCL Hockaday Abstracts, vol. XXXIX, 1556 (unpaginated).

[60] See chapter 4. A commission on church goods reported in 1556 that the only ornament in the city of Gloucester which had been sold was Our Lady Service of St Michael's, which had been purchased by William Hasard, draper, alderman and parishioner of St Michael's; however, this was contrary to the evidence contained in the St Michael's churchwardens' accounts. GCL Hockaday Abstracts, vol. XXXIX, 1556 (unpaginated); GRO P154/14 CW 1/5–1/6.

[61] Duffy, *Stripping*, pp. 543–8; G. J. Mayhew, *Tudor.Rye* (Hove, 1987), p. 73.

[62] William Bond is not listed as a purchaser; however, a number of the entries concerning the sale of church goods fail to name the buyer. GRO P154/14 CW 1/5–1/6.

[63] GRO P154/14 CW 1/7.

In addition, they had the organ mended, paid for a new banner cloth and a cloth to hang 'before the hye aulter', and purchased 'a homelye bocke'.[64]

In the parish of Minchinhampton, the churchwardens incurred similar expenses, although the overall cost of restoration there was lower than at St Michael's because fewer changes were required. The rector since July 1551 had been Gilbert Bourne, a noted, well-connected Catholic, who was one of Mary's chaplains and became Bishop of Bath and Wells in 1554. He was a nephew of Sir John Bourne, who in turn was knighted by Mary in 1553 and served as her principal secretary from 1553 to 1557. Gilbert Bourne preached the first official sermon at Paul's Cross after Mary's accession, and according to Foxe, he 'tended much to the derogation and dispraise of king Edward' on that occasion, causing such a stir that a dagger was thrown at him. Bourne was a non-resident rector, but he may still have influenced the liturgy practised and the theology espoused in Minchinhampton parish church.[65] Despite the preference for traditional religion espoused by their rector, the Minchinhampton church-wardens still had to construct the Easter sepulchre and pay for its watching, and purchase frankincense, a pyx, an 'antyfoner' and two other books, as did their counterparts at St Michael's and elsewhere.[66] Hence, the liturgical changes of the first years of Mary's reign were expensive for parishes, even if they had retained vestiges of traditional religion during Edward's reign.

The financial demands brought by the Marian Restoration continued in the second half of her short reign, but there were also more explicit requirements concerning lay liturgical practices. Bishop Brookes visited the diocese as Cardinal Pole's deputy in the latter's metropolitical visitation of 1556, and the injunctions for his visit shed some light on official expectations of lay participation in the liturgy, as well as on those relating to accoutrements of worship:

Parishioners having no lawful impediment . . . [were] at days and hours accustomably appointed duly [to] resort to their parish church, there to hear all Divine

---

[64] GRO P154/14 CW 1/7–1/8. The 'homelye bocke' was the *Book of Homilies*, officially titled, *A Profytable and Necessary Doctryne, with Certayne Homilies Adjoyned . . . for the Instruction and Enformation of the People*, which had been prepared by Bishop Bonner of London in 1555 to replace its Protestant predecessor. Duffy, *Stripping*, p. 534. This volume was required by Bishop Brookes's visitation articles of 1556. 'Brookes' Injunctions for Gloucester Diocese', in *VAI*, vol. II, p. 401.

[65] GRO GDR vol. Ib, p. 8; vol. IIa, p. 57; J. G. Nichols, ed., 'Autobiographical Anecdotes of Edward Underhill, One of the Band of the Gentleman Pensioners', in *Narratives of the Days of the Reformation*, ed. J. G. Nichols (Camden Society, vol. LXXVII, London, 1859), p. 142n; 'The *Vita Mariae Angliae Reginae*', pp. 252, 295n; *A&M*, vol. VI, pp. 391–2, 542; J. G. Nichols, ed., 'Summary of Ecclesiastical Events in 1554', in *Narratives*, p. 287; 'Visitation Booke', p. 61; Haigh, *Reformations*, p. 219.

[66] GRO P217 CW 2/1, pp. 2–3.

service, not in jangling or talking or walking commonly up and down, especially at mass time, but occupying themselves, according to the time and place, in godly meditation and prayer, either with beads or books for prayer allowed and appointed.[67]

In addition, at the time of the elevation of the consecrated host, all parishioners were to 'reverently kneel in such places of the church where they may both see and worship the Blessed Sacrament', and further, 'all godly ceremonies of the Church, as holy bread, holy water, bearing of palms, creeping to the cross, standing at the Gospel, [and] going on procession' were to be used once again. Those practices which had been so vehemently prohibited by Bishop Hooper in his visitation of 1551, but which had been such an important part of pre-Reformation lay piety, were, once again being encouraged and promoted. Furthermore, the churchwardens of parishes where services had previously been sung were charged to form new choirs made up of those parishioners who had previously sung, and anyone who was qualified but refused to do so was to be presented at the visitation. Finally, the churchwardens were to provide

a decent tabernacle set in the midst of the high altar . . . a decent rood of five foot in length at the least, with Mary and John, and the patron or head saint of the church, proportionate to the same, not painted upon cloth or boards, but cut out in timber or stone; a homily-book . . . and generally all other things, which after the custom of the place and the greatness of the parishioners, they are bound to find and maintain; and all these things to be provided with all convenient speed, upon their peril.[68]

The authorities perceived that changes made thus far by parishes had not been adequate, and while some allowance was to be made for the differences between parishes, certain things were to be provided in all cases. This was essential for the complete restoration of Catholicism in England. Unfortunately, however, the Crown's strategies for reclaiming the wealth of the church and using it to finance changes at the parish level were failing to generate appreciable revenues.

At St Michael's, Gloucester, these new requirements prompted the churchwardens to assess a special rate in 1557 to help defray the additional costs which would result from compliance. A number of individuals also gave money for torches, but John Webley charged the parish £2 13s 4d for a 'chesable of redde velvett'. Additionally, the churchwardens paid one William Sandes 1d 'for the puttynge up of a clothe on a Rodde', but also purchased 'Mary and John', presumably carved in wood, for 10s. Finally, in the following year, the last of Mary's reign, two 'yrons for Marie and John' were purchased, and Mary and John were painted and placed on the

---

[67] 'Brookes' Injunctions for Gloucester Diocese', in *VAI*, vol. II, p. 405.
[68] 'Brookes' Injunctions for Gloucester Diocese', in *VAI*, vol. II, pp. 405, 406, 408.

rood loft. That same year, 1558, the churchwardens also bought a tabernacle with lock and key, and purchased yet another mass book from Humphrey Walkeley.[69] Meanwhile, Minchinhampton faced similar financial challenges. The organ was mended and, as at St Michael's, the statues were placed on the rood loft. They also bought a pyx.[70] In addition, both parishes continued to have the Easter sepulchre built and watched, a recurring expense for the duration of Mary's reign. In each case, the churchwardens and other parish leaders seem to have done their best to conform to the more specific liturgical requirements of the 1556 visitation within the capacity of their parish chest. In the case of St Michael's, they even made special provisions for increased revenues to cover the anticipated rise in expenditures.

In addition to all the diocesan-wide modifications in worship, the cathedral made at least one change which went beyond the purview of the local parish church: it re-introduced the custom of the boy-bishop. Traditionally, a chorister (or choir boy) had been selected to serve in that capacity; he was elected on St Nicholas Day (6 December) and typically served until Holy Innocents' Day (28 December). The boy would be vested in the episcopal attire, with a mitre on his head and a crozier or bishop's pastoral staff in his hand. According to the Sarum Processional, he should not only dress like a bishop, but also perform numerous episcopal ceremonies, excluding the Mass, surrounded by others who were to act as prebendaries. At Salisbury he had traditionally senced the altar and the image of the Holy Trinity, led worship, and conducted a visitation of the diocese. The high-point of his tenure, however, came on the Feast of the Holy Innocents, when he preached a sermon in the cathedral. The custom of the boy-bishop had been forbidden by Henry VIII in 1541, but was restored by Mary.[71] In 1558, John Stubs, chorister of Gloucester Cathedral, preached a sermon on the text; 'Except yow will be convertyd, and made lyke unto lytill children, yow shall not entre in to the kyngdom of heaven.' It had been written by Richard Ramsey, sixth prebend there, and was at least in part a polemical attack on the 'new fanglyd doctrine' of Protestantism and on those who had been burned for that faith, describing the latter as 'far wyde of true martirdom'.[72]

Thus, many of the outward signs of the old religion were in place and in use in the diocese of Gloucester by 1558. However, it was not just the external manifestations of traditional religious beliefs and practices which

[69] GRO P154/14 CW 1/1, 1/9–1/10.   [70] GRO P217 CW 2/1, pp. 4–9.
[71] 'Altering Feast Days', in *TRP*, vol. I, p. 302.
[72] 'Two Sermons Preached by the Boy Bishop', in *Camden Miscellany*, vol. VII, ed. J. G. Nichols (Camden Society, new ser., vol. XIV, Westminster, 1875), pp. v–xxxvi, 14–29, *passim*.

had been restored: individual lay piety had also returned to the old ways to a significant extent. The Marian Restoration of Catholicism was not yet complete, but it was well on its way to achieving its goal, having made significantly more headway with the laity than had Edwardian Protestantism. The Protestantism which so many historians have seen as firmly in place by the end of Edward's reign had not yet been accepted in Gloucestershire by more than a small proportion of the populace.[73] Only a few individuals and parishes had embraced the new religion under Edward, while most had chosen the ambiguous, conformist middle way. During Mary's reign, however, over half of those who left wills, as well as most parishes, strove to express and practise the faith and worship of the old religion to the best of their ability, eschewing the option of quiet, unobtrusive ambiguity. Mary's death near the end of 1558 must, therefore, have brought the people of Gloucestershire both sadness and some fear of what the future might hold for their religious lives.

[73] A. G. Dickens, 'The Early Expansion of Protestantism', p. 189; G. R. Elton, *Reform and Reformation*, p. 371.

6

The early years of Elizabeth's reign (1559–1569)

Following Mary's death in November 1558, Elizabeth acceded to the throne. Religious uncertainty would be the watchword in the diocese of Gloucester and the rest of the realm during the first decade of her reign. The queen's apparent ambivalence regarding official religious policy during those years exacerbated an otherwise difficult situation locally. The Marian Bishop of Gloucester, James Brookes, had died just before the end of Mary's reign and would not be replaced for over three years. Thus the diocese of Gloucester was set religiously adrift.[1] Brookes, and before him, John Hooper, had set clear if contrasting standards of religious belief and behaviour during the preceding decade, but now the see of Gloucester was vacant. The eventual selection of Richard Cheyney as bishop would only compound the problem. With a theology that even his contemporaries had difficulty categorising, plus an administrative style which has been characterised variously as 'dreamy' and 'pathetically weak [and] irresolute', his elevation to the episcopacy did little to arrest the drift begun earlier.[2]

Initially, Elizabethan Protestantism was a restoration of most of the beliefs and practices of the last years of Edward's reign; but exactly what did that include? The liturgy of 1552 was modified by replacing the rubric concerning vestments in that book with the more traditional proviso on that subject contained in the Prayer Book of 1549.[3] In addition, confusion arose as a result of conflicting directives in the Prayer Book of 1559 and the Royal Injunctions of the same year concerning the approved form of communion bread and the official policy on images.[4] Compounding the apparent confusion in direction provided by official policy, the hotter sort of Protestants, especially those just returning from exile on the continent,

---

[1] Lambeth Registrum Pole, fo. 63v.
[2] P. Collinson, *The Religion of Protestants: the Church in English Society, 1559–1625* (Oxford, 1982), p. 63 ; Price, 'Bishop Bullingham and Chancellor Blackleech', p. 175.
[3] *Prayer Books*, pp. 212, 229, 347; *Liturgical Services*, p. 53.
[4] *Liturgical Services*, p. 198; 'Announcing Injunctions for Religion', in *TRP*, vol. II, pp. 118, 123, 131; Cardwell, *Annals*, vol. I, p. 210. Cf. M. Aston, *England's Iconoclasts*, pp. 302–24.

were looking forward to a continuation of the changes which had begun in England in the early 1550s, and which they had found in the churches of Zurich and Geneva. In 1559, John Jewel, former Marian exile and future Bishop of Salisbury, described the queen as 'exceedingly well-disposed; and the people everywhere thirsting after religion', and all the Precisians, or more godly Protestants, were looking forward to the convocation of clergy to be held in 1563. They expected that ecclesiastical gathering to approve further reforms. Anticipating that event, John Parkhurst, Bishop of Norwich, former Marian exile and former rector of Bishop's Cleve in Gloucestershire, expressed his desire that the convocation would lead to an improvement in religion along the lines of the church in Zurich, which he had experienced as an exile.[5] Meanwhile, others, perhaps including the queen, hoped for a return to more elaborate and colourful ritual, perhaps resembling Lutheranism or even Henrician Catholicism. This possibility was given additional credibility by the provision in the Act of Uniformity of 1559 that the 'ornaments of the church, and of the ministers thereof' were to be those used early in Edward's reign, rather than those stipulated in 1552, and by the queen's insistence that the lights and cross remain in her chapel.[6] The unresolved question of the queen's marriage also confused the religious picture as her reign began. It was of course assumed that she would marry and that her husband would influence matters of policy, as had Philip during his brief reign as king with Mary. Established religion, in particular, was seen as vulnerable to change, depending on the queen's choice of a mate. Elizabeth encouraged speculation concerning her possible marriage partners, which only increased the ambiguity already present in her religious policies.

In Gloucestershire, the religious uncertainty of early Elizabethan Protestantism was compounded by the vacancy in the bishopric and by the man who was ultimately chosen to hold the see. There are at least three undated extant lists of vacant sees and prospective bishops in William Cecil's hand, all prepared before the new Archbishop of Canterbury was chosen, and Richard Cheyney, who eventually became Bishop of Gloucester, was among those listed as 'spiritual men without promotion at this point'.[7] None the less, it would be over three years before he was selected. In the meantime, the leading magnates of the region were concerned about the spiritual

---

[5] Jewel to Peter Martyr, from London, 1 August 1559, in *Zurich Letters*, part I, p. 39; Parkhurst to Bullinger, from Ludham, 28 April 1562, *Zurich Letters*, part I, p. 108.

[6] The presence of images in the queen's chapel prompted Richard Cox, Bishop of Ely, to decline to minister there. Inner Temple Library MS, Petyt 538/47, fo. 555; printed in J. Strype, *Annals of the Reformation and Establishment of Religion* (Oxford, 1824), vol. I, part II, pp. 500–1.

[7] Lambeth Registrum Parker, vol. I, fo. 109; *Fasti Ecclesiae Anglicanae*, comp. J. Le Neve (Oxford, 1854), vol. I, p. 214; PRO SP 12/4/38.

health of the diocese. Early in the reign they prepared a document entitled, 'Consyderacions for a busshoppe to be placed in the Sea of Gloucester nowe vacant', in which they described the virtues of the diocese and lamented the absence of a bishop. They described Gloucestershire as

greately furnished with nobel men, knightes esquiors and gentlemen as anye other . . . and bysyde that muche inhabyted by merchantes, clothiers, wevers, ffullers, tuckers and men not allwey most easely ruled, yf they be not well instructed and framed by knowledge and good religion to lyve in thorder of good subjectes . . . [Unfortunately,] the ministers theare for lacke of a busshop growe farre oute of order, and the countie of late yeres is ill infected with suche vices as cannot be corrected but by ecclesiasticall auctorytie, nor well be subdued, without the countennaunce of a busshop in place.[8]

The see was not filled until 19 April 1562 when Archbishop Matthew · Parker consecrated Cheyney at Lambeth Palace. Despite his early mention in lists of episcopal prospects, the tardiness of his appointment may indicate reluctance on the part of the Crown to entrust the implementation and enforcement of religious policy to one known to be an unwilling Protestant.

'If ever the hand of authority had placed a round man in a square hole', comments F. O. White, in his *Lives of the Elizabethan Bishops*, 'it was when Cheyney was sent to Gloucester as its spiritual overseer'.[9] Indeed, Richard Cheyney's episcopate was in sharp contrast to those of his immediate predecessors, Hooper and Brookes, both in terms of his theology and his administration. It was perhaps more akin to that of the first Bishop of Gloucester, John Wakeman. Hooper's episcopate had been characterised by the vigorous personal style of his administration and his clearly delineated theology, and although Brookes's vigour seems to have been directed largely outside the diocese, his theology was as well defined as Hooper's. In contrast to Hooper and Brookes, Wakeman's theology had shifted in unison with that of the Crown, and had thus been difficult to define. Additionally, for a number of reasons he was not an energetic implementor of Henrician religious policies. Cheyney, like Wakeman, had a theology that was difficult to interpret, although he certainly did not lack vigour in expounding it, and it did not change significantly during his clerical career, which spanned three major shifts in official theology. Cheyney had received preferments under Henry VIII, Edward VI, Mary and Elizabeth, including at least one of significance in each reign. Furthermore, in the case of Mary and Elizabeth, the Crown was listed as the patron.[10] In his beliefs, at least, he had integrity. As a result of his

---

[8] PRO SP 12/20/53.
[9] F. O. White, *Lives of the Elizabethan Bishops of the Anglican Church* (London, 1898), p. 174.
[10] C. H. Cooper and T. Cooper, *Athenae Cantabrigienses 1500–1609* (Cambridge, 1858–61),

administrative style, however, Cheyney did not command the respect of his contemporaries, not even of the clergy who served under him in the diocese of Gloucester. He is, therefore, an enigma. Although determined to present his beliefs energetically, he did not appear willing to devote similar vigour to the administration of his diocese.[11]

Bishop Cheyney's beliefs were undeniably conservative, albeit idiosyncratic. He believed in the Real Presence, but not in transubstantiation.[12] When he took part in a disputation held in Convocation in 1553, he asserted that the bread and wine remained bread and wine throughout the mass, even though the body and blood of Christ were really and truly present.[13] Then, when the Articles of Religion were debated in Parliament in the mid-1560s, John Jewel, Bishop of Salisbury, reported that 'one alone of our number, the bishop of Gloucester, hath openly and boldly declared in parliament his approval of Luther's opinion respecting the Eucharist'. That is, although he did not believe in transubstantiation, Cheyney still believed in the Real Presence of Christ's body and blood in the sacraments at the time of the administration, a position which put him at odds with most of the bishops and leading clerics in England.[14] However, on the crucial matter of free will, Cheyney said: 'I coulde better like the judgement of Erasmus then Lutheres on the controversie of freewyll'.[15] Thus his

---

vol. I, p. 400; J. Peile, comp., *Biographical Register of Christ's College, 1505–1905* (Cambridge, 1910), vol. I, p. 16; A. A. Wood, *Fasti Oxonienses: Annals of the University of Oxford*, ed. P. Bliss (London, 1815), cols. 169–70; *Fasti Ecclesiae Anglicanae*, vol. I, p. 481; vol. III, p. 352; A. T. Bannister, comp., *Diocese of Hereford Institutions, etc. (AD 1539–1900)* (Hereford, 1932), p. 12; PRO E331 Gloucester/1, p. 8; *Calendar of Patent Rolls, Philip and Mary* (London, 1939), vol. I, p. 450; GRO GDR vol. Ib, p. 150; *Calendar of Patent Rolls, Elizabeth* (London, 1939), vol. I, pp. 397, 438.

[11] For further discussion of the theology and diocesan administration of Bishop Richard Cheyney, see C. Litzenberger, 'Richard Cheyney, Bishop of Gloucester: an Infidel in Religion?', *SCJ* 25 (Fall 1994), pp. 567–84.

[12] Although there is no record of direct contact between the two men, Andrew Perne and Richard Cheyney espoused similar, anomalous theological beliefs during the reigns of Mary and Elizabeth, and both had Cambridge connections. Perne never left, serving as master of Peterhouse from 1555 until his death in 1589, having enrolled at St John's College in 1535. Cheyney was a student, and then a fellow, of Christ's College, receiving his Bachelor of Arts degree in 1529, and serving as a fellow from 1534 to 1547, with the intervening years spent as a fellow of Pembroke. P. Collinson, 'Andrew Perne and his Times', in *Andrew Perne: Quartercentenary* (Cambridge Biographical Society Monograph No. 11, Cambridge, 1991), pp. 1–13, *passim*; J. Venn and J. A. Venn, comps., *Alumni Cantabrigienses Part I, to 1751* (Cambridge, 1922), vol. I, p. 329; Peile, *Biographical Register of Christ's College*, vol. I, p. 16.

[13] *The Trew Report of the Dysputacyon Had and Begonne in the Convocacyon Hows at London . . . In the Yeare of our Lord MDLJJJJ* (Basel [Emden], 1554), STC 19890, sigs. Diiv, Dvi–v.

[14] John Jewel to Henry Bullinger, from Salisbury, 24 February 1567, in *Zurich Letters*, pt. I, pp. 185–6.

[15] Richard Cheyney to William Cecil, from Gloucester, 15 October 1569, PRO SP 12/48/16; printed with some inaccuracies in R. H. Clutterbuck, 'Bishop Cheyney, and the Recusants

beliefs defied simple categorisation, but statements he made in sermons after he became bishop leave no doubt that his sympathies were closer to the old religion than to the new. In a sermon in a Gloucestershire parish, he called into question the reliability of the Calvinist Geneva Bible. He asserted that the Gospel according to St John in the Geneva Bible had been translated incorrectly, and therefore the whole volume's reliability was in doubt.[16] Additionally, during a series of sermons in Bristol in 1568, he allegedly described the leading reformers as

not yet throughlye tryed and approvyd as the Catholyke ffathers are . . . [and as being] at dyssentyon amonge them sellves . . . Therfor [he said] . . . follow the olld ffathers and doctours. Although Mr Calvyn denyethe some of them.[17]

Ultimately, Cheyney's beliefs led to his brief excommunication in 1571 for insubordination. Although he had subscribed to uniformity in common prayer in 1570, he refused to attend convocation the next year, because attendance was predicated on subscribing to the more specific Articles of Religion, which included an article on the Eucharist that left little or no room for the Real Presence. The Articles had originally been approved by the convocation of 1563, but had not been ratified by Parliament. Over the intervening years changes had been introduced, including a modification to Article Twenty-Eight, which addressed the Real Presence. The word 'only' was added so that it read: 'The body and blood of christe is geven, taken, and eaten in the supper after an heavenly and spirituall maner only.' This was the article to which Cheyney so strongly objected. He was excommunicated on 20 April 1571 and absolved two months later after pleading illness as the cause of his absence. He had been excommunicated for his insubordination, rather than his 'heresy'; however, his beliefs had motivated his behaviour. All the other bishops subscribed to the Articles in 1571; there is no record that Cheyney ever did.[18] Thus, Gloucestershire was in the paradoxical position of having a bishop with his own idiosyncratic but conservative beliefs whose primary responsibility was the im-

of the Diocese of Gloucester', *TBGAS* 5 (1880–1), pp. 228–9. He made a similar statement in one of his sermons in Bristol before an apparently hostile congregation. 'Citizens of Bristowe' to the Privy Council, from Bristol, 21 October 1568, PRO SP 12/48/22; printed with some inaccuracies in R. H. Clutterbuck, 'Bishop Cheyney', p. 231.

16 GRO GDR vol. XXI, p. 304.

17 'Citizens of Bristowe', PRO SP 12/48/22; printed with some inaccuracies in R. H. Clutterbuck, 'Bishop Cheyney', p. 231.

18 Wilkins, *Concilia*, vol. IV, pp. 261–2; Inner Temple Library MS, Petyt 538/38, fo. 54, printed in J. Strype, *The Life and Acts of Matthew Parker* (Oxford, 1821), vol. III, pp. 182–3; Cardwell, *Synodalia*, vol. II, p. 530, 531; GRO Furney MS B/1, p. 70; W. Laud, *The History of the Troubles and Tryal of the Most Reverend Father in God, and Blessed Martyr, William Laud* (London, 1695), p. 83; C. Hardwick, *A History of the Articles of Religion* (London, 1904), pp. 329–31; Edmund Guest to William Cecil, 1565, PRO SP 12/ 41/51, printed with some inaccuracies in R. H. Clutterbuck, 'Bishop Cheyney', pp. 226–7.

plementation of Elizabethan Protestantism, which he did not completely accept.

Cheyney may, thus, have used the potential inefficiencies inherent in the diocesan administrative structure in Gloucestershire to conceal his true reluctance to carry out his responsibilities to the Crown, especially the promotion and enforcement of official policy. During Edward's reign the reluctant, haphazard administration of the diocese by the chancellor, John Williams, had prompted Bishop Hooper to take personal control of the diocesan courts. However, Williams seems to have been more diligent in enforcing official policy under Mary, a trait not shared by his Elizabethan successors. Following Cheyney's consecration, he named John Lowth as his chancellor. Lowth served until inhibited in 1565, and, although little is known of his performance in Gloucester, the Archbishop of York, Edmund Grindal, was to find him difficult to manage when he served as archdeacon of Nottingham after leaving Gloucester. However, it is possible that Lowth's removal by Cheyney was based on their conflicting religious beliefs, since he may have been too zealous a Protestant for Cheyney's taste. He appears to have considered himself as such when, a few years later, he wrote his reminiscences of the years of Mary's reign and submitted them to John Foxe for inclusion in the latter's *Book of Martyrs*.[19]

Lowth's replacement, Thomas Powell, who was also chancellor of Worcester, served for a substantial portion of Cheyney's episcopate, presiding over the consistory court at a time when its reputation and authority were in a steady decline, a decline for which he was primarily to blame. Cheyney had known Powell before, as chancellor of Worcester, and consequently knew he was choosing someone with experience, though he may have misjudged Powell's standards and ethics.[20] The chancellor was relieved of his commission in January 1571 for unspecified reasons, which may have been related to the accusation made a year earlier that he was a 'wicked judge', and to his alleged willingness to accept bribes, which would be revealed in great detail a few years later.[21] His replacement was Richard Grene, with whom he had shared the chancellorship of Worcester since March 1566.[22] Grene then served for five years, until Powell was myster-

---

[19] GRO GDR vol. XII, p. 121; P. Collinson, *Archbishop Grindal, 1519–1583: the Struggle for the Reformed Church* (London, 1979), pp. 210–11; R. A. Marchant, *The Church under the Law: Justice, Administration and Discipline in the Diocese of York, 1560–1640* (Cambridge, 1969), pp. 150–1; Louth, 'Reminiscences', pp. 1–59.

[20] GRO GDR vol. XIII, p. 121; F. D. Price, 'Thomas Powell', p. 96; Cheyney to Archbishop Matthew Parker, from Halford, 24 January 1561, Corpus Christi College MS 114, p. 797; printed in part in C. G. Bayne, 'The Visitation of the Province of Canterbury, 1559', *Historical Review* 28 (1913), p. 640n.

[21] See chapter 7.

[22] GRO GDR vol. IX, p. 9; GDR vol. XXVII, pp. 113–14; 'Indenture of Agreement', GRO D48/Z2; F. D. Price, 'The Administration of the Diocese of Gloucester', p. 72.

iously reinstated. Perhaps the furore surrounding the latter's previous tenure had died down and it was once again safe for Cheyney to bring back his preferred chancellor. An examination of the consistory court records shows that Grene was significantly more conscientious and methodical in his administration of the court than was Powell.[23]

Bishop Cheyney's conduct, however, was not without its price, as he was not able to please either followers of the old religion or supporters of the new. Writing in 1568, Archbishop Matthew Parker lamented the 'rule [the bishop of] Glocester maketh in his people', while Edmund Campion, an earlier protégé of Richard Cheyney and future Jesuit martyr, criticised Cheyney from the opposite perspective in 1572, when he asserted, '[You are] the hatred of heretics, the pity of Catholics, the talk of the people, the sorrow of your friends, the joke of your enemies'.[24] Comments made by Gloucestershire priests and lay people support these assertions, as Cheyney's theology was viewed with suspicion and his authority flaunted. In October 1570, Arthur Blunt, a Gloucestershire priest, asserted that 'The bishopp is an Infidill of his Religion', and the vicar of Newent declared 'that my Lord Bissop had nothing to do in his [the vicar's] church and he would preach in his owne cure whether my Lord wold or no'.[25] Similarly, Thomas Westfield, who had previously been excommunicated but had refused to stay away from church, stated in May 1571 'that he did not care for the Bishoppes absolucion', and Richard Rowles of Leonard Stanley laughed when Cheyney made his assertion concerning the accuracy of the Geneva Bible.[26] This disregard for episcopal authority seems to have derived in part from Cheyney's theology, and in part from extreme dissatisfaction with Thomas Powell's chancellorship, exacerbated by Cheyney's apparent inability to rectify that situation. The result of the bishop's administrative style, combined with his choice of subordinates, resulted in the ineffective implementation of official policy, as the diocese was allowed to continue to wander in the religious wilderness.

Hence from the perspective of parishioners in early Elizabethan Gloucestershire, leadership in implementing reform had to come from the most exalted levels of the ecclesiastical hierarchy, that is, from the Crown or the Archbishop of Canterbury; it certainly was not coming from their bishop. The first such direction came in 1559, and a second would come in 1576; but in neither case was the diocese being singled out for special attention.[27]

[23] F. D. Price, 'Thomas Powell', pp. 96–7.

[24] Matthew Parker to William Cecil, from Lambeth, 19 August 1568, PRO SP 12/47/43; 'Campion the Martyr to Cheney, Anglican Bishop of Gloucester', *The Rambler: a Catholic Journal and Review*, new ser., 8 (1857), pp. 61–2. I would like to thank David Crankshaw for this reference.

[25] GRO GDR vol. IX, pp. 9–11.   [26] GRO GDR vol. IX, p. 106; vol. XXI, p. 304.

[27] There is no evidence that Matthew Parker ever conducted a metropolitical visitation of the

In 1559, Gloucestershire was visited as a part of the Royal Visitation to inaugurate the use of the new *Book of Common Prayer* and to encourage adherence to the Acts of Supremacy and Uniformity approved by Parliament in April of that year.[28] The royal visitors reached the western diocese in mid-August 1559, and conducted a thorough visitation based on the recently promulgated royal articles and injunctions.[29] All parsons were to preach against images and 'works devised by man's fantasies . . . as wandering of pilgrimages, setting up of candles, praying upon beads, or such like superstition', and parishes were to 'utterly extinct, and destroy' all images. Further, the parishes were to procure 'within three months next after this visitation . . . one booke of the whole Bible of the largest volume in English', and within twelve months they were to have the *Paraphrases* of Erasmus as well. As noted earlier, these directives were significantly stronger than the corresponding references to images in the Royal Injunctions of the same year, but it was this more forceful version that was impressed on local parishioners by the royal visitors.[30] By these and other similar actions, parish worship and individual lay piety were to be restored to their late Edwardian form; however, the changes would not be accomplished that easily.

As was true elsewhere in England, the initial flurry of liturgical changes in Gloucestershire in 1559 seem to have begun during or after the royal visitation of the county, Easter 1559 having been observed in the traditional manner, with the erection of the Easter sepulchre and the lighting of the Easter taper.[31] By autumn St Michael's, Gloucester, and Minchinhampton had purchased the new *Book of Common Prayer*. Before the end of the year, St Michael's also bought a psalter and paid two carpenters 14d 'to take downe the rode with Mary and John', thus removing statues which had been completed and set up less than a year earlier.[32] Two years later, St Michael's sold a large quantity of church goods, many to the same individuals who had purchased them eight years earlier, during Edward's reign. William Bond, the sometime mayor, purchased 'twoo of the best vestementes and the olde coope' for 36s, while another alderman and former mayor, Henry King, obtained 'one albe iij corporas cases ij endes of torches a canape to hange the sacramente in foure poundes of waxe foure

diocese of Gloucester, in spite of his disapproval of Richard Cheyney's performance as bishop.

[28] The visitors to the diocese of Gloucester included John Jewel, former Marian exile and future Bishop of Salisbury, William, Earl of Pembroke, and two lawyers. J. Strype, *Annals of the Reformation*, vol. I, pt. I, p. 248.

[29] Jewel to Peter Martyr, from London, 1 August 1559, in *Zurich Letters*, pt. I, p. 39; *TRP*, vol. II, p. 117; Bayne, 'The Visitation of the Province of Canterbury, 1559', pp. 636–69.

[30] *TRP*, vol. II, pp. 117–32, *passim*.   [31] R. Hutton, 'Local Impact', pp. 133–4.

[32] GRO P154/14 CW 1/11; P217 CW 2/1, p. 12.

bookes and a barre of yron' for 17s 4d, and a chalice for just over £4. Other parishioners purchased 'the oyle boxe', banners, a cushion, other vestments and books, and 'the roode postes'. Receipts totalled over £10. The evidence from the surviving wills of purchasers is too sparse to allow any general statement as to their motivation. However, the two who bought the largest share of goods, William Bond and Henry King, both left Protestant wills.[33] During that three-year period from 1559 to 1562, most congregations also seem to have acquired English Bibles, psalters, both volumes of the Homilies, and the *Paraphrases* of Erasmus, the essential texts of Protestant worship. Minchinhampton purchased a new Bible in 1560, the *Paraphrases* in 1561, and the books of Homilies in 1563. Tewkesbury bought the Homilies and a communion book in 1563, although this may not have been their first purchase of the 'service book' of 1559.[34] None the less, there is little evidence of the relatively thorough elimination of vestiges of the old religion suggested by a wider survey of contemporaneous churchwardens' accounts from all over England.[35]

Before the end of the decade, many parishes had made further modifications in their worship and liturgical space. St Michael's replaced their chalice with a communion cup, bought a new Bible, two communion books, the *Paraphrases* and a volume of the Homilies, and paid upholsterers for two carpets for the communion table. They also had the earth hauled out of the chancel once again to lower the area where the altar had been so they could pave it, and they hired one John Perser, carver, for 'makynge and carvynge of the frame in the quere', possibly for the communion table.[36] In addition, both St Michael's, Gloucester, and St James, Dursley, hired carpenters to build seats 'about the communion table', and St Michael's and Lechlade hired painters, as the Lechlade accounts said, 'for wrytynge of the churche', that is, painting the Ten Commandments, the creed and the Lord's Prayer on the walls of the church. At Dorsington, on the other hand, the churchwardens reported in 1572 that 'they have not sentences of scripture written in places where ymages were'. One wonders, given the cost of such painting (14s 4d at Lechlade) and the financial straits of many parishes, if there were not other parishes which were like Dorsington but just kept quiet on this point.[37] St Michael's and St Aldate's in Gloucester and the parish of Dursley were also among the parishes that whitewashed the interiors of their churches to

---

[33] GRO P154/14 CW 1/13; GRO Wills, 1565/116; PRO PROB 11/54, fo. 74.
[34] GRO P217 CW 2/1, pp. 15–16, 21; GRO P329 CW 2/1, pp. 1–2; printed in *Tewkesbury*, pp. 1–2.
[35] Hutton, 'Local Impact', pp. 133–7.   [36] GRO P154/14 CW 1/17, 1/18, 1/21–1/24.
[37] GRO P154/14 CW 1/25; P124 CW 2/4, fo. 6; P197 CW 2/1, fos. 3–3v; GRO GDR vol. XXIX, p. 197.

cover up the pre-Reformation paintings. There is little evidence that Gloucestershire parishes scraped the paintings off their church walls, possibly owing to the cost as much as to a desire to preserve the images. The parish of Kempley was one of the few exceptions. The alternative, whitewashing, had to be repeated frequently, as the pictures bled through and the whitewash could be rubbed off. A number of parishes reported that their wall-paintings were visible as late as 1572, either because the whitewash was no longer effective, or because they had yet to attempt to cover them.[38] Such whitewashing, while nominally compliant in that it hid the images, may have been motivated by a desire to preserve rather than eliminate the paintings, either because of a continued preference for traditional religion, or simply because of the value and beauty of the artwork thus concealed.

The provision of special sermons appeared even more slowly in Gloucestershire than did writing on church walls. These sermons were usually (though not always) a manifestation of the newly established faith, and were intended to be given in addition to the quarterly sermons required of each parish priest or his substitute. The only evidence of their occurrence before 1580 comes from the city of Gloucester, where on occasion the inhabitants assembled in the cathedral for such sermons. In his will dated August 1561 John Hichins, a woolen draper, left £25 'towardes the fyndinge [funding] of a preacher that shalbe able to instructe the people in Godes Booke and that he shall preache ones a daie for one whole yeare . . . within the citie of Glocester'.[39] Later that same year, probably in response to Hichins's largesse, the corporation paid a joiner 'for makynge the seates in the cathedrall churche' for the mayor and recorder of the city to occupy, and the next year a Mr Eton of Worcester, who was probably Guy Eaton, the former archdeacon of Gloucester and Marian exile, preached 'dyverse sermons within the sayd citye'. Then, in 1564/5, the city spent 20d 'for a fourme for the stewardes [of the city] to sitt upon in the mynster church and for a plancke to lye under their feet in the sermon tyme'. Two more seats and a number of cushions were added two years later, and in 1568/9 one William Ballard began receiving an annual fee 'for leienge upp the cussins in the colledge [cathedral]'.[40] While the corporation's funding of Mr Eton's sermons was the only entry of its type to appear in their records

[38] St Michael's whitewashed its walls in 1567 and 1574; Dursley did so in 1566 and 1571; and St Aldate's did it in 1568. GRO P154/14 CW 1/19, 1/25; P124 CW 2/4, fos. 5v, 10; P154/6 CW 1/5; Verey, *Gloucs.*, vol. II, pp. 279–80; GRO GDR vol. XXIX, pp. 94, 182, 188, 189, 229.

[39] PRO PROB 11/47, fos. 97v–98.

[40] GRO GBR F4/3, fos. 83v–202, *passim*.

prior to 1580, preaching appears to have been a regular feature of Elizabethan Gloucester by the end of the 1560s.

Civic preaching was a generally accepted manifestation of Protestantism, even if it was slow to become established in Gloucestershire. However, other manifestations of the new religion did appear, some of which moved beyond the bounds of official policy. In the early 1560s, in Alderly in the Cotswolds,

ther parsonne . . . preacheth unto [them] on a monethe or oftener . . . and [in the absence of a curate] at the requestes of the parishioners [a stipendiary priest] did minister and in the ministration did not use suche ornamentes as are appoynted, not in contempte of the lawe, nor beinge requyred to use them by any of the paryshe, nether to thoffence of any of them . . . [and he] did omit somme parte of the service appointed by the boke of commen prayer onely at suche tymes as he preachethe.[41]

However, clergy were not the only people who deviated from the Prayer Book. Richard Tracy, the Protestant pamphleteer, had 'for the space of twelve monithes declared the gospell and pistell or els a salme' during Sunday services in the parish of Stanway, in violation of Prayer Book rubrics but apparently with the approval of those present.[42]

Moreover, Tracy did not limit his rhetoric to the promotion of Protestantism within his parish church; he also addressed the danger of images in a letter to William Cecil, secretary to the queen. In pursuing this cause he was in illustrious company with John Jewel, Bishop of Salisbury, Edmund Grindal, then Bishop of London, and Richard Cox, Bishop of Ely. Cox wrote directly to the queen in the early 1560s respectfully declining to preside at the Eucharist in her chapel because of the images on her altar. Writing in 1565, Richard Tracy reminded Cecil that,

In the holy scryptures God threteneth to roote owte all ymages, and sayeth that he abhorrethe them and commaundeth hys people to destroy all the pyctures, and to breake asynnder althe ymages.

He then continued, saying he hoped the queen would destroy her images,

consyderynge that God off the other parte commaundeth not any magystrate to have any graven or molten ymage ne commaundethe any graven ymage or molten ymage to be seting upon any aulter.

Like his more illustrious counterparts, Tracy was probably distressed by the continued presence of images in local parish churches as well as in the royal chapel, and hoped the queen could be persuaded to take the lead in

---

[41] GRO GDR vol. XX, p. 18. This type of liturgical innovation was probably one of the factors which led in 1573 to the proclamation 'Prescribing Book of Common Prayer; Ordering Surrender of Admonition of Parliament', in *TRP*, vol. II, pp. 375–6.

[42] GRO GDR vol. XX, p. 81. Richard Tracy had held the lease of the manor of Stanway since 1533. See chapter 2.

eradicating them once and for all. Not surprisingly, he was no more successful than the bishops in pursuing this cause. Images would stay in the queen's chapel, although restrictions on them in parish churches would be enforced with increasing rigour in the next decade.[43]

Disputes and divisions among those responsible for creating and implementing official policy were also reflected at the parish level. Religious homogeneity may have characterised some parishes (whether traditional, conforming or more radically Protestant), but often that was not the case. In fact, parishes where there was total unanimity of opinion and belief probably did exist, but seldom appeared in the records, since no one would have necessarily seen fit to report suspect actions. In addition to the various manifestations of nonconformity by parish leaders and clergy which were recited to official visitors, the laity occasionally complained about practices which actually conformed, but of which they disapproved. Thus, in Minsterworth some parishioners disapproved of the actions of their curate, protesting in 1563 that

the curate refusathe to weare a cope at the mynistration of the holy communion and sayethe no man shall make him use any suche or like supersticion, further on Sondayes he dothe wearie the parrishe with over longe prechinge . . . not beinge graduate or licensed otherwise.[44]

This case and others like it may provide evidence of the presence of individual lay people with strong religious convictions which went beyond official policy. On the other hand, such presentments may indicate that some parishioners lacked sufficient knowledge to report accurately on nonconforming practices. In a number of cases, however, nonconformity was too obvious to miss. For instance, a number of men demonstrated resistance to local liturgical practices and called public attention to the fact by their presence right outside the church doors during services. In addition, a number of parishioners of Chipping Camden, Ruardean, Tewkesbury and Maisemore were presented in 1563 because they did '[walk,] taulke and jangle at servyce tyme'. In 1569, fourteen men were presented for walking and talking loudly during divine service. In the parish of Hinton-on-the-Green, located in the northern-most portion of the diocese, 'the youthe . . . will not tarye in the church at the tyme of service but will go out of the church before it be doen', and probably before communion. However, this may have been due to their youth, rather than to their church papistry. Similarly, Richard Myllarde the younger, of

---

[43] SP 12/36/37; Inner Temple Library MS, Petyt MS 538/47, fo. 555, printed in J. Strype, *Annals of the Reformation*, vol. I, pt. II, pp. 500–1.

[44] GRO GDR vol. XX, p. 32. Some parishes, however, responded to change with greater unanimity, as did the parishioners of Southrop, where the rood loft was still standing in 1563. GRO GDR vol. XX, p. 67.

Cowley, and John Colles, of North Cerney, left the church before the distribution of the bread and wine.[45] At Tewkesbury, in 1563, three men of the parish 'did walke with ther cappes on ther heades at the tyme of the holy communion before the chauncell doore' (that is, across the front of the nave or body of the church where the door to the chancel or choir was located), in an action which indicated both their disapproval of the form of worship being practised and their refusal to communicate. This latter case is all the more remarkable, because those walking in front of the chancel door were the bailiffs of the town, John Butler and Thomas Godwin, accompanied by William Cole, gentleman. In addition, since the bailiffs of Tewkesbury were ultimately responsible for that parish, they were further implicated when the same set of presentments also disclosed a number of 'not defaced relics' still in the possession of the parish. These included a pax, candlesticks, censors, incense, a mass book, processionals, and two 'clappers to go about with on Good Friday', all items which should have been destroyed by this date. In the same parish at about the same time two other men 'were sittinge behinde the church doore with ther cappes on ther heades at the common prayer'.[46]

In any case, conforming to the established religion was only one of the concerns of parish leaders. Cardinal Pole's archiepiscopal visitation in 1556 had revealed an alarmingly high incidence of dilapidated churches throughout the realm, owing at least in part to parishes' struggling to meet the combined demands of building maintenance and changing liturgical requirements in the face of decreasing gifts and increasing costs.[47] Such was the case in Gloucestershire. If the corporate response to Elizabethan Protestantism was generally one of reluctant limited acceptance, at least during the first decade of the reign, then perhaps part of that reluctance was prompted by the cost of the liturgical changes used to measure conformity, rather than by parishioners' religious beliefs. In the instances where compliance with official religious policy was given priority over building maintenance, the physical condition of parish buildings probably suffered. There may very well have been too many requirements placed on the limited means at parishes' disposal. In 1563, half of all the parishes in the diocese needed to make urgent repairs to some aspect of their properties, and a quarter had broken windows.[48] In the small parish of Barnwood, on the outskirts of the city of Gloucester, the church was in such 'great

---

[45] GRO GDR vol. XX, pp. 44, 79, 82; vol. XXVI, pp. 54–6; vol. XXXX, fos. 125v, 161, 251. For a discussion of youth and the church, see P. Griffiths, *Youth and Authority: Formative Experiences in England 1560–1640* (Oxford, 1996), pp. 178–200, *passim*.

[46] GRO GDR vol. XX, p. 44.   [47] Haigh, *Reformations*, p. 212.

[48] Slightly fewer parishes in the northern vale had 'ruinous' structures or needed glazing than in the rest of the diocese. GRO GDR vol. XX, *passim*.

decay . . . [that] yf it be not remedyed in tyme it will fawle'.[49] However, even in a reasonably large, substantial and conscientiously conforming parish like St Michael's, much-needed repairs to the church tower consumed parish financial resources in 1560, causing that parish to defer a number of liturgical changes until the following year.[50] Similarly, Minchinhampton spent a great deal on its steeple in the early years of the reign, finally paying to have its top dismantled at that time.[51] The steeples of other parishes were also in need of immediate attention in 1563.[52] However, Tewkesbury missed its chance. Saddled as they were with a huge edifice, the churchwardens regularly spent a large proportion of their parish funds on maintenance, but did not act promptly enough to save their beautiful, lead-clad steeple, which came crashing down on Easter Day 1559.[53]

During the first ten years of Elizabeth's reign, however, several parishes made physical changes requiring substantial funds, as well as devoting significant sums to ordinary maintenance. At Dursley, masons worked on the wall by the chapel in the church and re-pointed the steeple.[54] To the east in the Cotswolds, the parish of Lechlade paid carpenters to build a partition between the chancel and the north aisle to create a 'scole howse'.[55] Meanwhile, at Tewkesbury a large new chancel window was installed, presumably partially filling the arch which had previously led to the pre-Reformation Lady Chapel at the east end of the church.[56] Similarly, Teddington built a new stone tower in 1567 to incorporate a window and arch acquired from Hailes Abbey.[57] Thus, some parishes were still able to raise funds for projects which were deemed to be important enough to warrant special effort, even if they could not fund full compliance with official religious policy. On the other hand, such responses may have been manifestations of covert resistance to change, rather than simply conflicting priorities. As with individual actions and expressions of beliefs, the motivations for such representations of faith are inherently multi-faceted and hence difficult to discern with any certainty.

When these complex parish responses are overlaid with the actions of individual lay people, the kaleidoscopic nature of lay religion in Gloucestershire under Elizabeth begins to emerge. Official policy did not translate

[49] GRO GDR vol. XX, p. 6.   [50] GRO P154/14 CW 1/12.

[51] GRO P217 CW 2/1, pp. 13–15, 20–1.

[52] These parishes were Lower Guiting, Naunton and North Cerney in the Cotswolds, Ruardean in the Forest, and Tortworth in the southern vale. GRO GDR vol. XX, *passim*.

[53] GRO P329 CW 2/1, fo. v.   [54] GRO P124 CW 2/4, fos. 6, 10.

[55] GRO P197 CW 2/1, fos. 4v, 5v.

[56] GRO P329 CW 2/1, pp. 15–18, 43; printed in *Tewkesbury*, pp. 10–13, 27–8. The Lady Chapel had been demolished shortly after the dissolution of the Abbey. See chapter 3.

[57] Verey, *Gloucs.*, vol. II, p. 356.

directly into consistently observed liturgical practices, as the diocesan religious drift continued to include a wide range of conservative customs, as well as aspects of conformity. Thus, those who objected to the forms of worship they found in their parish churches were not necessarily disagreeing with official religious policy; rather, in some cases, they may have been trying to draw attention to the lack of local conformity. Parish liturgy across the diocese stretched from the use of copes by some priests and of beads and Latin primers by church papists, to Protestant rectors preaching too long for some people's taste. This spectrum of responses had been prompted by the ambiguous official pronouncements of the established Church. Through the 1560s, Catholics were finding it increasingly difficult to conform, and Puritans were growing more and more aware of the limits beyond which Elizabethan Protestantism was unlikely to go. Meanwhile, the majority who were trying diligently to conform, at least outwardly, did not always have a clear understanding of the specific rubrics of that conformity, given the variety of its local manifestations and conflicting directives from the queen and her archbishop. However, when the forms to which they were expected to adhere were made clear, those trying to conform were frequently reluctant to give up all of the vestiges of the old religion for practices which seemed strange and different or devoid of valued aspects of the old.

None the less, actions were only one way in which lay people responded to the policies of Elizabethan Protestantism. They also used words, the words of their wills, and by these statements frequently revealed an initial reluctance to give up traditional beliefs quite similar to that manifested in parish responses to official policy during the same period.

The swing from traditional to ambiguous statements of faith in the wills of non-elite lay people during the first year following Elizabeth's accession was both abrupt and pronounced, as it had been early in Edward's reign. Whereas in 1557 and 1558 approximately equal numbers of wills included traditional and ambiguous soul bequests, by 1560 the proportion of ambiguous preambles had jumped to 70 per cent, while the incidence of traditional statements had fallen to just under 30 per cent. This was a repetition of the change in the pattern of preamble preferences seen in 1547 and 1548, and the mirror image of that evident during the years under Mary.[58] Presented with the reintroduction of the new religion, Elizabethan

---

[58] See Figure 6.1, and Appendix B. Chi-square value = 525.95 with 8 degrees of freedom based on the total annual preambles in each of the three general categories is an extremely significant value. This analysis is based on a sample of 1,470 wills; 803 from women and 667 from men, with 118 traditional preambles, 1,237 which were ambiguous, and 100 distinctly Protestant, drawn from approximately 4,400 extant wills written between December 1558 and 1580, and proved in the diocese of Gloucester. Thus, assuming the highest possible variability of the sample from the population, the results of the analysis

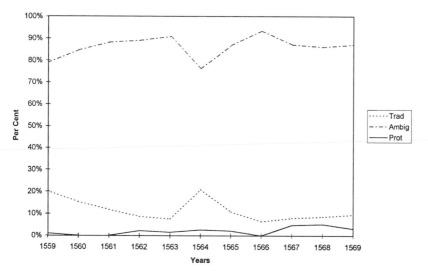

Figure 6.1   Non-elite will preambles (1559–1569)

testators and their scribes in Gloucestershire seem to have chosen to 'keep their heads down'. In this way, they could conceal their continued preference for the old religion.

Despite the predominance of ambiguous preambles, the complexity and variety of those statements of faith continued to increase. The trend begun under Edward and Mary continued with testators often using language that was their own, or was at most used by only a few other people. That is not to say that the previous formulas had vanished, but they now shared the stage with new, sometimes idiosyncratic, forms. Even the most common of these preambles became more varied. Whereas, the bequest of the soul 'to Almighty God' had been the dominant form during Edward's reign, it was now joined by several variations on that common theme. Richard Collier, a weaver from North Nibley, was quite typical in using a slightly expanded version of the standard ambiguous statement, in which he bequeathed his soul 'into the handes of Almightie God my creatour and redemer'.[59] Such variations also might incorporate expressions of a more Christocentric lay piety, as in the preamble used by Thomas Hemmynges, a labourer from Broad Campden, who declared: 'I bequeythe my soule to Allmightye God my maker and to Jhesu Christ his sone my redemer and saviour.'[60]

Similarly, Henry Drewrye of Tewkesbury combined a reference to the

will be within 1.31 per cent of that for the entire population at the 95 per cent confidence level. Schofield, 'Sampling in Historical Research', pp. 154–61.
[59] GRO Wills, 1570/155.   [60] GRO Wills, 1564/96.

passion with the passage from Job when he bequeathed his soul 'to Almyghtie God that boughte it with his most precyous blood', and left his body to the earth, 'ther to remayne tyll the later daye that it shall pleas theternall God to rayse it agen to be unyted with my sowle as I doo most fyrmely and assuredly beleve'.[61] Robert Horner, a shearman of St Michael's in Gloucester, and Margery Rigge, a single woman of Teynton, chose a slightly different emphasis when they described Christ as 'my only savior and reademer' in soul bequests, thus expressing their belief in salvation through Christ's death and passion without giving up their theological ambiguity.[62] These wills exemplify the move to use the word 'only' more often, even if the religious sense of the preamble was not changing, perhaps in an attempt to continue to hide the testator's true beliefs in the face of the generally increasing inclusion of the word 'only' and other changing conventions concerning such statements.

In addition, the formulas which invoked the passion were changed in more fundamental ways in certain cases, as belief in salvation through Christ's passion was replaced or augmented by references to his resurrection. The hope and joy of Easter were apparently replacing the sense of despair and unworthiness of Good Friday for some lay people. Writing in 1569 and 1573, respectively, Dorothy Evett and Elizabeth Sowthern, both of Mickleton in the northern Cotswolds, used the same formula: 'I bequethe my soule to Almighty God my maker and redemor Jesus Christe trustinge by the merites of hys glorius resurreccion and assention to be saved.'[63] Not only were expressions of faith becoming more Christocentric, the Christ at the centre was often the resurrected saviour, rather than the Christ on the cross.

While the choice of language and theological emphases in elite wills was consistent with that found in the wills of their more ordinary neighbours, the pattern of religious preferences in the wills of early Elizabethan Gloucestershire gentry differs somewhat in one important respect. Whereas under 5 per cent of non-elite wills included Protestant preambles between 1559 and 1569, 19 per cent of the elite wills from the same period included such statements.[64] As was the case in Edward's reign, the gentry accepted Protestantism more quickly than did the ordinary inhabitants of the county, but the difference between elite and non-elite responses was slightly greater in this case. While declarations of Catholic or traditional faith were proportionally equivalent for the two groups, fewer of the elite opted for religious ambiguity. Thus, as the pattern of religious expression in non-elite wills in the first decade of Elizabeth's reign echoed that of Edward's reign,

---

[61] GRO Wills, 1561/33.   [62] GRO Wills, 1559/242, 1563/85.
[63] GRO Wills, 1570/22, 1573/36.   [64] See Figure 6.2.

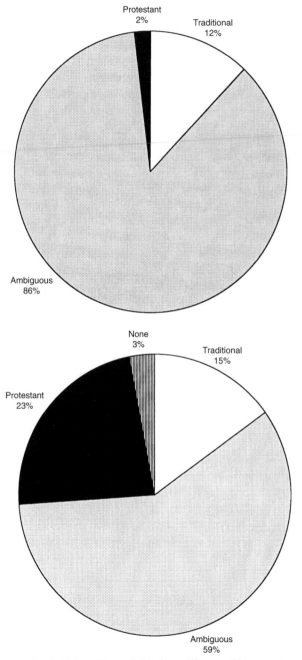

Figure 6.2   (a) Non-elite and (b) elite will preambles (1559–1569)

so too did the pattern among gentry wills; but in one case the trend was toward ambiguous statements of faith, while in the other it was at least tentatively toward declarations of Protestantism.

Shifts in lay religious beliefs are also manifested in the evolving preferences for different types of charitable bequests, both large and small. As in earlier times, these included bequests to parishes, municipalities and to the poor. After Elizabeth's accession, the decline in ritualistic parish bequests begun during the previous decade continued through the 1560s, before stabilizing in the 1570s.[65] The most common parish gift at that time was a few pence to a few shillings toward unspecified expenses, but by the mid-1560s an increasing proportion of testators were designating such bequests for repairs, perhaps having recognised the desperate condition of their parish churches. In 1564, Jone Blount bequeathed 12d for the repair of the parish bells, and a year later Arthur Crewe, a clothier of Hawkesbury, gave 40s 'towardes the pavinge and makinge of a convenient place for the comunion to be ministred in within the parishe churche', presumably the paving of the area where the altar had been.[66] Many others left sums ranging from 12d to £10 for the more general maintenance of their parish churches. On the average, by 1570, just under 10 per cent of all testators were leaving something to their parish church, with a slightly higher proportion of women than men making such gifts. Small or ritualistic municipal bequests also suffered somewhat at this time, although the decrease was less pronounced. The annual proportion of wills including such gifts had been quite erratic, at least since 1541, and continued in like manner through the 1560s, before settling down to appear in an average of only 2 per cent of wills in the 1570s.

Bequests to the poor were another matter, however. Perhaps the most generous of these gifts came from Sir Thomas Bell, former Mayor of Gloucester and opponent of Bishop Hugh Latimer so many years earlier, whose will is dated 20 September 1559. It begins with an ambiguous but Trinitarian soul bequest, and then goes on to leave a number of recently constructed buildings

unto the maior and burgesses of the citie of Gloucester and theire successors for ever to the entent purpose and use . . . susteynaunce and maytenaunce of fyve poore and impotente folkes to abyde and inhabite in the . . . howsen by me buylded.

The will then continues by stipulating the conditions of Sir Thomas's largesse, namely, that

every of the . . . poore folkes havynge no impedimente by sickenes daylie assemble them selfes to gether in to the bodie of the chappell there called sometymes Saunte Keneboroughes chappell in the mornynge betwene the howres of seven and eight of

[65] See Appendix B.   [66] PRO PROB 11/53, fos. 316–17v.

the clock and saye fyve pater nosters and a crede in the honor of the father the son and the holie goost.[67]

Thus Sir Thomas continued the traditional practice of including an explicit *quid pro quo* to be fulfilled by his impoverished beneficiaries, albeit in slightly modified form, since he did not request prayers for his soul. Other significant gifts to the poor during the first few years after Elizabeth's accession were less generous and less traditional in their motivation. An example of such a bequest was that of Margaret Hickes of Tewkesbury, who, having bequeathed her soul to Almighty God, left the rents from specified lands to aid the poor of her parish.[68] Meanwhile, the popularity of more modest provisions of this type increased sharply, while the percentage of testators leaving nothing to the poor declined steadily.[69] Such gifts achieved a new high of nearly 30 per cent among both elite and ordinary testators in the mid-1560s, a level that would be maintained at least until the late 1570s. While the popularity of the modest gifts to the poor may initially have been due to the fact that it was the only remaining traditional bequest condoned by the authorities, and therefore could be a further sign of preference for the old religion, the continuing high proportion of such gifts in the 1570s probably indicates that people were responding to the ideas of civic humanism combined with a scripturally based understanding of stewardship.[70] As they had done in Mary's reign, testators usually restricted their gifts in some way, such as designating the funds for poor householders in their parish or for householders within the parish who lacked ploughlands.

Even some Catholic testators give evidence of changing lay piety. Writing in 1565, Anthony Ayleworth of Naunton in the Cotswolds bequeathed his soul quite traditionally to 'almightie God, and to owre blessed Ladie Sainte Marie and to the whole cumpaignie of heaven', but then went on to restrict some of his charitable gifts. Each communicant of his parish, rather than each inhabitant, was to receive 4d, and every child that could recite the Lord's Prayer would get 2d, while those who could not would each get only 1d.[71] This will is quite revealing in several ways, and perhaps provides a glimpse of both the ambiguity and the complexity of beliefs in England in the 1560s. Ayleworth clearly valued at least a modicum of catechising among the young. Furthermore, while his choice of words to describe the fellow-parishioners who were to benefit from his generosity may have been coincidental, his reference to 'communicants' rather than 'inhabitants' is unusual. Thus, he may well have wanted to restrict his gifts to his more

---

[67] GRO Wills 1566/150.   [68] GRO Wills 1562/71.   [69] See Appendix B.
[70] Duffy, *Stripping*, pp. 504–5; Todd, *Christian Humanism*, pp. 133–8.
[71] PRO PROB 11/48, fos. 176–76v.

pious neighbours, excluding those residing in the parish who were not so classified. He is promoting receiving communion in the Elizabethan Protestant church while espousing his own Catholic beliefs, an apparent paradox, but one which was fairly common in Gloucestershire and elsewhere at that time, before the Crown clarified its religious policy and more carefully defined the nature of the established religion.[72]

As the 1560s came to a close, so too did the *de facto* tolerance of Catholics and radical Protestants or Precisians. Several forces converged to prompt the Crown and Council to clamp down on nonconformity of whatever stripe, although in some parts of England checks on Catholicism had been implemented somewhat earlier. In the diocese of Norwich, the godly Bishop John Parkhurst had moved against selected prominent priests and lay people with Catholic sympathies. A metropolitical visitation had taken similar steps in the diocese of Chester, where the conservative bishop, William Downham, had allowed Catholicism to flourish.[73] Somewhat surprisingly, the diocese of Gloucester, with its continuation of many traditional practices and its retention of many forbidden items, did not receive similar attention. Perhaps the extent of Catholic survival in Cheshire was greater than that in Gloucestershire.

In any case, the nature of Elizabethan Protestantism became much clearer throughout the realm at the end of the decade as a result of the Crown's responses to a number of separate events, some in support of Catholicism and others promoting additional Protestant reforms. Three developments were related to attempts to restore Catholicism. In 1569, the northern earls rose up against the Crown and demanded among other things a return to the old religion. In 1570, the Pope issued the bull *Regnans in Excelsis*, excommunicating Elizabeth and consequently placing English Catholics in a very difficult position. Their allegiance to their church and their monarch were now in conflict, and the penalties were great on both counts: some chose church papistry, which often included abstaining from communion, while others became determined recusants, increasing the numbers reported as absent. Finally, in 1571, the ill-fated Ridolphi Plot came to light. It would have restored Catholicism to England by replacing Elizabeth with her Catholic cousin Mary Stuart, and making the Duke of Norfolk her king. These developments prompted a more vigilant watch over papists. Meanwhile, manifestations of Puritanism, most notably the Vestiarian Controversy of 1565–6 which centred on the question of appropriate clerical attire, prompted the authorities to delineate more explicitly the bounds of acceptable Protestantism. The efforts to

[72] For further discussion of this behaviour, see A. Walsham, *Church Papists: Catholicism, Conformity and Confessional Polemic in Early Modern England* (Woodbridge, 1993).
[73] MacCulloch, *Suffolk*, pp. 192–3; C. Haigh, *Reformation and Resistance*, p. 259.

curtail and discipline both Catholics and Protestants would be supported in the early 1570s by the passage of statutes approving the Articles of Religion which clarified the bounds of Elizabethan Protestantism, and by associating reconciliation with the papacy with treason. Henceforth, the focus would be on outward conformity not private faith, but enforcement of acceptable worship practices and the like would be a significant change for the laity in dioceses such as Gloucester.[74]

Elizabeth's reign had begun rather tentatively, with some policies being held in abeyance as the Government waited to see whom she would marry. Furthermore, the queen's disagreements with the bishops and archbishop had resulted in the issuance of conflicting definitions of conformity during the first year of her reign. The lack of clear guidelines or consistent enforcement over the next ten years merely aggravated an already difficult situation. In Gloucestershire, Bishop Richard Cheyney would have welcomed that ambivalence and administrative neglect, given his hostility to the established religion, and the lay people, who had been happy with the restoration of Catholicism just a few years earlier, would have relished the lack of a clear, vigorously enforced policy. It may also have been welcomed by the more godly Protestants, who saw benign neglect as their opportunity to worship as they wished, emphasising preaching of the lively Word over ceremony and the Eucharist. Then, as the new decade began, the Crown's vision of the established church gained further definition: the rules were changed, and enforcement of outward conformity came to characterise Elizabethan religious policy.

[74] 13 Elizabeth, c. 2, 3, 13. Cf. J. J. LaRocca, 'Time, Death and the Next Generation: the Early Elizabethan Recusancy Policy, 1558–1574', *Albion* 14 (1982), pp. 103–17.

The clarification of the religious settlement (1570–1580)

After the ambiguity of the 1560s, official religion in the second decade of Elizabeth's reign was remarkably well focused and more energetically enforced that it had been previously. The emphasis would be on actions rather than thoughts, public worship rather than private prayer. Thus, attending church was more important to the Crown than taking communion, and priests' attire was more important than their knowledge (at least if one is to judge by the penalties for transgressing the rules). Not only did those in power have a relatively clear vision of acceptable Protestantism, but they also had the advantage over previous reigns of having a reasonably stable policy which had been in place for several years. They may have clarified and even narrowed the boundaries of acceptable religious expression, but at least the people had not been confronted by a swing of the religious pendulum in over ten years. In more and more parishes throughout the realm the externals of the new religion were becoming familiar. Elizabethan Protestantism was becoming a known quantity to increasing numbers of people; and yet, even in 1580, the movement toward full acceptance of the new religion would be just beginning.

In the 1570s, Elizabeth and her advisors were finding new means of enforcing conformity among the nobles and gentry. The saga of the Berkeley/Lisle land dispute and the related 'poaching war' provided such an opportunity. While ostensibly a dispute over land, it took on religious overtones during Elizabeth's reign, and seems to have involved a number of Gloucestershire gentry. Furthermore, some of the most heated exchanges occurred in this decade, key protagonists of which included Elizabeth's favourite, Robert Dudley (the Earl of Leicester), Katherine, Lady Berkeley (sister of Thomas Howard, the Duke of Norfolk, who was executed in 1572 for his involvement in the Ridolphi Plot), and Katherine's husband, Henry, Lord Berkeley. The Berkeleys were Catholics, while Leicester was a known supporter of godly Protestantism and had been an arch-enemy of the Duke of Norfolk. Leicester's supporters in this dispute included Sir Nicholas Poyntz, Sir Giles Poole, Sir Thomas Throckmorton, Richard

Berkeley (a cousin of Lord Berkeley), and Sir John Tracy (Throckmorton's son-in-law, grandnephew of the Protestant pamphleteer, Richard Tracy, and a Member of Parliament for the county), all of whom favoured the new religion.[1]

The dispute had begun early in the fifteenth century over rights of inheritance to the Berkeley holdings between the Lisles and the Berkeleys.[2] To complicate matters, the Crown had also gained an interest in the disputed lands through a series of convoluted exchanges earlier in the sixteenth century. In Elizabeth's reign, the standard-bearer for the Lisle family was none other than the Earl of Leicester. Prior to 1572, in an attempt to negotiate a settlement to the dispute, he had made overtures for the two Berkeley daughters to marry his nephews, Sir Philip Sidney and his brother, Robert, who would one day be Lord Lisle. Lady Berkeley had declined, but then her political position had changed for the worse after her brother's execution.[3] Leicester and the queen then moved to increase the pressure on the Berkeleys to give up their claims to the disputed lands, using both conventional law-suits and less conventional poaching to further their cause. In 1572, while on a royal progress which included Gloucestershire, Elizabeth, accompanied by Leicester, visited Berkeley Castle while Lord Berkeley was away. While there, they hunted Berkeley's deer without permission, killing twenty-seven the first day and more the next.[4] That same year several of the county elite, namely, Sir Nicholas Poyntz, Sir Giles Poole, Sir Thomas Throckmorton and Richard Berkeley, wrote to Lord Berkeley urging him to accept Leicester's marriage proposal, but to no avail.[5]

Thus, in Gloucester, with Leicester and his Protestant supporters pitted against the Catholic Berkeleys, poaching became a surrogate for battles over religion, as well as for disputes between rival elite families in the turbulent 1570s. As the suits continued in London, so too did the poaching war in Gloucestershire under the leadership of Leicester's energetic and well-connected representative, Sir Thomas Throckmorton, and there were now two goals. In addition to reclaiming lost land, this series of battles in the courts and the forests would send a message to the Berkeleys and others who might be hoping for a return to Catholicism. Covert Catholicism

---

[1] R. B. Manning, *Hunters and Poachers: A Cultural and Social History of Unlawful Hunting in England 1485–1640* (Oxford, 1993), p. 137; I. H. Jeayes, comp., *Descriptive Catalogue of the Charters and Muniments at Berkeley Castle* (Bristol, 1892), p. 333.

[2] J. H. Cooke, 'The Great Berkeley Law-Suit of the 15th and 16th Centuries', *TBGAS* 3 (1878), p. 305.

[3] J. H. Cooke, 'The Great Berkeley Law-Suit', p. 321.

[4] R. B. Manning, *Hunters and Poachers*, pp. 48–9; J. H. Cooke, 'The Great Berkeley Law-Suit', p. 321.

[5] I. H. Jeayes, *Descriptive Catalogue*, p. 330.

might be tolerated, but rebellions such as the Ridolphi Plot would not be, and the Berkeleys would not forget that. Religion and politics, as well as religion and revolt, had long been intertwined. In this instance, Elizabeth and Leicester used poaching along with more legitimate means of control to discourage another rebellion, but also to enforce religious conformity more rigorously, and in this effort they appear to have had the support of at least a few of the local gentry.

None the less, this and other more conventional strategies, such as the development of a more definitive religious policy early in the decade, did not bring either immediate ecclesiastical uniformity or religious conformity. The Crown and Council would continue to contend with recalcitrant clergy and lay people. In Gloucestershire, as elsewhere, those who clung to the old religion did so with increasing tenacity, while the more radical among the godly Protestants continued to resist the pressure to conform. However, Bishop Cheyney's episcopate created an atypical situation in that diocese. His lackadaisical approach to his responsibilities and Chancellor Thomas Powell's corruption combined to create an environment which nurtured religious diversity. Powell's tenure as chancellor was interrupted from 1571 to 1576, and it is difficult to understand why he was reinstated. His second term ran for almost three years before the sub-dean of Gloucester Cathedral brought suit against him before the High Commission in London. A survey of the records of the diocese, probably conducted in 1578 in preparation for filing the suit, revealed significant abuses of Powell's position. Of the 300–400 persons presented before Powell for moral offences such as incest, fornication and adultery during his chancellorship, fewer than thirty had confessed, done penance in public or had their penance properly commuted. It was alleged that Thomas Powell had commuted the sentences of the others in exchange for monetary payments.[6] He finally disappears from the records of the Gloucester consistory court after 28 January 1579, just months before Bishop Cheyney's death.[7] His removal in the first instance in 1571 may have been the result of a similar set of accusations, now lost, which Cheyney could not ignore. Certainly, the ineffective administration which resulted from his negligence would have hindered the promotion of Protestantism in Gloucestershire under Cheyney, and that may well have been the bishop's intent.

The ineffectiveness and corruption of the diocesan consistory court also

---

[6] PRO SP 12/146/82.

[7] The plaintiff's brief, which is the only surviving document from the litigation in the High Commission, contains twelve accusations, each supported by several individuals. Richard Cheyney appears as an accuser in four charges, including those alleging that Powell had commuted sentences 'without the Bushoppes consent . . . and against his will', and that he had commuted hundreds of sentences for money. F. D. Price, 'Thomas Powell', p. 104; PRO SP 12/146/82.

prompted the Crown to establish a Commission for Ecclesiastical Causes within the dioceses of both Bristol and Gloucester in 1574. Those who served on the Commission included Giles Lord Chandos, Sir Giles Poole, Sir Nicholas Poyntz, Sir John Tracy and Richard Berkeley, as well as Bishop Cheyney, Dean Laurence Humphrey of Gloucester Cathedral, the diocesan chancellor, and the recorder and successive mayors of the city of Gloucester. The Commission's powers were sweeping, including both the normal authority of the consistory court and the additional option of employing the civil authorities and penalties to enforce Commission judgments.[8] This new body was not intended to replace the consistory court, but rather to augment it and reinforce its powers. Although the enforcement of religious conformity was given as the primary reason for its creation, the Commission ultimately dealt with the same range of offences as the consistory court, with cases being referred back and forth between the two. In the final analysis, the opportunity for recourse to temporal as well as spiritual discipline enabled the Commission to deal effectively with moral offenders. However, not even those additional powers were sufficient to induce those charged with religious nonconformity or recusancy to submit to its judgments. The authorities kept trying, but faith was a strong motivator. Ultimately, then, this tribunal became just another embodiment of the ineffective administration which plagued the Elizabethan diocese of Gloucester at least through the 1560s and 1570s.

In the absence of effective episcopal leadership to promote and enforce Elizabethan Protestantism, there were two other ways in which the requisite changes could be effected: either through the work of the parish clergy or by the good offices of the Archbishop of Canterbury. Generally, as was true elsewhere in England, parish clergy in the diocese lacked the qualifications and authority necessary to promote Protestantism effectively. Although the quality of the clergy began to improve in richer dioceses in the 1570s, such was not the case in the diocese of Gloucester.[9] There, the clergy deprived in Mary's reign did not, for the most part, return to their livings in the diocese of Gloucester following her death, and parishes compensated for vacancies and non-resident rectors by hiring poorly trained stipendiary clergy.[10] A survey of the clergy, probably conducted in 1584, indicates that although some progress had been made in the level of

---

[8] *Commission*, pp. 44–7. For further discussion of the work of this commission in Gloucester, see Price, 'The Commission for Ecclesiastical Causes', pp. 61–184. For a more general discussion of the Elizabethan reliance on such commissions and their impact on the authority of the bishops, see Manning, 'The Crisis of Episcopal Authority', pp. 1–25.

[9] Haigh, *Reformations*, pp. 268–72, *passim*.

[10] John Parkhurst, the Oxford educated rector of Bishop's Cleve, Marian exile, and future Bishop of Norwich, was a notable exception. John Parkhurst to Josiah Simler, from Bishop's Cleve, 20 December 1559, in *Zurich Letters*, vol. I, p. 61.

skill and learning since Bishop Hooper's survey in 1551, the difference was not substantial.[11] The earlier survey had revealed that over half the clergy in Edwardian Gloucestershire lacked both knowledge of scripture and the learning expected of prospective communicants.[12] The later appraisal assessed the clergy on their knowledge of scripture and Latin, and revealed greater proficiency in Latin than in biblical knowledge. Only 96 of the 308 Gloucestershire parishes (just over 30 per cent) are represented in the returns, but of that number the clergy of over half (55) of the livings were described as 'well seen', 'sufficient', 'perfect' or 'learned' in Latin, or were characterised as understanding the language. Slightly fewer (48) were judged to be 'sound', 'zealous', 'well seen', 'mete divine[s]', or 'good scholar[s]' with respect to the scriptures. Just 11 of the 96 respondents were given poor ratings, such as having 'small skill', or 'indifferent' knowledge. The other 28 were described variously as 'meanly seen', having 'reasonable skill' or being 'so so'.[13] Thus, as late as 1584, many parishes still lacked adequate clergy. The leadership void which existed at the highest level in the diocese extended down to its lowest level, the individual parish.

Only with the archiepiscopal visitation of 1576 were parishes which still practised aspects of the old religion or had forbidden items in their inventories called to account for their ways.[14] Other dioceses had achieved a significant degree of parish conformity to Elizabethan Protestantism several years earlier. For instance, the diocese of Norwich had made at least a partial shift as a result of a special metropolitical visitation in 1567, organised to compensate for Bishop Parkhurst's lack of administrative abilities.[15] The visitation in 1576 was intended for the whole province of Canterbury, and thus was not in response to particular problems in the diocese of Gloucester. However, it may have had a greater impact on lay religion there than had any of the previous actions of the diocesan hierarchy. The articles of inquiry were probing and fairly detailed, and the archbishop's commissioned representatives, Laurence Humphrey and Arthur Saule, were particularly zealous Protestants, both having lived in exile during Mary's reign. Humphrey, who in 1576 was dean of Gloucester,

---

[11] D. M. Owen, *A Catalogue of Lambeth Manuscripts 889 to 901, Carte Antique et Miscellanee* (Gateshead, 1968), p. 9. Based on a comparison of the incumbents listed in the survey and the Bishop's Register for the years 1576 to 1584, it appears that the clergy survey for the diocese of Gloucester, which is described in that volume as a result of Grindal's directive of 1576, could not have originated that early, but was probably carried out in the summer of 1584. Lambeth Palace Library MS, *Carte Miscellanee XII/7*; GRO GDR vol. Ib, pp. 32–8.

[12] 'Visitation Booke', pp. 17–77.   [13] GRO GDR vol. XXXIX, unpaginated.

[14] 'Articles to be Enquired of Within the Province of Canterbury,' in *The Remains of Edmund Grindal*, ed. W. Nicholson (Cambridge, 1843), pp. 156–77.

[15] R. Houlbrooke, *Church Courts and the People During the English Reformation, 1520–1570* (Oxford, 1979), pp. 39, 190–1.

had returned from the continent to become regius professor of divinity at Oxford in 1560, and president of Magdalen College, Oxford, the following year. In the mid-1560s, he and his colleague, Thomas Sampson, dean of Christ Church, Oxford, were at the centre of the Vestiarian Controversy, for which the surplice and the square cap became the symbols.[16] He was installed as dean of Gloucester on 13 March 1571 and promptly reappointed the former Marian exile, Guy Eaton, as archdeacon of Gloucester. Meanwhile, in 1562, Saule had been installed as a prebend of Gloucester Cathedral. Three years later he was appointed by Thomas Bentham, Bishop of Lichfield and Coventry, to make a visitation of that diocese.[17] As the archbishop's visitors in Gloucester, the men discovered significantly more evidence of nonconformity than had been revealed by any of the regular episcopal visitations. In the mid-1570s, the diocese of Gloucester was still a long way from full acceptance of Elizabethan Protestantism.[18]

Five parishes, in particular, had clung to as much of the old as they could. At Aylburton in the Forest of Dean, the priest, described as 'a mayntayner of popish purgatorie and other papistries', used a chalice, even though the parish had purchased a cup, and did not read the homilies or preach, or read the Ten Commandments or the Lord's Prayer.[19] The Cotswold parish of Compton Abdale lacked the appropriate Bible, both volumes of the Homilies, the *Paraphrases*, a communion cup and cover, and a cover for the communion table. Furthermore, the priests of both Compton Abdale and Aylburton 'staieth at crosses and redeth gosples' during perambulations, and neither taught the catechism.[20] Both men also wore surplices in the perambulation, but at Compton Abdale, in addition, the parson wore a cope when celebrating the Eucharist. (Surplices were to be worn during regular worship services but not during perambulations of the parish, such as those traditionally conducted during Rogationtide; copes were not to be worn at all.) In Grindal's Articles of Inquiry for his

---

16 Collinson, *The Elizabethan Puritan Movement*, pp. 68–9; *DNB*, vol. XXVIII, pp. 238–9. Cf. Primus, *Vestments*, pp. 71–166, *passim*; J. K. Kemp, 'Laurence Humphrey, Elizabethan Puritan: His Life and Political Theories' (unpublished PhD dissertation, West Virginia University, 1978).

17 GRO GDR vol. IIa, p. 132; J. Strype, *The History of the Life and Acts of Edmund Grindal* (Oxford, 1821), p. 315; *DNB*, vol. L, p. 313.

18 Episcopal visitations of the diocese were conducted at least three times during Cheyney's episcopate: 1563, 1569 and 1572. GRO GDR vol. XX, pp. 1–83; vol. XXVI, pp. 7–143; vol. XXIX, pp. 10–232.

19 GRO GDR vol. XL, fo. 225.

20 From the reformers' point of view, perambulations of Rogationtide processions had traditionally been fraught with superstitious practices. The injunctions of 1559 had limited the rituals and words to be used on such occasions, in order to eliminate the possibility of the inclusion of forbidden ceremonies. The accusation of these two priests indicates that they had continued some of the old practices. *TRP*, vol. II, p. 122.

visitation of 1576, item 6 asks 'whether all vestments, albs, tunicles . . . and such other . . . monuments of superstition and idolatry be utterly . . . destroyed'.[21] Stroud was similar to Compton Abdale, lacking the *Paraphrases* and a cover for the communion table; additionally, it still had 'idolatrie in the church windoes and on tombes', their priest 'useth crossinge at baptisme', and there were no sermons 'at all'. The use of the sign of the cross in baptism was in fact required by the *Book of Common Prayer*, although the hotter sort of Protestants objected to it, so a complaint concerning this action indicates the presence of Puritans in that parish. Nearby, North Nibley was missing similar required items, but more significantly, 'the place of the wall where the altar stoode [had] not [been] made playne', and the chancel remained 'unpaved, full of duste and stones, verie filthy, no convenient place for the communion'.[22] This may be an indication of a desire on the part of the parish to set up their altar again and return to the old religion, because they had not touched the space since they had removed the altar, probably even retaining the wall paintings or reredos which would have adorned the area on the wall above the altar. The parish of Cubberly was also delinquent in that they still had 'parte of the roodelofte . . . undefaced'.[23]

Too much of the old remained for true conformity to be readily achieved as a result of this visitation alone. However, some parishes may have tried to anticipate the visitors' concerns, while others probably took steps to meet at least some of the requirements imposed by the visitors after they had left. In an action similar to that taken elsewhere in England, the churchwardens paid 'for plasteryng and whytyng the walles and wyndowes in the churche' to conceal forbidden images at Tewkesbury, and possibly Fairford, before the visitors arrived.[24] Then, shortly after the visitation, other changes were made. Tewkesbury and a number of other parishes replaced their chalices with the requisite covered communion cups. In all, 51 parishes (just under 17 per cent) were delinquent in this matter, and while none of the parishes in the southern vale reported this deficiency, 10 per cent of those in the Forest and approximately 20 per cent of those in the Cotswolds and the northern vale lacked the requisite cup. There were

[21] Thus, in this instance he seems to have intended to prohibit vestments which were authorised by the Book of Common Prayer in the rubric which defines acceptable vestments by referring back to the first Edwardian prayer book. 'Articles' in *The Remains of Edmund Grindal*, pp. 158–9.

[22] GRO GDR vol. XL, fos. 131v–32, 153–53v, 206v, 225; Moore, '"The Bruised Reed" (Is. 42:3): a Study of the Catholic Remnant in England, 1558–1603, with Special Reference to Gloucestershire' (unpublished MPhil dissertation, University of London, 1990), p. 41.

[23] GRO GDR vol. XL, fo. 190.

[24] GRO P329 CW 2/1, p. 59; printed in *Tewkesbury*, p. 38. The stained-glass images of saints were similarly concealed at Great St Mary's in Cambridge. Haigh, *Reformations*, p. 245.

also two parishes where the priest refused to use the cup which the parish had purchased, opting instead to continue to use a chalice.[25] The lack of such a cup would have made it more difficult to distribute wine to the laity. Thus, the regional differences in the incidence of this deficiency show that the southern vale may have been conforming more completely to the requirements of Elizabethan Protestantism than the other parts of the diocese, perhaps because of its proximity to the more Protestant city of Bristol.

Some parishes continued to hold on to a wider range of the accoutrements of the old liturgy, even though they may not have been using them. In 1577, after the metropolitical visitation, the parish of Tewkesbury still had a tall candlestick, 'one riche coape, . . . vij albes', and 'a pece of imagerye', and they had just sold a piece of velvet, some 'fryng and white sylke', old vestments and pieces of vestments, and 'vij stepes of steyer', probably the stairs to the rood loft, which would have been free-standing at Tewkesbury because of the wide space between the pillars at the entrance to the chancel.[26] A year earlier, the churchwardens of Bishop's Cleve listed a cross, a censor, two bells, two candlesticks, a pyx, and 'certen vestmentes and copes' in their inventory.[27] According to official policy, all of these items were to have been destroyed or disposed of soon after Elizabeth's accession, so that they could not be used to convert the liturgy of the *Book of Common Prayer* into something more akin to traditional, pre-Reformation worship.

Tewkesbury, at least, would slowly begin to accept Protestantism after the visitation. Coincidentally, the town had been transformed in two important ways in the preceding years. In the early 1570s, followers of the new religion had begun to emerge as parish leaders, and they were responsible for whitewashing the walls before the visitation. Then, through the good offices of the Earl of Leicester, Tewkesbury had obtained a much-prized, new royal charter in 1575. The acquisition of the charter resulted in

[25] GRO GDR vol. XL, fos. 2–265, *passim*; GRO GDR vol. XL, fos. 156, 225. These statistics are in sharp contrast with those of the diocese of Norwich, where chalices were replaced by cups in many parishes in the late 1560s following Matthew Parker's metropolitical visitation to the diocese in 1567. R. A. Houlbrooke, *Church Courts*, p. 170.

[26] In most parishes the rood stairs would have been built into the masonry of the chancel arch. GRO P329 CW 2/1, pp. 55, 62; printed in *Tewkesbury*, pp. 35–6, 40. An inventory made eight years later, and presented to the diocesan visitors on 4 May 1585, contains a similar, though not identical, list of items, some of which were entirely in keeping with the established religion while others certainly were not. Items include 'the best coope of tynsell with redd roses', 'iij Awbes of lynnen', 'one Amyce', 'the best pawll for the communyon boorde', 'one other pawll of redd and grene satten with a fronge', 'one other of checker worcke', 'a table clothe with a frynge of golde', 'a blacke pawll of vevytt', and cushions of velvet and satin. GRO P329 CW 2/1, p. 87; printed in *Tewkesbury*, p. 58.

[27] GRO GDR vol. XL, fo. 50v.

the reorganisation of the town's government and the creation of a number of new offices in addition to the customary two bailiffs. These positions were filled predominantly and increasingly by Protestants, who would provide more impetus for adherence to Elizabethan religious policies in both the parish and the town. Three years later, in 1578, the Cordwainers' Guild in the town indicated their support for an even more Protestant local religious policy by adopting an ordinance forbidding members to open their stores during Sunday services 'under payne of iiii d for everie defaulte'.[28] Such an edict would have been consistent with the Sabbatarian leanings of many Elizabethan Protestants at that time. None the less, all this movement toward more comprehensive acceptance of the established religion did not result in the complete rejection of all aspects of the old religion; that would only happen over a much longer period of time.

However, not all Gloucestershire parishes were holding on to aspects of pre-Reformation worship as had Tewkesbury and Bishop's Cleve. In some places the religious drift permitted by Bishop Cheyney moved in a Protestant direction, as the endowed sermons by Mr Eton in Gloucester in the 1560s had demonstrated. In addition, some parish inventories of church goods contrasted sharply with those of Tewkesbury and Bishop's Cleve. In 1576, St Aldate's, Gloucester, had a silver communion cup with cover, a surplice, a communion table, two linen tablecloths, two silk carpets for the table, a Bible, two communion books, a table of the Ten Commandments, three books of articles, and three books of injunctions.[29] The church goods held by Dursley that same year included two Bibles, two volumes of the *Paraphrases* of Erasmus (one on the Gospels, and the other on the Epistles), two Books of Common Prayer, a psalter, a New Testament, two additional prayer books with paper covers (possibly small books of special prayers, such as those issued against plague and the Turks), a register book, a prayer for the queen, 'the communion cup of silver and gilt with a case thereto', a cloth for the communion table and two platters.[30] St Aldate's was missing several items, but had disposed of all vestiges of the old, while Dursley's inventory was that of a model conforming parish. Thus, some congregations had taken the steps necessary to provide for worship in accordance with the standards of official policy. Based on the returns from the visitation in 1576, most parishes were probably conforming. Between half and three-quarters did not report any religious misconduct, although this statistic could be misleading; while most parishes may have been in complete compliance with the archbishop's visitation articles, others may have chosen to conceal such discrepancies. Small

28 GRO TBR D1/1, p. 17.   29 GRO P154/6 CW 1/10a.
30 GRO P124 CW 2/4, fo. 14.

deviations from the official standard could have been ignored in a parish with either a strong sense of religious unanimity or very powerful leadership.

None the less, there was even confusion concerning the clergy's liturgical practices among conforming parishes, and the cause of the difficulty had been put in place shortly after Elizabeth's accession fifteen years earlier. As noted earlier, there was a discrepancy in the description of proper communion bread between the Prayer Book and the Royal Injunctions of 1559. The injunctions stipulated that wafer-bread was to be used, while the Prayer Book called for bread that 'is usual to be eaten at table'.[31] The impact of this difference was felt through the first half of Elizabeth's reign, and violations even prompted Bishop Cheyney to take occasional action, although apparently not before 1570. In March of that year, he heard cases involving three priests who were charged with administering the communion improperly, and in these cases that meant with loaf bread rather than wafers. Then, in 1576, the priest of Barnsley in the Cotswolds was similarly presented for refusing 'to minister with bread accordinge to the injunctions'. Not all parishes wanted wafers, however; the churchwardens of North Cerney complained that their priest 'refused to minister with usuall bread', again indicating a lack of clear direction concerning the approved practice. However, this aspect of the problem was felt throughout the realm. In Norwich, Bishop Parkhurst was perplexed as to how to proceed, and was concerned about the 'ernest disputacions [that] are maynteyned abrode for the breade'. After an exchange of letters, Archbishop Parker wrote, advising Parkhurst, 'for peace and quietnes heare and theare to be contented therwith' with the use of both wafers and 'lofe bread'. Similarly, in 1580, the Privy Council advised the Bishop of Chester to allow both practices to continue, rather than stir up controversy by trying to enforce the use of loaf bread. Once again Bishop Cheyney was marching to his own tune, vigorously enforcing the Injunction's requirement that communion wafers be used.[32]

Meanwhile, a slightly different complaint was made against Mr Tailor, the rector of the parishes of Woodchester and Minchinhampton in the Cotswolds, where his tenure may have brought abrupt change. At Minchinhampton, at least, he appears to have been the first minister who openly and enthusiastically embraced Protestantism, and he not only embraced it,

---

[31] *TRP*, vol. II, p. 131; *Liturgical Services*, p. 198.

[32] GRO GDR vol. XXIV, pp. 709, 722; vol. XL, fos. 160v, 167; Parkhurst to Matthew Parker, 6 June 1574, from Ludham; Parker to Parkhurst, 14 June 1574, from Lambeth, in *The Letter Book of John Parkhurst, Compiled during the Years, 1571–5*, ed. R. A. Houlbrooke (Norfolk Record Society, vol. XLIII, Norwich, 1974/5), pp. 243, 247; K. R. Wark, *Elizabethan Recusancy in Cheshire* (Chetham Society, 3rd ser., vol. XIX, Manchester, 1971), p. 18n. I would like to thank Dr Walsham for this reference.

he went beyond conformity to promote his own hotter version. His parishioners complained that he thought too much rather than too little of the commination against sinners. Furthermore, he declined to teach the catechism, because he thought he could do a better job of instilling the essentials of the faith through his sermons. Other effects of his presence became evident shortly after his institution at Minchinhampton in 1575. Two men were hired for the 'pullynge downe dystroyenge and throwynge out of the church sundrye superstycyous thinges tendinge to the maynte-nance of Idolatrye', and the annual payment to the diocese which had previously been called 'Penticost Money' in the churchwardens' accounts, was now described as 'Peter's Pence or smoke farthinges sometyme due to the Antecriste of Rome'.[33] This type of language was not typically used in churchwardens' accounts, and does not appear either before or after these entries in Minchinhampton's records. Thus, it appears that Mr Tailor's energies in converting the parish to Protestantism extended even to the pages of this rather mundane record of the parish's financial matters, albeit only in this one instance.

At Woodchester, Mr Tailor had refused to teach the catechism, thinking he could do better on his own; however, more generally, the practice of instructing the youth of the parish in a standard set of basic beliefs was seen as the most fundamental way of instilling the essentials of Protestantism in the laity. Teaching the catechism had been promoted by official policy since the 1530s, but compliance was still a problem in Gloucestershire at the time of the metropolitical visitation of 1576.[34] Item 14 of the Visitation Articles asked 'whether all fathers and mothers, masters and dames of your parish, caused their children, servants, and apprentices, both mankind and womankind, being above seven years of age and under twenty, which have not learned the Catechism, to come to church' to learn from the minister. He, in turn, was directed to instruct them every Sunday and holy day 'for half an hour at the least, before or at the Evening Prayer'.[35] In fully 30 per cent of the parishes, however, this was not happening, at least not regularly, and Woodchester is the only parish to suggest that instruction was still considered important, even if it did not use the officially approved form. The southern vale was doing somewhat better in this respect than the rest of the diocese with only 20 per cent of the parishes being remiss. The Forest of Dean, on the other hand, was doing significantly worse, as in that remote region 45 per cent (17 of the 37 parishes) lacked any regular catechetical instruction.[36] As with the 'litmus test' of the communion cup,

[33] GRO GDR vol. XL, fo. 189; P217 CW 2/1, p. 54.
[34] *VAI*, vol. II, pp. 6–7, 36–7, 402; *TRP*, vol. I, p. 394.
[35] *The Remains of Edmund Grindal*, pp. 161–2.
[36] GRO GDR vol. XL, fos. 2–265, *passim*.

it appears that the highest level of conformity in the diocese could be found to the south of the city of Gloucester.

Again, using the returns of 1576, it is possible to identify regional patterns of corporate response to official religious policy. In the Forest of Dean, 65 per cent of the parishes lacked both regular sermons and the reading of homilies. In addition, a large proportion of the Forest parishes still had some undefaced vestige of pre-Reformation piety, used traditional vestments and did not teach the catechism regularly. Meanwhile, in the southern vale, no parish was presented for lacking a communion cup, a higher proportion of the region's parishes were teaching the catechism regularly than in any other, and less than 5 per cent of the priests there persisted in wearing traditional vestments in contravention of the visitation articles. In general, then, the Forest of Dean was the region with the least conformity to Elizabethan Protestantism in 1576, while the southern vale had the most. The legal and religious independence of the Forest of Dean in this instance may have been a continuation of the problems which had plagued those who had attempted to impose external regulations on that region for hundreds of years, rather than a simple instance of the people clinging to Catholicism. The inhabitants valued their way of life and distrusted outsiders. Thus, as the Forest had been home to at least one group of evangelicals meeting in a mill in the late 1530s, so it was now a safe area for the continuation of traditional liturgical practices.[37] Meanwhile, in the southern vale, the portion of the county containing the highest concentration of cloth manufacturing, perhaps frequent communication with London or proximity to the much more Protestant city of Bristol encouraged the spread of reformist ideas. That being said, however, this region was just barely conforming, not rabidly Protestant, and the Cotswolds, which were potentially subject to the same influences as the southern vale, appear to have lagged behind in terms of basic conformity. Again, it is possible to see the lack of direction which resulted from Cheyney's benign neglect of the implemention of Elizabethan Protestantism.

The leadership void created by Cheyney's approach to his office could have been filled by the Gloucestershire gentry, but that does not appear to have been the case, their involvement in the Berkeley/Leicester 'poaching war' notwithstanding. They may have influenced and even controlled those who were in their service, but there is little evidence to indicate that they involved themselves in the religious leadership of the county in anything but a pro-forma way. In addition, extant parish records contain no hints of gentry influence on beliefs at that level. The prime exception is Sir Giles

---

[37] See chapter 2.

Poole, who seems to have stepped into the breach in 1573 when as a justice of the peace he learned of 'a secte of disordered personnes' in the county. The group had allegedly appointed a minister and developed an order of worship 'according to their owne fantasies'. He and his fellow-justices had committed them to the gaol and informed the Privy Council, prompting that body to prod Bishop Cheyney to take some action to persuade those in custody as well as others still at liberty to conform. Tellingly, the letter to Cheyney further stipulated that the reforming attempts by the bishop or other learned preachers should occur 'in the hearing of some of the justices'.[38] As noted above, Poole was also one of the members of the Commission for Ecclesiastical Causes established in the county the following year, perhaps partially as a result of Cheyney's lack of vigilance regarding that disorderly sect. In his role as a commissioner, Poole was joined by Sir John Tracy. Others also served, but these two members of the gentry were the most active.[39]

A more comprehensive examination of the returns from the various visitations, both episcopal and archiepiscopal, reveals some other interesting patterns of responses. First, it appears that the types of problems being reported changed over time. In 1563, the typical nonconforming parish was one which lacked the *Paraphrases*, had few, if any, sermons, and did not have services at convenient times, generally because their priest was a pluralist.[40] Nine years later, the lack of sermons and the *Paraphrases* were still key problems; however, now the typical delinquent parish also lacked a Bible 'of the largest volume' and a proper communion cup, and their communion table was not carpeted.[41] By the time of the archiepiscopal visitation in 1576, most communion tables apparently were appropriately covered, but the long delinquent sermons, *Paraphrases*, communion cup and Bible were now joined by the omission of the regular reading of the Homilies and the comminations in the typical nonconforming parish. Furthermore, surplices were being worn during the perambulation in violation of article thirty-eight of the archbishop's visitation articles. The proportion of parishes reporting some type of liturgical nonconformity grew from 25 per cent in 1563 to 55 per cent in 1576, and those without regular sermons climbed from less than 5 per cent of the parishes in 1563 to over 30 per cent in 1576.[42] It appears that while some parishes were having increasing difficulty meeting the basic standards of building maintenance and liturgy, these standards were also being raised, and, at least in 1576, the visitors were more vigilant than in recent previous visitations.

---

[38] *APC*, vol. VIII, p. 132; vol. X, pp. 428–30.
[39] GRO GDR vol. XXXV, *passim*, printed in *Commission*, pp. 44–136, *passim*.
[40] GRO GDR vol. XX, pp. 1–83, *passim*.
[41] GRO GDR vol. XXIX, pp. 10–232, *passim*.   [42] GRO GDR vol. XL, fos. 2–265.

Parishes were apparently not asked about either communion cups or the coverings for their communion tables in 1563, while the regular reading of the comminations and the details of the ceremony attendant upon the perambulation of the parish were ignored until 1576. Thus, it is possible to see a shift in the definition of conformity during the first half of Elizabeth's reign.

Additionally, some of the visitation queries revealed an anomaly. In each instance there were questions about the presence of Bibles and books of homilies, and prior to 1576 most parishes had them; then, during the last visitation, many parishes reported them missing. The responses of a small number of parishes to the questions about the requisite books, combined with entries in churchwardens' accounts, may provide a partial explanation for this aberration. It appears that the books needed frequent repair or replacement, and it is possible that the expenses pressed on parishes by the successive sets of religious changes, plus ongoing building maintenance, consumed all available funds, leaving none for the repair of these texts.[43] Thus, in some cases the nonconforming parish in 1576 may have reached that state after having previously complied, having used the books until they literally fell apart, could no longer be used, and thus were reported as missing. However, a number of parishes probably had just not taken more than the minimal steps toward the establishment of a fully Protestant liturgy, and had not yet obtained all the necessary books. The widespread lack of the *Paraphrases* reported in all the visitations may be a case in point.

Financial strain may also explain why over half the parishes in the diocese lacked quarterly sermons in 1576. If the parish clergy were unable to preach, the parish was supposed to hire a preacher, as did Dursley in 1567, but not all could afford to do so.[44] In addition, the lack of sermons may have been due to the absence of sufficient qualified parish clergy or specially licensed preachers in the diocese, as a consequence of Bishop Cheyney's *laissez-faire* administrative style. It may also reflect the lack of a zealous Protestant presence among the priests of the diocese, since the hotter sort of Protestants, had they been present, would have been more likely to insist on regular sermons.

In addition, the problem of financing reform still loomed as a major impediment to both religious conformity and responsible stewardship of church buildings. In some parishes fund-raising was typically associated with the continuation of traditional activities, such as church ales and

[43] GRO GDR vol. XL, fos. 2–265; P124 CW 2/4, fo. 16v; P154/14 CW 1/17, 1/18, 1/21, 1/22, 1/24, 1/27, 1/29, 1/31; P197 CW 2/1, fos. 4v–5; P217 CW 2/1, pp. 36, 44, 57; P329 CW 2/1, p. 7; printed in *Tewkesbury*, p. 4.

[44] GRO P124 CW 2/4, fo. 8.

plays. Such pastimes were frowned on by godly Protestants, who were beginning to gain positions of leadership in other parts of the realm. However, through at least the first half of Elizabeth's reign, rural Gloucestershire parishes, such as Minchinhampton and Tewkesbury, continued to raise substantial sums for the parish chest from Whitsun ales, and at Tewkesbury additional revenue came from renting space for 'standinges in church howse on Bartlmew daye' for the fair, as well as 'at Saynt Mathuse fayre', another sign of diocesan-wide religious drift.[45] Tewkesbury had other diversions and sources of income as well, thanks to the 'players gere' held by the parish and hired out from time to time, usually to parishioners. The parish apparently had a long tradition of religious drama dating back to the fourteenth century, involving both clergy and laity.[46] The 'gere' (gear) was loaned once in the late 1560s, but its recorded use actually increased substantially in the 1570s, with some performances given in the church.[47] The gear was even rented out twice during 1576, the very year of the archiepiscopal visitation. At that time, it included 'five players gownes, iiij jackets, iiij beardes, [and] two heades'.[48] Over the next eight years it would be refurbished and augmented to include eight gowns, seven jerkins, four caps of green silk, eight 'heades of heare for the apostles', ten beards, a 'thunder heade', a 'face or vysor for the devyll', and 'Christes garments' made from six sheepskins.[49] The gear would continue to be used, maintained and expanded at least into the early 1600s, when a series of three plays were performed in the church to raise money for a new church tower to replace that which had fallen at Easter 1559. Financially, the plays presented in 1600 were a disaster, losing over £20. Perhaps most people had lost their taste for such activities by then. The churchwardens made one final attempt to recoup their losses, requesting permission from the bailiffs and burgesses of the town for a church ale. However, their request was denied because 'of abuses accustomed to be reformed', another sign of growing Protestantism among the leaders of the town, but this was in

---

[45] Minchinhampton held an ale almost every year at least through 1583. GRO P217 CW 2/1, pp. 10, 14, 17, 19, 20, 26, 34, 40, 42, 46, 62, 64, 66; printed in J. Bruce, ed., 'Extracts from Accounts of the Churchwardens of Minchinhampton, in the County of Gloucester, with Observations Thereon', *Archaeologia* 35 (1853), pp. 432–3. Tewkesbury's church ales were held more sporadically, but they continued until at least 1577. The fairs continued until at least 1575, St Bartholomew's fair occurring around August 24 and St Matthew's fair around September 21. GRO P329 CW 2/1, pp. 14, 15, 20, 21, 33, 35, 41, 45, 50, 63; printed in *Tewkesbury*, pp. 10, 14–15, 22–3, 26, 29, 32, 41.

[46] T. Hannam-Clark, *Drama in Gloucestershire* (Gloucester and London, 1928), pp. 20–1.

[47] GRO P329 CW 2/1, pp. 21, 41, 55, 57, 63, 66; printed in *Tewkesbury*, pp. 15, 26, 36, 37, 40, 43. In 1575/6, shortly before the archiepiscopal visitation, the brand new bailiffs' seat was 'brokene downe at a playe'. GRO P329 CW 2/1, p. 51; printed in *Tewkesbury*, p. 33.

[48] GRO P329 CW 2/1, pp. 55, 57, 62; printed in *Tewkesbury*, pp. 36, 37, 40.

[49] GRO P329 CW 2/1, pp. 65, 88; printed in *Tewkesbury*, pp. 42–3, 58.

1600, long after all such practices had been abolished in most parts of the realm.[50]

In the city of Gloucester, where entertainment was more often a municipal than a parish responsibility, plays as well as sermons were presented. In fact, plays were the mainstay of entertainment in Gloucester at least until 1580, a time when other municipal authorities were beginning to curtail such diversions. None the less, travelling companies of players retained their popularity throughout the realm at least to the end of the sixteenth century, and the corporation records give evidence of play productions in Gloucester as late as 1640/1.[51] Other types of entertainment were also offered, as musicians played, jugglers and puppeteers performed, and bears were baited; even so, plays (generally presented by itinerant groups or individuals) were the dominant form of entertainment.[52] On some occasions the productions seem to have been quite simple, with few props or costumes and no stage on which to perform; however, such was not always the case. During the queen's visit in 1574, lavish preparations were made for a variety of productions, including 'makeinge of twoe Scaffoldes with the furniture of the pagentes at the utter northgate and at the highe Crosse' (near St Michael's), providing 'hornes for the Antelap and unicornes and the tonge for the Dragon' for a play, and hiring waits from Shrewsbury 'for plaienge aboute the Citie everie moreninge'.[53] At about the same time, almost surely in the 1570s, the play, *The Cradle of Security*, was presented in the boothall at Gloucester, and was attended by a young child, one R. Willis, who watched from the safety found between his father's knees, and only wrote about it in 1639 when he was some seventy-five years of age. That production was sponsored by the mayor, and admission was complementary. The play depicted a prince, who represented sinfulness, being distracted from sober pursuits by three women, 'Pride, Covetousnesse, and Luxury', and ultimately falling from grace. 'This sight tooke such impression in me', said Willis, 'that when I came towards mans estate, it was as fresh in my memory, as if I had seen it newly acted.'[54] An initial attempt was made in 1580/1 to limit the activities of musicians and the production of plays in the city of Gloucester, but that action seems to have

[50] GRO P329 CW 2/1, pp. 74, 75, 79, 80, 81, 86, 130–1; printed in *Tewkesbury*, pp. 48, 49, 53, 54, 56, 93–4; GRO TBR A1/1, fos. 15, 24.
[51] E. K. Chambers, *The Elizabethan Stage* (Oxford, 1923), vol. I, pp. 278–88, 331–6; H. C. Gardiner, *Mysteries End: an Investigation of the Last Days of the Medieval Religious Stage* (New Haven, CT, 1946), pp. 74–5, 83–6; *REED*, p. 253.
[52] Beginning in 1578/9, the corporation retained their own musician when they hired Garrette Barneyes and began paying him an annual fee. GRO GBR F4/3, fos. 83v–218, *passim*. Excerpts are printed in *REED*, pp. 298–308, *passim*.
[53] GRO GBR F4/3, fo. 162.
[54] R. Willis, *Mount Tabor, or Private Exercises of a Penitent Sinner* (London, 1639), STC 25752, pp. 110–14; excerpts reprinted in *REED*, pp. 362–4.

had little effect, at least over the next few years, as adherents of Puritanism who would have vigorously suppressed such entertainment had not yet gained control of the city's ruling oligarchy. The activities of common players and players of interludes were restricted, but not those with exalted patrons, such as Leicester or the queen.[55]

In contrast to practices in the city of Gloucester, rural parishes offered different types of entertainment, sometimes as part of long-standing traditional parish celebrations, and sometimes as forbidden alternatives to divine services. At Huntley, 'the may lorde and morice dauncers' came into the church in the spring of 1576, while at Aldesworth there was dancing in the churchyard at Whitsuntide.[56] More often, however, dancing and other pastimes, such as gaming, eating and drinking, lured people away from worship, rather than on to consecrated ground. For instance, Robert Came and Robert Partridge were presented in 1576 for 'sufferinge daunsinge at service tyme' in the parish of Rangeworthy.[57] Others, such as Elizabeth Daniel of Horsley and Elizabeth Egberg of Stroud, both widows, and William Jones of Randwick sold meals during services, while still others, including Thomas Baker and the alewives of Huntley and Horton, offered people the opportunity to drink and gamble instead of worshipping.[58]

The sale of foodstuffs and other household commodities was also a common unauthorised activity during services in parishes of all sizes. This was especially true in the Forest of Dean, where it had been going on for over 100 years, as that area once again demonstrated its resistance to outside regulation.[59] Thomas Phillips, Geoff Weithen and John Chenitle of Staunton were presented in 1571, because they '[do] kepe market on holyday in tyme of divine service', and in 1576 Thomas Wylse of Dymock was charged with the same offence.[60] However, the most organised Sunday market in early Elizabethan Gloucestershire must have been that which had occurred 'at the churche walle' at Westbury in the Forest of Dean in 1563, when four men from Littledean, one from Flaxley and one from Churcham sold meat, and three from Longhope, and one each from Blaisdon, Flaxley and Westbury sold bread.[61] Clearly, money was to be made from others absenting themselves from worship or on their way home from services.

[55] GRO GBR B3/1, fos. 71v–72; excerpts printed in *REED*, pp. 306–7. For a contrasting interpretation of the development of Protestantism in Gloucester, see P. Clark, '"The Ramoth-Gilead of the Good"', pp. 167–87.

[56] GRO GDR vol. XL, fos. 166, 261v.

[57] GRO GDR vol. XL, fo. 143v. Rangeworthy is adjacent to Iron Acton, the family seat of the Poyntz family. Sir Nicholas Poyntz hosted Henry VIII and Anne Boleyn there in 1535, and one of his sons later became a Marian exile. See chapters 2 and 5.

[58] GRO GDR vol. XL, fos. 20, 109v, 188, 208, 253v.

[59] GCL Hockaday Collections, vol. XVIII, *passim*.

[60] GRO GDR vol. IX, p. 60; vol. XL, fos. 249–49v.   [61] GRO GDR vol. XX, pp. 26–7.

More frequently, however, parishioners' absences from church or from communion were not due to their retail activities; rather, in most cases the true basis for such action was a profound personal difference with official policy, even though the excuses offered often rested on claims of being 'out of charity' with one's fellow-parishioners or fearing attachment for debt. The number of those reported as habitually absent from church rose steadily from 47 to 82 between 1563 and 1572, before more than a doubling in 1576 to a total of 178 recusants, an increase of sufficient magnitude to indicate an actual increase in absenteeism, rather than just reflecting the greater thoroughness of the last investigation.[62] By contrast, the pattern for not receiving Easter communion (which could have included some of those who were present as well as those who were absent) shows very low numbers being reported in 1563 and 1572, with the intervening visitation in 1569 showing a much higher total, and the number reported in 1576 being still higher.[63] By 1576, the nature and perhaps the magnitude of the problems of failure to receive communion and absenteeism seem to have changed, as non-receipt of communion had become much more pervasive than had been the case earlier.[64] It was no longer an act of nonconformity found in a few parishes and prompted by dissatisfaction with parochial liturgical practices. Now a significant proportion of the parishes in the diocese could name at least one individual who was guilty of either not receiving communion or being absent from services, indicating that the complaints were being directed more generally toward official policy by the mid-1570s, rather than toward local parish manifestations of that policy, as had been the case earlier.

In 1577, addressing the problem of church absenteeism, or recusancy, Bishop Cheyney described three types of recusants: those who 'savour of papistrie', but allege sickness; those whose debts keep them away for fear of proceedings against them; and 'the thirde sorte, communelie called puritans, [who] wilfullie refuse to come to churche, as not lyking the surplas, ceremonies and other service now used in the churche'. Cheyney's focus on radical Protestants as recusants paralleled similar actions taken at about the same time by Edmund Freke, Bishop of Norwich, and John Aylmer, Bishop of London. There is evidence indicating that Freke and Aylmer may have been operating under specific instructions from the queen

---

[62] See Figure 6.2. GRO GDR vol. XX, pp. 1–83; vol. XXVI, pp. 135–7; vol. XXIX, p. 201; vol. XL, fos. 207–8, 241–2.

[63] See Figure 6.3. GRO GDR vol. XXVI, pp. 60–3, 122–5; vol. XXVIII, pp. 189–89a, 194–5; vol. XL, fos. 22–26v, 112v–13v, 231–31v.

[64] The returns from 1576 had the highest total, but include specific problems in only four parishes, while a great many more parishes named just a few individuals for non-receipt. In earlier presentments the total number of offenders were divided between a small number of parishes.

to give equal attention to all recusants, whether Catholic or radically Protestant.[65] Perhaps Cheyney had received a similar directive; however, the treatment in Gloucester was not equal. Very few Catholics were called to account for their absence from church during Cheyney's episcopate, while a number of Puritans were.[66] Even so, parishioners at both ends of the spectrum chose to absent themselves completely from divine services. Similarly, individuals of both persuasions were among those accused of not having received Easter communion. Of those who 'savour[ed] of papistrie', some were Catholic recusants and some were, as their detractors called them, 'statute Protestants' or 'church papists'. For the latter group, not receiving the sacrament was just one of a number of ways in which they might attempt to reconcile their Catholicism with their duties as loyal subjects of the Crown. They might have chosen, instead, to sit as far as possible from the pulpit, as did John Rekes, Thomas Mondy and Parrys of the Lode at Tewkesbury. On the other hand, they might have covered their ears so that they could not hear the sermon, or they might have brought Latin primers or other 'papistical' books to the service and read them rather than participating in parish worship. Similarly, they might have brought beads and prayed privately during the service, a common pious act in the pre-Reformation church.[67]

While most of those accused of either recusancy or not taking communion did not provide an explanation, there is some evidence of the presence of both church papists and recusant Catholics in Elizabethan Gloucestershire prior to 1580. In December 1562, Edward Heydon of Tortworth affirmed his belief in transubstantiation, and, when pressed, denied that such a belief was scandalous.[68] A year later, one Richard Mote of Berkeley was presented for saying that 'he dothe hope to see the masse up agayne', and John Bower of the same parish had 'certayne ymages decked withe roses set up in his chamber'.[69] Then, in 1576, Thomas Wylkins and George Baskerville of Tewkesbury were reported to the archbishop's visitors for, respectively, using beads and using a 'papist primer in church'. Thomas Dwofield and Lewys Bathan may have been guilty of similar practices, as they were described as

[65] P. Collinson, *The Elizabethan Puritan Movement*, pp. 201–2; MacCulloch, *Suffolk*, pp. 193–7; A. H. Smith, *County and Court: Government and Politics in Norfolk, 1558–1603* (Oxford, 1974), pp. 211–15, 225; *DNB*, vol. I, p. 754; vol. VII, pp. 670–1.

[66] Cheyney to the Privy Council, from the Vineyard in Gloucester, 24 October 1577, PRO SP 12/117/12; printed with some inaccuracies in R. H. Clutterbuck, 'Bishop Cheyney', pp. 232–3.

[67] GRO P329 CW 2/1, pp. 9, 14, 31, 45; printed in *Tewkesbury*, pp. 5–6, 10, 20, 29. Cf. A. Walsham, *Church Papists*; F. R. Raines, ed., 'A Description of the State, Civil and Ecclesiastical of the County of Lancaster about the Year 1590', in *Chetham Miscellanies V* (Chetham Society, old ser., vol. XCVI, Manchester, 1875), p. 3. I would like to thank Dr Walsham for this last reference.

[68] GRO GDR vol. XIX, p. 77.   [69] GRO GDR vol. XX, p. 51.

'suspected of papistry' in that same year. Additionally, John Whyte, the elder, although he may not have used them in public, was accused of keeping 'privelie ij masse bookes, one of parchment and a portesse and manuell . . . [and holding] opinions erroneous'.[70] One of the few women reported for an overt and public demonstration of traditional beliefs was Alice Huddleston, gentlewoman, who 'founde faulte with [the] curate for not wearinge a surplesse in perambulacions [and] called him [a] hunter' because he was wearing ordinary clothes rather than the vestments traditionally associated with such processions, but now prohibited.[71] Other people were slightly less direct in expressing similar beliefs. In the mid-1570s, six men at Coaley in the southern vale were accused of not coming into the church; rather, they 'lye under the church wall . . . at the tyme of service'. Similarly, Richard Robertes of the neighbouring parish of Berkeley was presented 'for standinge in the churchyarde at service tyme and [he] refused to come in at the warninge of the churchwardens', and at Maisemore in 1575 'there was suche hurleyburley that the minister could not proceed'.[72]

In addition, the records of the diocese during the first twenty years of Elizabeth's reign contain evidence indicating that church papistry and Catholic recusancy may have received indirect support from Bishop Cheyney's diocesan administration. Edmund Campion claimed in 1572 that Cheyney had not persecuted Catholics in his diocese, and the records support his assertion.[73] In the cases of non-receipt and recusancy involving church papists and Catholics, after the initial presentment and perhaps a single appearance before the consistory court, such cases just disappear from the record.

Church papistry may also have manifested itself on a corporate level, as a number of parishes failed to list the names of those who were either absent from services or guilty of not having received. In 1563, the churchwardens of the conservative parish of Stroud had alluded to 'some who have not receaved the communion this yere whose names you shall knowe yf admonition will not reforme them shortely'. Thirteen years later, before the archbishop's representatives, Titherington's parish leaders said that the whole 'parishe [was] slacke in cominge to churche', and those from Wickwar reported that 'certen of the parishe . . . resorte to other churches', but did not name them.[74] True, such an oversight could have been due to

[70] GRO GDR vol. XL, fos. 27, 47, 261v. Cf. Duffy, *Stripping*, pp. 117–20, 213; Reinburg, 'Liturgy and the Laity', pp. 529–33.
[71] GRO GDR vol. XL, fo. 51. Wearing a surplice in the perambulation of the parish was prohibited by the archbishop's visitation articles of 1576. *The Remains of Edmund Grindal*, p. 168.
[72] GRO GDR vol. XXXVII, fos. 17–17v; vol. XL, fos. 125, 139.
[73] 'Campion the Martyr to Cheney', pp. 61–2.
[74] GRO GDR vol. XX, p. 13; vol. XL, fos. 105, 120. Similar presentments were made in 1576

negligence on the part of the parish leadership; however, they need not have lied to avoid implicating their neighbours. Admonitions were called for before presentments were made, especially in cases of recusancy, and churchwardens were urged to exercise discernment and only present significant cases. Furthermore, both lay and clerical parish leaders occasionally chose to define the terms used to describe offences quite narrowly, thus limiting their applicability.[75] Of course, failure to supply this information would certainly have benefited those who were guilty of the offences, and this kind of result may have motivated sympathetic parish leaders to participate in such collusion, thus protecting the church papists. As a further motivation for the leaders, such a united front in the face of external control could have been used to create a special boundary and transform a normally public parish into a private space from which outside authorities could be excluded.

Cheyney's letter to the Privy Council concerning recusants, focused on 'Puritans' rather than Catholics, and in Gloucestershire Puritans generally seem to have received less protection from parish leaders and been subject to more attention from the consistory court than followers of the old religion. Like the church papists, some followers of the new religion chose to express their displeasure with the liturgy by publicly disrupting services, rather than by staying away. However, they were not as subtle as their more conservative counterparts. In the mid-1570s, in the parish of Compton Abdale, one of the places which had retained as much of the old liturgy as possible, Thomas Townsende signalled his impatience with the pace of change when he 'troubled the priest at communion and tooke awaie the cupp and wyne from him perforce'.[76] At the end of the 1570s, there were other, similarly motivated, confrontations. A number of parishioners of Sandhurst, including two women and three men, disturbed the divine service, while three of the leaders of the parish and town of Tewkesbury challenged the authority of the bishop by insisting that their chosen preacher, rather than the curate sent by the bishop, should officiate at a funeral.[77] The incident at Sandhurst was one of the few cases where

---

by the leaders from Duntisbourne Regis, Stonehouse, Saperton, Horsley, Edgeworth, Tetbury, Shipton Moyne, Bisley and Lydney. GRO GDR vol. XL, fos. 166v, 184, 184v, 186v, 193–93v, 198v–99v, 257.

[75] E. Carlson, 'The Origins, Functions, and Status of the Office of Churchwarden, with Particular Reference to the Diocese of Ely', in *The World of Rural Dissenters 1520–1725*, ed. M. Spufford (Cambridge, 1995), pp. 170–4; *TRP*, vol. II, p. 127; M. Ingram, *Church Courts, Sex and Marriage in England, 1570–1640* (Cambridge, 1987), pp. 328–9.

[76] GRO GDR vol. XL, fo. 153v.

[77] GRO GDR vol. XLIV, pp. 110–11. The Tewkesbury parishioners who defied the bishop in this case were Richard Rudgedale, the town chamberlain, Edward Baston, a burgess and friend of one of the local Protestant will scribes, and James Greene, a future churchwarden. GRO GDR vol. XLIII, fo. 41v.

women publicly expressed their opinion concerning the nature of the established liturgy. It was much more common for women to demonstrate their disapproval by simply being absent, thus being invisible, while the men were very visibly present in or near the church behaving in a disruptive manner. They had each found a way within society's behavioural norms to register their complaints, one considered appropriate to their gender.[78]

In a few cases, while the behaviour was not in and of itself disruptive or particularly public, the motive was clearly and explicitly religious, and the individuals involved stubbornly resisted all attempts to bring them into conformance with official policy. These were the people Cheyney seems to have been thinking about when he wrote his letter to the Privy Council, as they all would have counted themselves among the godly, and they certainly received a great deal of attention from both the consistory court and the Ecclesiastical Commission to the diocese. The individuals involved included Edmund Batte of Moreton Valence, William Drewett and his wife, of St Nicholas in Gloucester, and William and Elizabeth Whiting, Agnes Long, Anne Cole, and Thomas and Anna Bradford, of Cirencester, all of whom were accused of recusancy, although in some cases there were other charges as well.

In 1565, Edmund Batte had refused to 'come to the churche nor eate or drynke withe them that comme to the churche'. He was repeatedly presented for being absent and was required to appear in court, which he dutifully did each time. Eventually, his case was referred to the Commission for Ecclesiastical Causes, where, in August 1574, he asserted that he had not attended his parish church, because the minster 'wereth a sarples and other popish robes not correspondent to Godes worde'. Six months later he was still absent, saying 'that the churche the which is so termed in these daies ought not to be so called, for it is nothing else . . . but a place of supersticion and idolatrie'; he was then placed in the custody of the sheriff. He appeared once more the following June, but he had not changed his mind, and was duly sent back to the castle.[79]

William Drewett and his wife's reasons for staying away from church

---

[78] Marie Rowlands has observed that it was very difficult to punish recusant wives. She says that as a result married women had more freedom than their husbands to stay home during service times. Alexandra Walsham, however, sees the presence of a high proportion of females among recusants as a manifestation of a division of the labour of nonconformity. It was the wife's responsibility to be absent, while the husband was to function as a church papist. The latter analysis fits with the evidence from Gloucestershire, except in that diocese it applies to the hotter sort of Protestants, as well as to Catholics. Societal considerations seem to have been the fundamental determinants in these responses to official policy. M. B. Rowlands, 'Recusant Women, 1560–1640', in *Women in English Society, 1500–1800*, ed. M. Prior (London, 1985), pp. 151–2. Cf. A. Walsham, *Church Papists*, pp. 77–81.

[79] GRO GDR vol. XXVI, p. 31; vol. XXIX, p. 88; vol. XXXV, pp. 4, 9, 24, 64, 80; printed in *Commission*, pp. 49, 52, 60, 78, 85.

were very similar to Batte's. However, the crux of their case concerned the baptism of their child. Drewett's first appearance before the Commission resulted in him being jailed, after he 'skoffinglie . . . called the busshopp of Gloucester sittinge in commission goodman pope that sittes there with whitt sleves, the popes robes will begin scripture and confounde us anon, and because you loke to be called Lord Busshopp, then geve me leave Mr Busshopp, you shalbe called Lord Busshopp'. Subsequently, Drewett was released, but he and his wife still refused to have their child baptised. At his next appearance, with his wife also present, the mayor and sheriffs of the city 'and the hedd men of the parishe' were ordered to enter their house 'and take the chylde and bringe yt to churche . . . and there the minister to christen it'. However, Drewett and his wife insisted that if their child was taken from them by force and baptised 'they wolde never receave yt againe nor take yt for their chylde any more'; but that was not the end of the matter. Some three weeks later, the couple were back before the Commission with the baby in its father's arms. A midwife who was present was ordered to take the child from him:

Whereupon the commissioners forewarned hym that they intende to commytte him to one prison and his wyffe to another, wyshinge and commaundinge him to deliver his chylde to his wyffe to remayne with her that she maie geve yt sucke in prison. And he saide he wolde carie yt with hym to prison and not deliver yt to his wyffe . . . Furder the comissioners commaunded Sir David Walter clerk [curate of St Michael's, Gloucester] than present to requyre the chylde of the saide Drewett . . . and to goe and christen yt; but he aunswered that the father of the chylde ought to requyre him for to christen yt . . . The commissioners requyred him [Drewett] once agayne . . . to deliver his chylde out of his armes unto his wyffe . . . but he wold not . . . The commissioners [then] commaunded the churchwardens of St Nicholas . . . to take the chylde from him and to deliver yt to the mother then standinge by; but Drewett wolde not lett yt goe . . . Whereupon they committed him [and the child to prison].

Two days later, both father and infant were released, and Drewett was subsequently sent to London to appear before the Privy Council to answer for his actions.[80]

In most cases, the more obstinate recusants were single individuals or couples, as were Edmund Batte and the Drewetts, but such was not the case in Cirencester. Between 1570 and 1574, forty-three individuals of that parish were presented either for absence or for not receiving holy communion, and in a few instances the authorities were still trying to reform the transgressors during the archiepiscopal visitation in 1576. This case of mass nonconformity appears to have first come to the attention of diocesan

---

[80] GRO GDR vol. XXXV, pp. 65, 110–11, 114, 116–17; printed in *Commission*, pp. 78, 103, 105, 107–8.

authorities in July 1570, just a month after one faction within the town had sent a letter to the Privy Council describing three members of the local elite, Nicholas Phillips (sergeant of the town and once a servant to the Marian Privy Councillor, Sir Henry Jerningham), Robert Strange (justice of the peace) and Christopher George (clerk of the peace) as 'wicked and traitorous papists'.[81] Strange was indeed a Catholic, as he attested in his will in 1587, and Christopher George was his son-in-law. The latter's will, written in 1597, is complex and ambiguous, but its emphasis on internal contrition may reflect the teachings of the post-tridentine Catholic Church. In his official capacity, Christopher George would become involved in attempts to force conformity on some of the most intransigent of Cirencester's nonconforming recusants five years later.[82] The presentment to the diocese reported that seventeen men were staying away from their parish church, including John George, brother of Christopher.[83] Two years later, many of the same individuals were still successfully resisting pressure to return to their regular parish services.[84] In the subsequent visitation it was alleged that 'the curate did not bid the holydayes fastinge and ymber dayes' and therefore, a number of individuals, some of whom had been among the original group of recusants, kept their shops open on those days. For the first time, a woman was also presented. Agnes Long was subsequently ruled to be contumacious for her refusal to obey the court's order that she attend her parish church.[85] The situation seems to have continued to deteriorate, and a special set of interrogatories was addressed to the leaders of the parish on 27 November 1573. At the time the leaders of the parish alleged that their curate, Mr Aldworth, and the other clergy serving the parish 'doe alter and vare . . . thorders appoynted by the booke of comen prayer', including ignoring the prescribed lectionary, and omitting portions of the service on occasions when there was no holy communion. Furthermore, Aldworth did not use the sign of the cross in baptism or wear a surplice when celebrating the Eucharist. The leaders of the parish then listed seven people who never came to church, nine who only came when Mr Aldworth was present, and 'divers [other] whoe doe not use to receave the communion'.[86]

The various allegations reveal a division within the parish of Cirencester involving a substantial number of individuals at each end of the religious spectrum. On the one hand, a number of people appear to have favoured Catholicism, including Thomas Rastell and Andrew Phelpes. Rastell would bequeath his soul quite traditionally to 'Allmightie God and to the blessed

[81] PRO SP 12/71/30.   [82] PRO PROB 11/72, fos. 33–33v; 11/93, fos. 323–5.
[83] GRO GDR vol. XXVI, pp. 135–7; GRO Wills 1556/67.
[84] GRO GDR vol. XXVIII, pp. 168–70.   [85] GRO GDR vol. XXIX, p. 71.
[86] GRO GDR vol. XXXI, pp. 81–7.

vurgine Marye and to all the holye companye of sainctes in heaven' when he wrote his will in 1574.[87] Phelpes also left a will which indicated his Catholicism. Rastell and Phelpes were among those who justified their absence from church by the fact that the clergy did not adhere strictly to the Prayer Book. The complaints and explanations offered by others included in the presentments indicate, on the other hand, frustration with the limited form of Protestantism being practised in their parish. Not even Aldworth, with his refusal to wear a surplice or make the sign of the cross in baptism, was godly enough for them. He had even obtained permission from the High Commission in London to use common loaf bread rather than wafers for communion.[88] This group of dissenters included a number of people, both women and men, who would prove very difficult to bring to conformity over the next several years. There was, however, a third group included in the presentments, a group that wanted a more reformed liturgy than that prescribed by official policy, but was not prepared to separate from the church. These were the parishioners who refused to attend church unless Aldworth was presiding. This division within the parish was similar to that found in other Elizabethan parishes, such as East Hanningfield in Essex. However, in that instance the minister was one of the hotter sort of Protestants, who led a quasi-separatist group within the parish, whereas in Cirencester the minister seems to have been godly, but not extremely so.[89]

In the autumn of 1574, Cirencester's case was referred to the Commission for Ecclesiastical Causes, in the hope that the extra powers available to that body could be used to compel the Cirencester parishioners to conform. Although the complaints remained the same, some of the individuals involved had changed. Those required to appear included four women. Two separate groups came before the Commission in October 1574, and each gave different reasons for their actions, indicating the division within the parish. One group reiterated complaints made earlier concerning their minister's lack of adherence to the *Book of Common Prayer*. Meanwhile, members of the second group gave a variety of related reasons for not attending services, all of which signified a preference for the hotter sort of Protestantism. One man said he stayed away because the minister 'dothe bid holidaies and fastinge daies the whiche is supersticion' (an interesting assertion, given that previously others had complained of the priest's failure to bid those days). Another wanted 'malefactors and papistes excluded out of the churche'. One of the women, Elizabeth Whiting, in a complaint which was similar to that of the Drewett's of St Nicholas in Gloucester,

[87] PRO PROB 11/59, fos. 187–8.
[88] GRO GDR vol. XXXV, p. 33; printed in *Commission*, p. 65.
[89] P. Collinson, *The Elizabethan Puritan Movement*, pp. 349, 352–3.

would not have her child baptised in the font 'for that it is supersticion'. As with the Drewetts, the Commission did attempt to have the child seized and baptised, but with equal lack of success; however ultimately she did have it christened in the parish of Hawkesbury by Mr Woodland, the minister there.[90] Another complainant asserted that the minster 'dothe followe mens tradicion and do not minister nor teache the word accordinge to Godes word'.

The members of this second group all resisted conformity, and the record of their appearance on this particular day concludes, 'Thus the said parties being very obsinat and not obedient . . . yt is therefore ordered they shalbe committed . . . [to prison] untill further order be taken.'[91] Members of this latter group reappeared several times before the Commission over the next year and a half. Some eventually conformed; others steadfastly refused. Among the most incorrigible were four women: Agnes Longe, Anne Cole, Anna Bradford and Elizabeth Whiting, and the husbands of two of the women, Thomas Bradford and William Whiting. Anne Cole refused to receive communion; Agnes Longe, Thomas and Anna Bradford and William Whiting refused to come to church. Some were accused of using conventicles rather than participating in their parish worship. Elizabeth Whiting, in addition to her resistance to baptism in the font, refused to come to church regularly. Her husband, William, was so obstinate in his refusal to go to church and so obstreperous in court that he was eventually sent to London to appear before the Privy Council, along with William Drewett, in March 1579. Whiting then disappears from the records; Drewett was still a prisoner in Newgate in November 1581.[92] Meanwhile in Cirencester, the divisions continued until at least 1588, when the town preacher, Philip Jones, delivered and published three sermons on the first chapter of the Epistle of James, referring in his dedication to continuing disputes within the town.[93]

These most difficult cases are but one indication of the growth of resistance to official religious policy in Gloucestershire in the 1570s. The sharp increase in that same decade in the total numbers of recusants and individuals refusing to take communion provides further evidence of the

---

[90] The officials delegated to seize the child included two prominent townsmen with contrasting religious leanings. Accompanying Christopher George was William Partridge, who would leave a decidedly Protestant will just two years after this event. GRO GDR vol. XXXV, p. 48, printed in *Commission*, p. 70; PRO PROB 11/61, fos. 22v–23.

[91] GRO GDR vol. XXXV, pp. 31, 48; printed in *Commission*, pp. 64, 70.

[92] GRO GDR vol. XXXV, pp. 45, 46, 48, 56, 59, 60, 63, 65, 68, 74, 114; printed in *Commission*, pp. 68, 70, 74–8, 80, 83, 106; *APC*, vol. XI, p. 77; GRO GDR vol. XL, fo. 164; vol. XLIII, fo. 94.

[93] P. Jones, *Certaine Sermons Preached of Late at Cicester . . . upon a Portion of the First Chapter of the Epistle of James* (London, 1588), STC 14728.

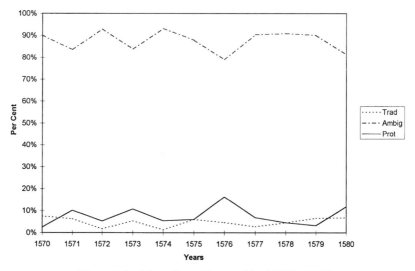

Figure 7.1   Non-elite will preambles (1570–1580)

Figure 7.2   Elite will preambles (1570–1580) (three-year rolling average)

same phenomenon. Some allowance must be made for the difference in character between the visitation in 1576 and those conducted earlier in Bishop Cheyney's episcopate; however, other factors also contributed to the increase in numbers in the 1570s. As Elizabethan Protestantism became more clearly defined, there was something more definite which one could oppose, and this may have prompted some to act on their personal beliefs, either by absenting themselves from church or by refusing to receive communion. This would have been especially true of those who had hoped for more reform, rather than less.

As with the evidence of nonconforming behaviour, the pattern of beliefs made evident in will preambles and charitable bequests changed significantly in the 1570s. During this decade, the proportion of ordinary testators declaring their Protestantism increased from an average of under 5 per cent in the 1560s to approximately 13 per cent by 1580, while among the gentry those favouring the new religion rose on average from approximately 25 per cent to 40 per cent.[94] In addition, the two groups had a very similar percentage of traditional or Catholic wills (down from 15 to approximately 6 per cent). As in the previous reigns since the break with Rome, the difference was in the proportion of individuals opting for ambiguous religious preambles; fewer of the elite chose that option.[95]

The type of language used in will preambles also continued to evolve. In 1577, Jone Apowell of Newent in the Forest of Dean, bequeathed her soul 'in to the handes of the Allmyghtey God, trusting to be saved by the deathe passion and resurrection of my alone advocate Jesus Christe my onely savyor and redemer'.[96] She thus combined Christ's passion and resurrection in her unique faith statement, and, by further adding the word 'alone' to her description of Christ as advocate, she transformed an otherwise ambiguous statement into one which, while still ambiguous, had Protestant overtones. As is so often the case, individual beliefs and actions defy clear precise and mutually exclusive categorisation. Invoking Christ's resurrection, for instance, may not in and of itself indicate clearly Protestant beliefs. That focus is, none the less, found in a number of wills of followers of the new religion. For example, it was, included in William Tracy's will, written in 1531. Following Tracy's lead, as did others all over England, Thomas Priden, a husbandman of South Cerney declared:

I commite me unto God and his mercye tristinge without eny dout or mystruste that by his grace and the mertes of Jesus Christe and by the vertue of his passion and of his resurrection I have and shall have remyssion of sines and resurrection of bodye and soule accordingle as hit is written, Job xix, I belive that my redemer lievethe

---

[94] See Figures 7.1 and 7.2. [95] See Figure 7.3. [96] GRO Wills, 1578/87.

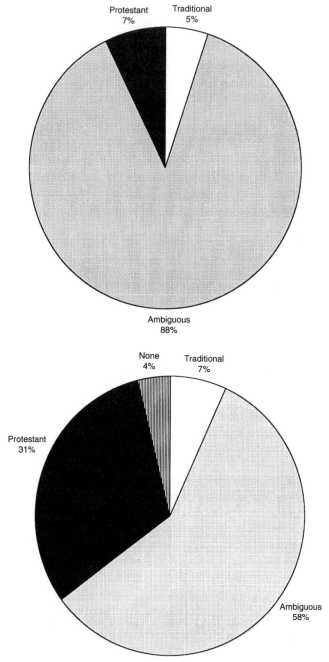

Figure 7.3   (a) Non-elite and (b) elite will preambles (1570–1580)

and that in last day I shall rise out of the earthe and my fleshe shall se my saviour. This my hope is layd up in my bosum.[97]

Key Protestant phrases included in this preamble appeared increasingly in Elizabethan wills in Gloucestershire after 1570. For instance, Jane Jones of St Michael's in Gloucester, after giving her soul to Almighty God through the merits of Jesus Christ, declared: 'I beleve I have and shall have perfect forgevenes of all my synnes.'[98] Jullyan Frape of Slimbridge combined references to both Christ's passion and resurrection with a similar assertion of the certainty of her salvation. Her preamble stated 'that by the vertue of his deth and patione and of his rising ageyne I have and shall have forgevnes of my synes'.[99] A number of wills included statements similar to that used by William Allen, a tucker from Tewkesbury, who declared that by Christ's passion he was 'fully assured to have pardon and remyssyone . . . [of his sins] by that most swet and comfortabell Chryst Jesus Amen'.[100] Others went a step further in asserting their assurance of salvation, as did John Pyrry, a husbandman of Rudford, when he bequeathed his soul to Almighty God, 'not doubtinge but that God for his mercies sacke sett forth in the precious bloude of his derely beloved sonne Christ Jesu our alone saviour and redeamer will receve my soule into his glory amongst his heavenly and blessed aungells'.[101] Still others chose to deny their belief in traditional means of achieving salvation more explicitly. The widows, Eleanor Sutton and Elizabeth Robartes of Stanway, both declared: 'I geve and bequeth my sowll into the handes of Jesus Christe my savioure by whose [death] and passion I trust to be saved and non other wise.'[102] Richard Whittingham, a baker from Gloucester, similarly, gave his soul to Almighty God and to Jesus Christ, his son, 'trusting by his deathe and passyon to be savyde and by no other meanes'.[103]

Some testators, meanwhile, addressed God directly, another indication of Protestant beliefs, with the clear sense of a personal relationship with God which did not necessarily require any intermediary. Elinor Heaven of Dursley commended her soul 'unto thy handes O Lord for thow hast redemed me thow God of truthe'.[104] Similarly echoing Psalm 31, William

---

[97] GRO Wills, 1573/195. See chapter 4 for the discussion of the wills of Jone Davis and Jone Tymmes.

[98] GRO Wills, 1581/42.   [99] GRO Wills, 1570/93.

[100] GRO Wills, 1580/201. Other wills similar in their assertion of assurance of salvation include GRO Wills, 1563/4, 1563/23, 1565/56, 1575/18, 1578/145, 1580/4.

[101] GRO Wills, 1575/75.   [102] GRO Wills, 1571/34, 1573/23.

[103] GRO Wills, 1573/166. These three testators were not alone in defining their theology in terms of what they did not believe. For examples of such statements of faith see the wills of Thomas Goodman, Jone Androwes, Elizabeth Redberde, Elizabeth Fortey, Martin Raye and Thomas Lugge. GRO Wills 1570/176, 1571/88, 1573/29, 1577/98, 1577/176.

[104] GRO Wills, 1562/16.

Berry of Dursley, yeoman, confessed his faith 'to be according to the Christian and apostolicall creede' in that he trusted to be saved by the merits of Christ's death, renouncing 'all other meanes' of salvation. He then concluded: 'And therefore I commend my soule O Lorde into thy holy handes for thowe haste redemed me O God of truethe.'[105] The statement of Margery Purnell of North Nibley was more mixed in its references to God. Her preamble reads:

I commend my sowle into the hands of Allmightie God my maker and redeamer trustinge to be saved by the merytes onelie of Jesu Christe my onelie saviour and redeamer, in his bloud shedd for my synnes and for the synnes of all his elect uterlie renouncynge all other meanes. And therefore I commende my sowle O Lord into thy holy hands.[106]

Such statements, even without the exclusion of 'all other meanes' of achieving salvation were clearly declarations of Protestant faith.

The rich variety of Gloucestershire preambles affirming the new religion can, however, be misleading. As late as 1580, only 13 per cent of all non-elite wills included such expressions of faith. That same year 8 per cent employed traditional soul bequests. The most traditional form, bequeathing the soul to Almighty God, the Blessed Virgin Mary and the holy company of heaven, last appears in the will of Peter Raynollde of Southrop written in 1563.[107] However, an edited version which bequeathed the soul 'to Almyghty God and to all the blessed company of heaven' continued in use throughout the first half of Elizabeth's reign, and it in turn spawned a new form, which combined the standard ambiguous statement with a reference to the saints.[108] Thus Richard Wattes of Badgeworth gave his soul 'to Almyghtie God my onlie creator and redemer to be associate withe the holle companye of heaven'.[109] Meanwhile, an increasing number of testators and their scribes opted for statements which invoked the Trinity, the most traditional of all the ambiguous preamble categories. This was the form Bishop John Wakeman had employed, and some still followed his lead, using simple statements of faith in salvation through the Trinity in their wills.[110]

Not all groups of Gloucestershire testators, nevertheless, followed the general pattern already described. Among ordinary testators, most references to belief in salvation through Christ's resurrection can be found in women's wills, and more women than men addressed God directly.

---

[105] PRO PROB 11/59, fos. 167v–68.   [106] GRO Wills, 1579/115.
[107] GRO Wills, 1563/96.   [108] GRO Wills, 1573/20.
[109] GRO Wills, 1569/103.
[110] PRO PROB 11/32, fo. 343v. For example, see the wills of the labourer, Thomas Balye, of Littledean, and the yeoman Thomas Hawle, of Minchinhampton, written in May 1562 and July 1576, respectively. GRO Wills, 1562/127, 1576/109.

However, the greatest discrepancy between men's and women's wills was in their uses of ambiguous forms as compared with their continued reliance on traditional statements.[111] By 1580, traditional soul bequests were almost non-existent in women's wills. Women and their scribes seem to have opted for ambiguous preambles in place of the traditional forms used earlier, as the popularity of ambiguous forms increased steadily through the 1570s. On the other hand, during the same period the popularity of each of the three groups of soul bequests remained nearly constant among male testators and their scribes. Ambiguous statements maintained their earlier level of appeal, and traditional forms did not disappear. In fact, the popularity of traditional preambles was roughly equal to that of Protestant statements in men's wills. The differences are slight and it is important not to overstate them, but perhaps women with traditional beliefs were choosing to conceal them behind ambiguous statements, while their male counterparts were not. Or perhaps scribes were treating women differently than they were treating men, making the decisions for them and choosing ambiguous preambles to protect them from some imagined punishment.

It is also possible to examine the wills of men from several levels of Elizabethan society to identify possible differences. As noted earlier, there were some differences between elite and non-elite wills, although the variations were not very significant.[112] The testator's status was seldom included in wills of the more humble testators written before the accession of Elizabeth, and was only included in half of the Gloucestershire wills of non-elite men during the first half of Elizabeth's reign. Therefore, the total number of such wills is fairly small; however, it is still possible to gain an impression of the pattern of religious preferences. Among the aldermen of the city of Gloucester and the county gentry, approximately 10 per cent left traditional wills, 20 per cent declared their Protestantism, and the remaining 70 per cent chose ambiguous statements. Meanwhile, approximately 14 per cent of the 200 husbandmen, yeomen and artisans leaving wills included a traditional soul bequest, while none of the 12 mercers or merchants and very few textile workers (18 of whom are included in this study) made similar choices. Instead, the cloth workers opted primarily for ambiguous formulas, while just over 13 per cent (5 of 36) of the artisans

---

[111] See Appendix B. Chi-square value of 26.7 with 4 degrees of freedom for ambiguous preambles divided by reign and gender is significant.

[112] Two hundred and seventy-five of the 647 non-elite Elizabethan men (42.5 per cent) who left wills included either their status or occupation. In addition, 254 elite men left wills which were proved in the Prerogative Court of Canterbury. It is not possible to analyse Elizabethan women's wills in this way, because most merely gave their status as 'widow' without further elaboration, and their wills seldom included material evidence of their social position or wealth.

and merchants chose Protestant statements.[113] Most notably, the preference for ambiguous preambles seen in the complete sample holds across all social levels below the gentry and other elite testators, with approximately 80 per cent of those testators choosing such statements. Meanwhile, ambiguous statements only appeared in approximately 73 per cent of the elite wills in the early 1570s and fell slightly to approximately 68 per cent in the last years of the decade. Traditional expressions of faith were falling from favour, but only the elite were showing any measurable readiness to embrace Protestantism, and even that was slight. Among ordinary testators the increase was very slow. Once again, as in Edward's reign, the predominance of ambiguous forms in non-elite wills seems to indicate that both established scribes and followers of the old religion were increasing their reliance on those forms. As with their actions, most of the laity were finding it possible to conform nominally in their wills, while still holding to aspects of the old religion.

In contrast to both the analysis by gender and that by social position, regional religious differences were significantly more distinctive among those below the gentry/aldermanic level.[114] In the northern vale and the Forest of Dean there was a substantial preference for ambiguous preambles combined with a sharp decline in traditional soul bequests, while Protestant preambles increased only very slightly. Once again, in those adjacent regions there is evidence of people turning from traditional to ambiguous preambles, suggesting the use of ambiguous forms to hide personal theology. In the Cotswolds and the southern vale the use of traditional statements decreased sharply during the 1560s, and levelled off in the 1570s. In addition, the southern valley was similar to the north in its strong preference for ambiguous preambles and minimal use of Protestant forms. In fact, throughout the vale Protestant statements were even less popular in the late 1570s than they had been earlier; only in the Cotswolds and in the city of Gloucester can we find notable signs of acceptance of the established religion. In the 1570s, 20 per cent of Gloucester testators and 10 per cent of those in the Cotswolds used clearly Protestant preambles. Among the elite, regional differences were less pronounced, but generally matched the pattern of their more humble neighbours.

Charitable bequests, unlike explicit declarations of faith, shed little light on the beliefs of the laity in the 1570s. However, the bequests themselves continued, although generally at the reduced level of the last years of the

---

[113] See Figure 7.4 and Appendix B. The level of preference for Protestantism was the only significant difference between the religious preambles of the elite and non-elite testators. Chi-square value of 15.79 with 4 degree of freedom.

[114] See Appendix B. Chi-square value of 46.05 with 16 degrees of freedom for non-elite ambiguous preambles by region and reign is significant.

previous decade. The proportion of wills including gifts to parishes remained low but stable, with a continuation of the focus on the maintenance of parish property established earlier in the reign. In 1570, Thomas Gower of Wotton-under-Edge left 40s for parish repairs, and seven years later Anthony Corbett of Berkeley left 10s to repair the neighbouring church in the village of Stone.[115] In the meantime, in the city of Gloucester, St Aldate's Parish, which had struggled to keep up with essential maintenance during the 1560s, was able to build a wooden steeple at considerable expense in the mid-1570s thanks to the generosity of numerous parishioners, both living and dead.[116] Exceptions to the general pattern of parish gifts without religious overtones were the occasional donations toward the purchase of Bibles, such as those of Walter Jordayne, yeoman, and Robert Basset, esquire. Jordayne gave his parish of Newland in the Forest of Dean 6d toward the purchase of a new Bible, and Basset designated 14s 4d 'towarde the buyeng of a newe Bible for the parishe chirche of Uley in the largest volume'.[117]

As with parish bequests, so too did gifts for the poor, both ritualistic and substantial, continue, with the smaller gifts maintaining the level achieved in the 1560s. In the city of Gloucester, William Goldeston, his brother, Richard, and Richard's wife, Jone, all left land, tenements or money to almshouses, or (in the case of Jone) for wood and coal to be distributed to the poor annually.[118] In none of these cases were the poor asked to pray for the dead, as they had been earlier in Elizabeth's reign, and, based on the religious preambles in these particular wills, it is clear that the Goldestons would not have wanted any such works on their behalf. These individuals seem to have been acting out of a belief in their own responsibility for the stewardship of God's creation, combined with a sense of civic duty, similar to that of Giles Geast in 1557 and their more humble fellow-donors.[119]

Civic duty also prompted a few testators to designate gifts in support of specific municipal projects, although the incidence of ritualistic gifts for the maintenance of highways and bridges continued to decline to a negligible level though the decade. Thus William Berry gave 10s to the 'repairinge of the market place comonly called the Crosse' in Dursley, and Thomas Gower contributed £20 toward 'the bringing of a conduyte to the markett crosse of Wotton[-under-Edge]'.[120]

Analysis of two other terms often included in traditional wills also helps

[115] PRO PROB 11/54, fo. 142; 11/59, fos. 271v–72.
[116] GRO P154/6 CW 1/8, 1/9, 1/10. St Aldate's also paid 10s 'for rearinge the ground in the chaunsell' in 1577, possibly in response to pressure from the archiepiscopal visitors the previous year. GRO P154/6 CW 1/11.
[117] GRO Wills, 1572/201; PRO PROB 11/54, fos. 195–95v.
[118] GRO Wills, 1569/156, 1574/143, 1579/107.   [119] See chapters 5 and 6.
[120] PRO PROB 11/54, fo. 142; 11/59, fos. 167v–68.

gauge the rate of change in Gloucestershire lay piety from the reign of Henry VIII. In traditional wills the parish priest was often referred to as 'my ghostly father', and the cathedral was called the 'mother church'. Having fallen from favour with Edward's accession and remained at a consistently low level through Mary's reign, such phrases became even less popular under Elizabeth. References to 'my ghostly father' disappeared by 1570, while those to the 'mother church' were appearing in only 2 per cent of wills by 1580. The diocese of Gloucester was slowly shedding some vestiges of traditional pre-Reformation religion, though not as a result of any specific direction from the ecclesiastical hierarchy.

During the first half of Elizabeth's reign the range of acceptable beliefs and practices exercised by the laity had moved very slowly from a mixture of outward conformity and private preferences for the old religion to an increasing acceptance of Protestantism, with the trend accelerating during the 1570s. However, the actual range of beliefs does not seem to have shifted very much; rather, it expanded as the preference for Protestant beliefs and practices gained favour, while some who preferred the old religion held their ground. The absence of any vigorous implementation or enforcement of Elizabethan Protestantism had left room for a wide range of responses to official policies at the local level, both corporately and individually, and the laity took full advantage of their options. The gentry were slightly more likely than the non-elite to stick with explicitly Catholic declarations later in the period, and opted for clearly Protestant statements earlier. In general, however, the proportion of individuals embracing the established Protestant faith began to increase in the 1570s, albeit without episcopal encouragement. On the one hand, church papistry seems to have been consistently condoned and Catholic recusancy ignored under Cheyney, while, on the other, the more godly Protestants were being subjected to repeated, if ineffective, discipline for their actions. Perhaps the 'osmotic process' of conversion by repeated exposure to the words of the Prayer Book and the Homilies, to which Patrick Collinson refers, was slowly having an impact on lay piety in Gloucestershire, but the predominant pattern of lay beliefs and practices in Gloucestershire was still generally one of nominal conformance combined with a marked degree of reluctance to give up aspects of traditional religion.[121]

---

[121] P. Collinson, 'The Elizabethan Church and the New Religion', in *The Reign of Elizabeth I*, ed. C. Haigh (1984; reprint, Basingstoke and London, 1991), pp. 179–80.

CONCLUSION

From the break with Rome to the middle of Elizabeth's reign, the laity in the diocese and the realm dealt with a series of different and often contradictory definitions of acceptable religious beliefs and practices, as officials of the Crown and church worked to implement the form of religion in favour at the moment. The actual result of these efforts, however, was not always what those in power had in mind, as parishes and parishioners interpreted and implemented official policies in ways which suited their circumstances, religious preferences and past experiences. Within Gloucestershire, each region responded in a distinctive way, but even within regions there were variations as neighbouring parishes and their individual parishioners differed in the degree and nature of their conformity to the established faith.

Exposed to the opposing beliefs of the last two Bishops of Worcester, Hugh Latimer and John Bell, witnessing the removal of shrines such as the Blood of Hailes, and presented with the dissolution of the monasteries, the laity generally seem to have welcomed the more conservative policies of the early 1540s and the respite from change offered by John Wakeman's equivocal, conforming and passive episcopal style. The relief was to be brief, however, as Henry's death and Edward's accession brought with it a renewed impetus for the implementation of Protestantism. While a few people exuberantly welcomed this definitive swing toward religious reform, most of the Gloucestershire laity appear to have 'ducked for cover' in an attempt to ride out this particular religious storm, as they opted for outward parish conformity and ambiguity in their wills. Under Mary, however, parishes appear to have tried to conform as fully as possible, despite the costs associated with the Catholic liturgy, while individuals, rather than continuing to express mere nominal acceptance of official religion, returned to full and heartfelt expressions of traditional faith in their will preambles. The earlier practice of lukewarm acceptance characterised by minimal conformity and ambiguous testamentary statements was repeated when, having actively welcomed the Marian restoration of

161

Catholicism, the laity were once again confronted at Mary's death by an official religious policy dedicated to re-establishing Protestantism.

With Elizabeth's accession official religious policy shifted once again, and this time the people of Gloucestershire resisted to an even greater degree than under Edward. Reluctance to embrace Elizabethan Protestantism can be seen both in the lethargic response of parishes to the full re-establishment of the reformed liturgy, and in the laity's predominant return to ambiguous statements of faith in their wills. Most, if not all, parishes seem to have acquired the new *Book of Common Prayer* by the time of the royal visitation to Gloucestershire at the end of the summer of 1559. However, the provision of other accoutrements of established Protestantism was typically delayed for up to three years, with some parishes still not having made the required physical changes to their churches at the time of the archiepiscopal visitation in 1576. The accumulated cost of successive liturgical changes or impatience with yet another shift in policy may have contributed to corporate reluctance. None the less, individuals also responded sluggishly to the reintroduction of the new religion, with testators in particular demonstrating their reluctance to assert Protestant beliefs. The first indication of resistance and scepticism was signalled by the abrupt swing back to ambiguous preambles. Later, the continued lack of enthusiasm for Protestantism brought a gradual expansion in the use of a variety of complex, but still fundamentally ambiguous, statements of faith mirroring the similarly complex but unequivocally traditional expressions of beliefs so popular under Mary. Again, as under Edward, the introduction of official Protestantism prompted the laity to conceal their beliefs behind ambiguous or marginally conformist statements and actions. Only by the mid-1570s did Protestantism begin to gain acceptance in certain parts of the diocese, and then only after a significant period of collective adjustment and apparent indecision. Throughout these years, as official policy was altered, the laity responded in a wide variety of ways. The modifications in lay beliefs and practices defy the rigid classifications desired by the state and the ecclesiastical authorities, and searched for by so many historians of the Reformation.

Too often scholars have allowed the articulate intelligentsia and clerical elites of the Reformation to define the paradigms by which the beliefs and actions of ordinary lay people are described and analysed. Thus, they have continued to employ a 'top–down' and even denominational approach to the study of sixteenth-century religious change, despite their apparent 'bottom–up' perspective. Lay religion cannot be portrayed in such cartoon-like, black-and-white images of Protestants and Catholics; rather we need a kaleidoscopic array of colours to depict accurately the countless shades of beliefs to be found. Protestantism was new and unfamiliar, and therefore typically unwelcome, and it was only natural that people would at first resist the new and grieve for the old. Furthermore, the Marian Restoration provided a reminder of what had been, and made acceptance of Protestantism that much more difficult. Hence, the reintroduction of Protestantism under Elizabeth must have been greeted with apprehension and regret by at least some of the laity, worn down as they were by continually shifting standards of acceptable religious beliefs and practices. A broad band of shades of belief would have been a natural outcome of the resulting process of gradual accommodation to the new religious norm, either by adopting some form of Protestantism or by finding a way to remain faithful to Catholicism within the increasingly Protestant realm.

The nature of early Elizabethan religious policy exacerbated the problem, given the conflicting official directives concerning liturgical practices, the expectation of additional reform being promoted by former Marian exiles, including Archbishop Grindal, and the confusion concerning the queen's religious preferences.[1] Should the communion bread be in the form of wafers or the common loaf? Was the priest to celebrate the Eucharist wearing a cope, or simply a surplice? Which ornaments could still be used in the church? Those who wanted either more reform or a return to Catholicism could each have found some cause for hope, but for the dutiful conforming majority of lay people, who were just tired of all the alterations, the confusion and apparent indecision of the 1560s provided little solace. Only with the coming of the 1570s were some of the uncertainties removed, following the suppression of the Northern Rebellion, the publication of the papal bull excommunicating Elizabeth, and Parliament's approval of the Articles of Religion. Thus, official policy once again became more explicit, and provided the laity with a more clearly articulated definition of religious conformity than they had known since Mary's reign.

While a more definitive religious policy undoubtedly contributed to an apparent acceleration in the pace of Protestantisation in Gloucestershire in the 1570s, other factors were also at work, most notably the archiepiscopal visitation in 1576, which vigorously sought to enforce conformity to Elizabethan Protestantism. However, more subtle influences were also active. Minimal conformity, including as it did the use of the *Book of Common Prayer*, would have gradually helped make the new religion familiar to the laity both in Gloucestershire and elsewhere across the realm. Then, as they worshipped, they could also have focused on aspects of the new liturgy which were most helpful to their private spiritual lives. Their

---

[1] Conflicting aspects of official policy included descriptions of the correct form of communion bread, and the appropriate vestments to be worn while celebrating the Eucharist. See chapter 6.

worship might also have been enlivened by psalm singing, as it was at Dursley, as more and more parishes purchased 'the psalter to be song'.[2] Signs of Protestantism were also becoming more prevalent outside the church. As Tessa Watt has pointed out, there was a proliferation of godly ballads and broadsides, sometimes printed on paper but appearing on painted cloths and walls as well. These frequently were used as decorations in homes and alehouses, and were often designed to reinforce aspects of Protestant doctrine, combining as they did both images and moral texts. The prodigal son and the Ten Commandments were both common themes of this genre, and the prodigal theme appears on a surviving painted cloth hanging in Owlpen Manor near Dursley. By such means as these, a predominantly Protestant atmosphere was created for the young, and the mature were further acclimatised to the established religion.[3]

Officially and unofficially, then, the promotion of Elizabethan Protestantism continued. However, the new religion still had to be accepted by the individuals and parishes of the diocese, and this brings us back to the process of effecting change. Having resisted the new and lamented the loss of the old, the laity began to accept the established religion only in the 1570s. The process by which they adopted Protestantism began with the internalisation of official expectations. This was followed by the highly personalised integration of the attendant beliefs and practices with valued vestiges of traditional religion which were specific to each individual. The differences between official Protestantism and the myriad of forms of that faith professed by individual lay people owed much to the relative value placed on various aspects of both the old religion and the new by each person. The result was a spectrum of conformist beliefs which extended from some forms of Catholicism to a preference for the hotter sort of Protestantism. It included both the church papists, who managed to avoid taking communion by always being out of charity with their neighbours, and the Puritans who encouraged their priest to leave the surplice in the cupboard and use loaf bread for communion. It also encompassed both those favourers of traditional religion who, like some of Thomas Farryngton's testators, used 'etc.' in place of references to the saints in their wills and zealous Protestants who provided long, assertively Calvinist statements of faith. The nature of conformity within the parishes was similar to that of their parishioners, although perhaps the portion of the spectrum spanned by corporate conformity was narrower than that reached by individuals.

By the middle of Elizabeth's reign, both parishes and individuals were thus transforming official policy to suit their particular circumstances and

[2] GRO P124 CW 2/4, fo. 7; Watt, *Cheap Print*, p. 55.
[3] Watt, *Cheap Print*, pp. 41, 48, 200–5, 217.

experiences. While parishioners of Dursley were seated to receive communion around their properly covered communion table, heard sermons, sang
the psalms, and had divested themselves of all the accoutrements of
traditional liturgy, those of Stroud, just a short distance to the north,
witnessed the Eucharist being celebrated at a table without the required
covering, heard no sermons, and still viewed images during worship.
Similarly, the interior of Lechlade church was adorned with scriptural texts
while in the neighbouring parish of Fairford they were probably worshipping in a darkened nave, having spread whitewash over their windows to
conceal the images in their stained glass. Inventories of church goods
further attest to a resistance to conformity on the part of some parishes,
while hedging their bets against a future return to Catholicism. Thus, both
Tewkesbury and Bishop's Cleve had retained copes, albs and other trap-
pings of traditional worship.[4]

Individuals, as well as parishes, presented a mixed picture of established
religion, as shown by the range of religious beliefs contained in lay wills.
Examples abound, but a few will suffice. Writing in March 1579, Margaret
Clarke, a widow from St Nicholas parish in Gloucester, bequeathed her
soul 'unto the mercy of Almightie God my maker soulie trusting to have
remission and pardon of all my synnes at the daie of judgment by the
merittes and deathe of Jhesus Christ my onlie savior and redemer', an
ambiguous statement which may or may not have concealed traditional
beliefs.[5] Others used different but equally ambiguous formulas. Meanwhile, some were expressing decidedly Protestant beliefs. In her will,
written in March 1580, Alice Nichols, a widow of Beverstone, bequeathed
her soul 'into the handes of Almightie God . . . with full assurance of
eternall salvation through the merites of Jesus Christ', and Richard Bubb,
husbandman of Badgeworth, whose will is dated just four months later,
declared: 'I geve and bequeth my soull to Allmyghty God and my savior in
whom onely I truste to be saved and by no other meanes.'[6]

Religious preambles were not the only manifestation of mid-Elizabethan
blended beliefs in wills; charitable bequests, in particular those intended for
parishes and the poor, provide additional evidence. Bequests to parishes
dropped in Gloucestershire until the mid-1570s, when they seem to have
stabilised, while gifts to the poor increased substantially under Protestantism, not just in Gloucester but all over England. Historians such as
Robert Whiting have interpreted the changes in such giving as indicative of
a secularisation of society. However, other explanations suggest themselves.[7] True, gifts to the poor were encouraged by civic humanism, but, as

---

[4] See chapter 6.   [5] GRO Wills, 1579/108.   [6] GRO Wills 1580/4, 1580/145.
[7] Whiting, *Blind Devotion*, pp. 98–101, 181–2, 186–7.

Eamon Duffy has asserted, they were also one of the few acts of charity from pre-Reformation Catholicism to be condoned and even encouraged under Protestantism.[8] Furthermore, they were promoted in scripture, which meant that the hotter sort of Protestants would have opted for them as well. Meanwhile, the decrease in gifts to parishes may have merely reflected a combination of common sense and good stewardship. Given the provenance of such benefactions during the previous thirty years, pious lay people may have sought other recipients and agents for their generosity.[9] It may also be a mistake to give too much credence to the existence of a dichotomy between the sacred and the secular. As Natalie Zemon Davis points out, this division 'may limit our historical insight unduly' by obscuring certain features of religious life.[10] Thus, lay charitable giving may have merely taken on new forms, rather than having actually disappeared, as a result of the Reformation.

Blurring of the division between the sacred and the secular can also be seen in the relationship between parishes and towns, both before and after the Reformation. David Harris Sacks has described the way in which the leaders of the city of Bristol paid for and led 'great public celebrations' in honour of St Clement and St Katherine prior to the Reformation to reaffirm spiritual and social civic unity, and similar pageants and celebrations were still taking place in Gloucester on Mid-Summer's Eve and St Peter's Eve as late as the 1570s.[11] Civic leaders, such as those of Tewkesbury and Gloucester, also positioned themselves prominently in churches for worship and special sermons. Robert Tittler has pointed out that the leaders of towns, bailiffs and burgesses, mayors and aldermen, used prominent seating in churches as a means of legitimating their power.[12]

The process of effecting religious change would have been difficult under the best of circumstances, and those of the sixteenth century had definitely

---

[8] M. Todd, *Christian Humanism*, pp. 133–8; Duffy, *Stripping*, pp. 504–5.

[9] This was certainly true of Giles Geast of Tewkesbury and of the Goldeston brothers, William and Richard of Gloucester. Geast established a charity to be administered by feoffees rather than by the churchwardens, while the Goldestons gave generously to the poor, and left nothing to their parish. PRO PROB 11/40, fos. 284v–87v; GRO Wills, 1569/156, 1574/143, 1579/107.

[10] N. Z. Davis, 'Some Tasks and Themes in the Study of Popular Religion', in *The Pursuit of Holiness in Late Medieval and Renaissance Religion*, ed. C. Trinkhaus and H. A. Oberman (Leiden, 1974), pp. 307–12.

[11] D. H. Sacks, 'The Demise of the Martyrs: the Feasts of St Clement and St Katherine in Bristol, 1400–1600', *Social History* 11 (1986), pp. 141–69, *passim*; GRO GBR F4/3, fos. 169v, 199. Cf. M. C. McClendon, '"Against God's Word": Government, Religion and the Crisis of Authority in Early Reformation Norwich', *SCJ* 25 (1994), pp. 353–69, *passim*.

[12] R. Tittler, 'Seats of Honor, Seats of Power: the Symbolism of Public Seating in the English Urban Community, *c.* 1560–1620', *Albion* 24 (1992), pp. 218–23; P329 CW 2/1, pp. 5–67, *passim*; printed in *Tewkesbury*, pp. 3–44, *passim*; GRO GBR F4/3, fos. 83v–202, *passim*. Also see chapter 6.

not been ideal. The swings back and forth between traditional and reformed religion between the early 1530s and the 1580s must have left those who wanted to conform conscientiously suffering from some form of spiritual whiplash, as they sought to adhere to each new set of policies. Meanwhile, those motivated by sincere pious convictions continued to practise their own faith, whether as Catholic or Puritan recusant, resisting all pressure to conform. Furthermore, the Marian restoration of Catholicism, however brief, would have provided a fresh reminder of what had been left behind. The local implementation of established Protestantism was further hindered in Gloucestershire during the first half of Elizabeth's reign by the theology and administration of Bishop Richard Cheyney. During the last twenty years of the sixteenth century, the city of Gloucester would be increasingly dominated by a godly oligarchy, which would include aldermen active in the city's leadership prior to 1580.[13] However, religious division and diversity would persist or reappear in some parts of the diocese through the next century and beyond. For instance, Tewkesbury's ruling elite would be religiously divided in the 1680s, and areas like Nailsworth near Minchinhampton would provide fertile ground for the development of nonconformity in the eighteenth and nineteenth centuries.[14] However, for those who lived through the 'years of uncertainty' brought by the English Reformation, external forces and circumstances, combined with natural human resistance to change and the need for individuals to personalise their faith, produced a broad spectrum of religious beliefs, albeit one with an increasingly Protestant accent. Eventually, as in the rest of England, the Reformation would transform Gloucestershire into a predominantly Protestant county and diocese, even at the level of the laity, but in 1580, at least in that western shire, the process of change had only just begun.

[13] Clark, '"The Ramoth-Gilead of the Good"', pp. 167–87.
[14] D. Beaver, 'Conscience and Context: the Popish Plot and the Politics of Ritual, 1678–1682', *HJ* 34 (1991), pp. 297–327; A. M. Urdank, *Religion and Society in a Cotswold Vale: Nailsworth, Gloucestershire, 1780–1865* (Berkeley, Los Angeles, CA, and Oxford, 1990).

Appendix A

Sources and methodology

Through the careful analysis of a large quantity of material on Gloucestershire, it is possible to create a picture of the past which accommodates a significant degree of variety and complexity.[1] The evidence on which this study is based includes wills, as well as parish, diocesan and state records, and surviving contemporaneous furnishings and decorations in the parish churches of the diocese. In particular, this study includes two parish case studies with the attendant reconstitution of the parochial leadership network for each, and a detailed theological and statistical analysis of the religious content of wills. Furthermore, the types of extant evidence has determined the amount of attention which can be given to different groups of Gloucestershire inhabitants. The middling sort and the more prominent townspeople, in particular, have the principal roles, while the bishops and other clergy and the gentry also receive attention. Meanwhile, people from the lower orders of society are relegated to 'bit parts' in the drama. However, even within these parameters religious beliefs and practices can vary significantly. David Palliser has asserted that lay religion 'can only with difficulty be forced into the strait-jacket of "Catholic" and "Protestant" labels'; indeed, humanity is much too complex for such simple categorisation.[2] An historical view which is derived from mountains of minutiae is likely to accommodate such complexity more easily than one which is fundamentally anecdotal. Rich and interesting accounts of specific incidents can then be used effectively to enliven that view.[3] In addition, in the use of detailed data I have delayed categorisations or generalisations until the last possible moment in the analytical process to avoid concealing evidence of diversity and to allow as much variety and complexity as possible to emerge in this representation of the past.

The sources used in this study can be divided into four rough categories: (1) miscellaneous textual material, including bishop's writings, other letters, and

---

[1] Earlier versions of this appendix appeared in C. Litzenberger, 'Local Responses to Changes in Religious Policy Based on Evidence from Gloucestershire Wills (1541–1580)', *Continuity and Change* 8 (1993), pp. 417–39, and in C. Litzenberger, 'Local Responses to Religious Changes: Evidence from Gloucestershire Wills', in *Religion and the English People, 1500–1640: New Voices/New Perspectives*, ed. E. J. Carlson (Kirksville, MO, 1998).

[2] D. M. Palliser, 'Popular Reactions to the Reformation during the Years of Uncertainty, 1530–70', in *The English Reformation Revised*, ed. C. Haigh (Cambridge, 1987), p. 113.

[3] This is in contrast to the way in which Robert Whiting combined a statistically constructed representation of the past with anecdotal material in his study of the Reformation in Devon and Cornwall. Seemingly, he relied heavily on anecdotal material, which was at variance with his general overview, drawing conclusions which were not consistent with the overall picture he had created. Whiting, *Blind Devotion*.

centrally held court and council records; (2) diocesan visitation and consistory court records; (3) parish, municipal and charity documents, including churchwardens' accounts, parish registers, guild and charity accounts, and borough and corporation records; and (4) wills. The first two sets of material contain information pertaining to the diocese, bishops, the county elite and official policy. The third and fourth sets correspond to the other two tiers in this study: the parish and the individual. Having identified these associations, however, we need to emphasise that within some of the categories, and indeed, within some specific sets of documents, more than one methodology was needed to gain full use of the contents.

The methodologies employed in analysing the majority of these sources are quite straightforward. The analysis of the religious content of wills, however, is more complex. Furthermore, wills are the single most significant source of information about individual lay piety employed in this study; therefore, the way in which they were used will be discussed in considerable detail.

Over 8,000 wills survive which were written by testators in Gloucestershire between the creation of the diocese in 1541 and 1580; this study is based on the analysis of over 3,500 of these.[4] That number includes all extant women's wills (which total 1,325) and a systematic sample of 1,285 lay men's wills drawn from the 6,000 extant male wills from the period proved in the Gloucester consistory court.[5] In addition, all the extant wills (approximately 500) of the county elite have been studied, as have all the surviving wills from the parishes of Tewkesbury and Cirencester. The latter provide further insight into local scribes' roles in determining the content of these documents.[6]

Despite the quantity examined, however, wills, and especially will preambles, must be used carefully and cautiously. In her 1971 article, Margaret Spufford asserted that unless the testator 'had strong religious convictions, the clause bequeathing the soul may well have reflected the opinion of the scribe or the

---

[4] While the terms 'will' and 'testament' legally refer to two different instruments, they are used synonymously in this work. For a discussion of the distinctions between the terms, see F. Pollack and F. W. Maitland, *The History of English Law before the Time of Edward I* (2nd edn, 1898; reprint, Cambridge, 1968), vol. II, pp. 314–56; S. Coppel, 'Wills and the Community of Tudor Grantham', in *Probate Records and the Local Community*, ed. P. Riden (Gloucester, 1985), pp. 72–4. For further discussion of wills, probate and testamentary cases in the consistory court, see Houlbrooke, *Church Courts*, pp. 89–116, *passim*.

[5] See Appendix B.

[6] All extant wills of female testators were included, along with 20 per cent of the wills of lay men. Since the wills were filed alphabetically by first name within probate year, it was possible to select the sample of male wills by identifying the first man's will in each year based on a random number (modular 5), and then reading every fifth man's will through the rest of that year. The resulting sample includes approximately equal numbers of women's and men's wills. In this case, assuming the highest possible variability of the sample from the population, the results of the analysis of the sample will be within 0.97 per cent of that for the entire population at a confidence level of 95 per cent. Further, chi-square tests, which measure the strength of relationships and the importance of differences, have been used to identify important patterns in groups of wills, at a significance level of 0.001. R. S. Schofield, 'Sampling in Historical Research', pp. 146–84, *passim*; H. M. Blalock, *Social Statistics* (rev. edn, London, Tokyo, Paris and Singapore, 1981), pp. 183–6; R. Floud, *An Introduction to Quantitative Methods for Historians* (2nd edn, 1973; reprint, London and New York, 1986), p. 136.

formulary book the latter was using', rather than that of the testator.[7] Furthermore, both Dr Spufford and Professor A. G. Dickens warned of the need to 'avoid statistical pedantry when attempting to derive doctrinal impressions from testamentary records'.[8] However, the real problem stems not from the use of statistics in general, but from the particular methods employed. Ignoring the complexity and variety contained in will preambles, codifying them too early in the analytical process, or relying on an inadequate sample can lead to inaccurate and distorted conclusions.

Scribal influence remains, however, a significant factor in wills analysis and many historians have contributed further to the discussion of its existence and the resulting implications since the publication of Dr Spufford's article.[9] Christopher Marsh, in particular, has added some useful insights to our understanding of this issue. Using testamentary evidence from several dioceses he demonstrated that testators typically devoted far less time and energy to their will preambles than they gave to their bequests of property and personal belongings, which were for most people the main, though perhaps not all-consuming, reason for preparing a will. In a majority of cases the scribe may have supplied the preamble with little or no consultation with the testator, and may also have supplied some or all of the

[7] M. Spufford, 'The Scribes of Villagers' Wills in the Sixteenth and Seventeenth Centuries and their Influence', *LPS* 7 (1971), pp. 28–43.

[8] A. G. Dickens, *Lollards and Protestants*, p. 221.

[9] Matlock Population Studies Group, 'Wills and their Scribes', *LPS* 8 (1972), pp. 55–7; R. C. Richardson, 'Wills and Will-Makers in the Sixteenth and Seventeenth Centuries: Some Lancashire Evidence', *LPS* 9 (1972), pp. 33–42; B. Capp, 'Will Formularies', *LPS* 14 (1975), p. 49; M. L. Zell, 'The Use of Religious Preambles as a Measure of Religious Belief in the Sixteenth Century', *The Bulletin of the Institute of Historical Research* 1 (1977), pp. 246–9; R. T. Vann, 'Wills and the Family in an English Town: Banbury, 1550–1800', *Journal of Family History* 4 (1979), pp. 346–67; L. C. Attreed, 'Preparation for Death in Sixteenth-Century Northern England', *SCJ* 13 (1982), pp. 37–66; G. J. Mayhew, 'The Progress of the Reformation in East Sussex 1530–1559: the Evidence from Wills', *Southern History* 5 (1983), pp. 38–67; R. Whiting, '"For the Health of my Soul": Prayers for the Dead in the Tudor South-West', *Southern History* 5 (1983), pp. 68–94; C. Cross, 'Wills as Evidence of Popular Piety in the Reformation Period: Leeds and Hull', in *The End of Strife*, ed. D. Loades (Edinburgh, 1984), pp. 44–51; N. Evans, 'Inheritance, Women, Religion and Education in Early Modern Society as Revealed by Wills', in *Probate Records and the Local Community*, ed. P. Riden (Gloucester, 1985), pp. 53–70; S. Coppel, 'Wills and the Community of Tudor Grantham', pp. 71–90; D. Cressy, 'Kinship and Kin Interaction in Early Modern England', *P&P* 113 (1986), pp. 38–69; C. Cross, 'Northern Women in the Early Modern Period: the Female Testators of Hull and Leeds 1520–1650', *Yorkshire Archaeological Journal* 59 (1987), pp. 83–94; J. D. Alsop, 'Religious Preambles in Early Modern English Wills as Formulae', *JEH* 40 (1989), pp. 19–27; C. Burgess, 'Late Medieval Wills and Pious Convention: Testamentary Evidence Reconsidered', in *Profit, Piety and the Professions in Later Medieval England*, ed. M. A. Hicks (Gloucester, 1990), pp. 14–33; C. Marsh, 'In the Name of God? Will-Making and Faith in Early Modern England', in *The Records of the Nation*, ed. G. H. Martin and P. Spufford (Woodbridge, 1990), pp. 215–49; M. Prior, 'Wives and Wills, 1558–1700', in *English Rural Society, 1500–1800*, ed. J. Chartres and D. Hay (Cambridge, 1990), pp. 201–25; M. Takahashi, 'The Number of Wills Proved in the Sixteenth and Seventeenth Centuries. Graphs, with Tables and Commentary', in *The Records of the Nation*, ed. G. H. Martin and P. Spufford (Woodbridge, 1990), pp. 187–213; M. K. McIntosh, *A Community Transformed: the Manor of Havering, 1500–1620* (Cambridge, 1992), pp. 85–91, 188–94; Duffy, *Stripping*, pp. 504–23, *passim*; 'Wills as Propaganda', pp. 415–31.

charitable bequests. However, Dr Marsh went on to assert that even the possibility of apparently independent scribal action in will-making does not invalidate sixteenth-century English wills as statements of the testators' religious beliefs. As God's steward on earth it was the Christian's duty to use the last will and testament as a means of promoting and supporting God's work in the world. Testators did view will-making as an important devotional act, and therefore probably approved the preamble and charitable bequests, even if the latter were initially supplied by the scribe. Furthermore, a testator could express personal beliefs by selecting or simply approving a suitable formula, or by choosing a scribe who would employ a preamble consistent with those beliefs; creativity was not required.[10]

The quantitative methods employed in wills analysis have also typically been problematic. Often insufficient wills survive from the region and period being studied to constitute a representative sample. On other occasions the methods used in drawing the sample from the surviving wills have been flawed. Then, having determined the sample to be studied, categorisation is often based on only a cursory evaluation of the language employed, rather than on a consideration of the contemporaneous theological implications of the phrases and sentences included there. Finally, inadequate use has often been made of database capabilities and statistical procedures. This study employed both a text-based database and a spreadsheet program in the collection and analysis of the Gloucestershire wills.[11] A database of wills information was collected, including verbatim transcription of religious preambles; the textual content of the preambles was analysed for the theological implications; codes were assigned; and statistical information was extracted and used to test hypotheses. Software selection and database design for the investigation of wills were based on an analysis of both the contents of typical wills and the nature of the investigation being conducted. Most wills from the period contain a basic set of information; however, even within that set, the lengths of the fields needed to record each item differed dramatically from will to will, and the other information contained in the wills varied widely. Thus, the selected database had to be able to handle variable-length fields, and allow for the presence or absence of specific fields within each record, in order to minimise the disk space required to hold all the wills data. In addition, analysis of the data would be facilitated by the ability to search for words or phrases within fields. Of the available software products, ASKSAM came closest to meeting these requirements. The ASKSAM database allows for the use of up to ten pre-defined input screens for ease and flexibility in data entry, seven of which were used to record the wills information for this study. The first includes the information common to every will: name, sex, date of will, parish, region, spouse, social status or occupation, religious preamble, burial instructions, and any additional comments. Other input screens were used to capture sets of information not found in every will, including names, roles and relationships of individuals, and information on various types of charitable bequests.

This study used a very detailed set of soul-bequest categories to record the complex range of beliefs articulated in the preambles. These were then used with various types of charitable bequests to perform the desired analysis. By applying

---

[10] Marsh, 'In the Name of God?', pp. 219, 238, 243.
[11] The text-based database used was ASKSAM, a product of ASKSAM Software of Perry, Florida. The spreadsheet program was QUATTRO, produced by Borland International of Scotts Valley, California.

Table A.1. *Will preamble categories*

Traditional
    References to the blessed Virgin Mary and/or the holy company of heaven;
    Use of 'only' with references to the blessed Virgin Mary and/or the holy company
    of heaven;
    References to being associated with the blessed Virgin Mary and/or the holy
    company of heaven (or the word 'elect' used in place of a reference to the saints);
    Otherwise traditional bequests which include references to Christ's passion;
    Otherwise traditional bequests which include statements of trust in salvation
    through Christ's death.
Ambiguous
    Bequests to the Holy Trinity;
    Bequests to Almighty God and/or Jesus Christ (the most ambiguous form);
    References to God's mercy (without any mention of the blessed Virgin Mary or
    the holy company of heaven);
    References to the merits, precious blood and/or passion of Jesus Christ or
    Almighty God;
    Use of 'only' (e.g. 'My only redeemer') with bequests to Almighty God and/or
    Jesus Christ;
    References to Christ's resurrection and/or ascension;
    References to 'reigning with the elect', or being one of the 'number of the elect'.
Protestant
    References to assurance of salvation (without any doubt or mistrust);
    Testator directly addressing God;
    Use of the phrase, 'I have and shall have' salvation or forgiveness of sins;
    Use of the phrase, 'and by no other means';
    Use of the phrase, 'not by any work of works of mine'.

textual content analysis to individual soul bequests found in the wills, it is possible
to study the changing usage of key phrases and gain some knowledge of responses
to changes in official religious policies.[12] By such means seventeen categories of
religious will preambles have been identified, describing a spectrum of beliefs which
range from very traditional to distinctly Protestant. However, labelling them further
can be quite problematic. In order to gain a view of the 'forest', rather than just a
few trees, it was necessary to group the categories, but where does one draw the
lines? For purposes of this analysis I have identified five categories as 'traditional'
and five as 'Protestant', and have labelled the remaining seven as 'ambiguous'.[13] I
chose to classify those preambles which fell between traditional and Protestant on
the religious spectrum as 'ambiguous' rather than 'neutral', the more common
designator for this group, because the former more accurately describes the faith of
those in the middle. These testators' statements (and the related actions of their

[12] For a general discussion of textual content analysis see K. Lindkvist, 'Approaches to
Textual Analysis', in *Advances in Content Analysis*, ed. K. E. Rosengren (Sage Annual
Reviews of Communications Research, vol. IX, London and Beverly Hills, CA, 1981), pp.
23–41.
[13] See Table A.1.

fellow-parishioners) seem to indicate equivocation rather than a lack of interest, vagueness rather than impartiality. This point is made most dramatically by examining the wills written between 1547 and 1569, and comparing declarations of faith with the actions in parishes at the same time.[14]

Hence, three sets of categories have been established for this study. All the categories grouped as traditional are distinguished by the inclusion of a reference to the Blessed Virgin Mary, to the company of heaven or both. Additionally, these preambles may also describe Christ's passion as a means of their salvation, and may even refer to Christ or God as 'my only saviour' or 'my only creator', but mention of the Virgin Mary or the saints is the determining factor in their classification as 'traditional'. The most standard of these preamble formulas is of course, 'I bequeath my soul to Almighty God, to our Lady and to all the whole Company of Heaven'. At the other end of the spectrum all the categories labelled 'Protestant' explicitly repudiate traditional means of salvation, such as the efficacy of works or prayer for the soul of the testator, express unqualified assurance of the salvation of the testator, or address God directly. Thus, declarations of faith in salvation by the death and passion of Jesus Christ, 'and by no other means', or 'without any doubt or mistrust' have been designated as 'Protestant'. The remaining collection of categories have been grouped under the rubric 'ambiguous', and consist of those forms which could be used in good conscience by individuals espousing a wide range of beliefs, including people leaning toward either Protestant or traditional faith. This subset comprises preambles which bequeath the soul to the Holy Trinity, as well as those which refer to God's mercy. Also classified in this group are statements which mention Christ's passion or resurrection, or describe God or Christ as 'my only redeemer', all of which could be (and were) used comfortably in wills which otherwise expressed the full range of beliefs. While it is true that preambles which refer to the passion or the resurrection, as well as those which use the word 'only' and omit all reference to the Virgin Mary or the saints, often go on to make explicitly Protestant statements, they occasionally continue by asking St Mary and all the saints to pray for the soul of the testator. Hence, lacking language which is explicitly traditional or Protestant, they have been included in the 'ambiguous' group.

Additionally, the use of the word 'elect', so often associated with Protestantism, has required special attention. In some cases it is clearly used in place of a reference to all the saints, and thus that preamble is categorised as 'traditional'. In other cases, however, it is employed more ambiguously in phrases such as 'reigning with the elect' or being 'one of the number of the elect', and therefore is labelled as 'ambiguous', albeit at the Protestant end of the ambiguous spectrum. Finally, the 'ambiguous' category includes the standard form, 'I bequeath my soul to Almighty God', and its slightly more expansive offspring, 'I bequeath my soul to Almighty God my maker and redeemer', which seems to have gradually superseded the shorter form in popularity by 1580. The demarcation lines in this forest of expressions of faith can indeed be quite vague and difficult to establish, and have been included here to facilitate the discussion of lay religion, a tool to help us understand the past. In the final analysis, it must be remembered that we are dealing with a spectrum of beliefs, rather than with three clearly defined 'boxes' into which we can place people and their wills.

Yet, even with careful categorisation, scribal influence could still distort the

---

[14] See chapters 4, 5 and 6, and Appendix B.

picture of lay religion which emerges from the Gloucestershire wills. Analysis of all the extant wills (not just those in the sample) from the parishes of Tewkesbury and Cirencester indicates, however, that testators may indeed have had a good deal of preamble choice if they wanted to exercise it. The 188 wills from Tewkesbury are divided among 27 different preambles, while in Cirencester 106 wills included 26 separate soul bequests. In each case a substantial proportion (25 to 50 per cent) give evidence of the variety of soul bequests. In Tewkesbury, the wills of 52 testators employed 23 additional preambles. In Cirencester 51 wills are divided among 24 preambles. Clearly, those testators desiring a non-standard soul bequest, and a wide variety at that, were capable of achieving that end. Further study reveals that the reason for the choice lies in the number of scriveners functioning within each town and the number of preambles each employed. In Gloucestershire during this period, will scribes seldom explicitly identified themselves as such. However, by examining hand writing, spelling and the use of particular phrases, and then combining that analysis with the witnesses listed for each will, it is possible to make informed judgments as to the identity of the scribe.[15]

In Tewkesbury, eleven scribes have been identified for this period, with three emerging as the town's primary will-writers: John Cole, Nicholas Crondale and John Gase. John Cole was the longest functioning scribe of the three, active from 1546 to at least 1586. He was the parish clerk, responsible for making the baldrics for the church bells, as well as writing wills. As a scribe he was responsible for forty-four wills and employed eleven different preambles. During the last years of Henry's reign, the earliest years of his time as parish clerk and scribe, Cole wrote preambles of the standard ambiguous form. Then, during Mary's reign, he retained this ambiguous preamble, while adding the standard traditional soul bequest. These two options continued into Elizabeth's reign, when he added an additional ambiguous preamble which referred to the passion. Finally, he replaced the standard ambiguous formula with his own variation: 'I bequethe my solle into the handys off Allmyghty God the father of our Lorde Jhesus Chryste.'[16] As religious policy changed over the forty years of his scribal activity, John Cole's preamble repertoire grew. Meanwhile, in 1553, Tewkesbury's curate, Nicholas Crondale, had begun writing wills. He wrote at least twenty-nine between 1553 and 1572, usually employing the ambiguous form, which bequeathed the soul 'to Almighty God my maker and redeemer'. More choice was added for Tewkesbury testators in 1556 when John Gase appeared as a scribe. During the ten years of his activity he wrote eighteen wills, all of which were either traditional or ambiguous. Those seeking Protestant preambles in the 1570s could also summon Thomas Freebank, Richard Rogers or Richard Coxe. Likewise, it was possible to look outside the town for a suitable scribe, as the appearance of a Cirencester scribe as the writer of at least one will attests. In Tewkesbury, during the period from 1540 to 1580, a growing number of preamble formulas were available for use as the number of scribes, as well as their individual repertoires, increased. Clearly, those testators wishing a degree of control over the nature of their soul bequest had the means at their disposal, and the fact that individual scribes employed a variety of forms supports

---

[15] This is similar to the methodology employed by Marjorie McIntosh in the identification of will scribes, although her approach differs somewhat due to differences in the information available for analysis. M. K. McIntosh, *A Community Transformed*, p. 88.

[16] GRO Wills, 1559/216.

the supposition that at least a portion of the populace did give some attention to their preambles.

In Cirencester, as in Tewkesbury, the variety of preambles is evidence of the availability of options for testators there. In contrast to Tewkesbury's eleven, only four scribes have been identified for Cirencester, of whom only two wrote more than two wills each. Peter Gery wrote at least eleven wills between 1545 and 1557, using either the standard traditional form or his own distinctive but decidedly ambiguous statement, bequeathing the soul 'to Almighty God, the Lord and giver of all goodness'.[17] Gery disappeared as a scribe in 1557, and Thomas Faryngton, a tucker, began to function in that capacity. Faryngton can be associated with at least twenty-two Cirencester wills between 1557 and 1578, as well as one for a Tewkesbury testator in July of 1573. His first wills in Cirencester in 1557 used standard preambles, either traditional or ambiguous. However, only a year later, in the will of Thomas Turner, weaver, Faryngton used a new, albeit traditional, form: 'I bequeth my sowle vnto Almyghty God the Father, to Jesu Chryst his onlye sonne our redemer, and to the Holye Goost the Comforter and to all the blessyd company of hevyn.'[18] For the following fourteen years Faryngton relied upon his own variant of a traditional soul bequest. Then, in 1571, he began to modify it. In the will of Alice Adys, dated January 1571, Faryngton changed his preamble by replacing the reference to the company of heaven with an 'etc.' as she bequeathed her soul 'to Allmightyte God the Father, to Jhesus Christ my onely salvyor and to the Holy Ghost the comforter etc'.[19] Technically, Faryngton's new preamble was no longer traditional but ambiguous, since only the testator and scribe could have been sure of the exact meaning of 'etc.'. He continued to use his original formula, but also employed the newer ambiguous version of 1573, and more changes would follow. Later, in 1573, he shortened his personal preamble even further in one case, making it even more ambiguous by omitting the 'etc.' entirely.[20] The next two years saw him abridge his original formula still more, so that it appears to be nothing more than the most standard ambiguous form of a soul bequest. Significantly, however, he retained the 'etc.' at the end so that it read, 'I bequeath my soule to Almighti God etc.'[21] Not only did Faryngton provide a variety of traditional and ambiguous preambles, but he modified his own traditional formula in such a manner as to provide a welcome solution to Elizabethan followers of the old religion who were anxious to appear conformist but did not want to misrepresent their true faith, even in their wills.

The use of 'etc.' was not, however, the sole province of either the Cirencester scribes or those with traditional beliefs. The first appearance of 'etc.' in the wills examined in this study pre-dates Faryngton's first modified preamble by nearly two decades, and does not appear to be concealing the testator's beliefs. In August 1554, Marian Samson, whose parish was not given, bequeathed her soul 'to God etc.'.[22] Likewise, Jane Harbell of Minchinhampton's use of 'etc.' on 4 October 1559 seems equally unambiguous, as she bequeathed her soul 'to Almyghtye God my maker and redemer trustyng withoute doute or mystrust to be savyd onlye by his passyons and death, etc., and by none other'.[23] In both cases 'etc.' may have been used merely to save space, time or money. Yet, clearly, as the evolution of Thomas Faryngton's

[17] GRO Wills, 1555/29.   [18] GRO Wills, 1558/223.   [19] GRO Wills, 1571/18.
[20] GRO Wills, 1573/93.   [21] GRO Wills, 1575/124, 1577/80.
[22] GRO Wills, 1554/78.   [23] GRO Wills, 1560/103.

preamble demonstrates, the well-placed use of 'etc.' could conceal whole theological systems in a seemingly ambiguous soul bequest.

Scribal manipulation of ambiguous preambles is not the only aspect of their creation that warrants further investigation. Depositions from testamentary cases contain descriptions of the actual process of will-writing, which also contributed valuable evidence to this inquiry. In most cases, the will was originally drafted with only the testator, or testatrix, and scribe present. Only later was it read before witnesses, and the public reading of the will followed by the subscription of witnesses' names seems to have been a normal part of the preparation for death in sixteenth-century Gloucestershire. John Bubbe of King's Norton was typical when, in the late 1540s, he sent for Edmund Robyns of the same town and Richard Shot of Barnwood to come to his house to hear his will. Thus, the day before he died 'the testator cawsed one to goe for his gostly father and to cawse him to bryng the testament withe hym to thintent that . . . [these men] might here it redde'.[24] Similarly, in 1551, Richard Conwey, rector of Stowell, wrote the will of Margerie Collet on one occasion, and then returned to read it at another time in the presence of Robert Lumes of Hampnet.[25] In these and many other cases the scribe, having been summoned, would either take notes for a formal will and draft it later, or prepare a draft while its contents were being dictated by the testator or testatrix. He would then return later to read the completed testament before witnesses.[26]

However, some wills had a more convoluted provenance. For example, the will of Alice Lynet of Charlton Kings was the subject of a testamentary case in July 1551. William Hall, her curate, testified that her servant, Jane Fynche, had been sent to summon him to the testatrix's house to write her will. 'In the hall at the chimney before the fyre and about x of the clock aforenoen . . . [with the] deponent sittyng at the high table fowre yardes or there aboutes distant from the said chimney' he wrote her will, but it was not read to her at that time. A month later Alice sent for him and he read the will to her, 'noon other bodie beyng [present]'. Then she took it, saying she would show it to her children. A second will was also apparently made, since Walter Coriar, also of Charlton Kings, testified that he was present when the writing of a will was completed on the Monday following Palm Sunday. In that instance, 'the testatrix [then] said she wold have no more at that tyme but she said in case it be nedfull hereafter at any tyme to amend it she said she wold. Than the priest wrappyng up the testament departed.' Approximately two months later, on 5 June, Nicholas Holder, a boarder in Alice's house, asked if she had heard her will read, since she had taken it from the priest, and when she said no he urged her to hear it. She sent him to find someone who could read it, and he returned a half hour later with his son, John, 'and than she rose from the fyre and went to a cupbord in a table bord and fetched out thense a white boxe wherein was the testament', and heard it read. She died eight days later.[27]

In only two extant testamentary cases was evidence presented of a will being dictated to a scribe in the presence of witnesses. In August 1578, Margaret Brooke,

---

[24] GRO GDR vol. III, pp. 65–7.   [25] GRO GDR vol. VIII, p. 67.

[26] GRO GDR vol. VIII, p. 253; vol. XIX pp. 94–5, 133; vol. XXV, pp. 65–7; vol. XLVI, p. 55.

[27] This case illustrates one of the principal reasons for a will to be contested in court: a dispute over which of two or more surviving wills is the true last will and testament of the deceased. In this case, it appears that it was the first will that was read in the presence of Nicholas Holder by his son, John, and that Alice intended that to be her true testament. GRO GDR vol. VIII, pp. 87–91.

the daughter of the city recorder of Gloucester, Richard Pates, made her will 'at about one of the clock at night' in the presence of twelve people, and died nine or ten days later.[28] Ten months later, Margaret Grodie was sick with the plague and, wanting to make her last will and testament, employed an ingenious means of accomplishing the task without exposing the scribe to that dreaded illness. 'She cawsed Thomas Key [her neighbour] to be called for and in the windoe of his owne howse the saide Key stoode, and she being in her awne chamber did make her will and Thomas Key did wryte yt and at any tyme when he dowted . . . [the] word she spoke he wold aske the women that were [caring for her] . . . and they wold tell him in her heeringe.'[29] Hence, the testator normally sent for a scribe after becoming ill and then dictated the will. Often in the testamentary cases which survive, the act was completed some time before the death of the testator or testatrix. Hours, days, weeks or even months later, the will would be read before witnesses. It is possible, however, that this picture of the timing of will-making is skewed by the source of the evidence: testamentary cases. Most, if not all, of these cases concerned a dispute over whether the will which had been filed for probate was in fact the true last will and testament of the deceased. Wills made some time before death, and especially those originally dictated without witnesses being present, would be more likely to have been suspect and thus the subject of litigation. However, in at least some cases the pattern above was followed. Furthermore, the references in the depositions to 'the reading of the said testament before' witnesses would tend to indicate that the writing and the reading were, indeed, two separate acts, with a 'fair copy', rather than a rough draft, being publicly read. However, the timing of both acts appears to have been controlled by the testator, who also usually named his or her own witnesses.

The scribe's role in will-making is not the only factor which has led historians to doubt the accuracy of the will preamble as a representation of the testator's faith. For example, the will of William Tracy of Toddington in Gloucestershire was refused probate and his bones exhumed from consecrated ground and illegally burned, allegedly because of the religious content of his preamble. This incident has typically been cited by historians as a deterrent to the inclusion in wills of sincere statements of faith which were contrary to official religious policy, and the church courts did have the right to refuse probate on such grounds. The granting of probate by the church, however, only affected the disposition of goods contained in the will; it had no effect on the devising of land. Thus, refusal to grant probate was not as strong a deterrent to expressions of unauthorised beliefs as it would have been if it had affected land. However, there are no other known examples of that prerogative being invoked again before the seventeenth century.[30] Protestant preambles were included in Gloucestershire wills written during the reigns of Henry and Mary, and traditional soul bequests can similarly be found in both Edwardian and Elizabethan wills; none of them was refused probate. A number of individual testators and their scribes who were willing to include religious statements which expressed un-authorised beliefs were thus able to do so without penalty. None the less, the

---

[28] GRO GDR vol. XLV, fo. 108.   [29] GRO GDR vol. XLV, fo. 138v.

[30] S. Coppel, 'Wills and the Community', p. 72. For evidence of the Edwardian reformers' view of wills and their preambles as expressed in the 1552 draft revision of the canons, see J. C. Spalding, *The Reformation of the Ecclesiastical Laws of England, 1552* (Sixteenth Century Essays and Studies, vol. XXIX, Kirksville, MO, 1992), pp. 286–300. The other will refused probate was that of Humphrey Fenn, a Presbyterian preacher in Coventry, written in 1631. Craig and Litzenberger, 'Wills as Propaganda', p. 431.

choices offered by some scribes do appear to have been influenced by official policy, at least in Tewkesbury and Cirencester. There testators had the opportunity to pick their scribe and then to select a specific formula from those in his repertoire, and some of those who performed such services do seem to have been influenced to some extent by the religious policies of the regime. Thus, under Henry and Mary the options offered by some scribes included traditional and ambiguous forms, while under Edward and Elizabeth those same individuals only employed ambiguous statements. Other scribes, on the other hand, offered more distinctively traditional or Protestant formulas, apparently without much regard for the authorised religion. However, they did not produce substantial numbers of Protestant wills, as only testators with strong, clearly defined reformed beliefs seem to have opted for explicitly Protestant preambles. Thus, the wills of some testators would have been influenced to some degree by the authorities while others would not. Official policy, then, may have dampened enthusiasm for declarations of faith which contravened the established religion, and probably did contribute somewhat to assertions of traditional beliefs when the old religion was officially sanctioned, and to ambiguous statements under Protestant regimes. However, the rich array of over 350 specifically different preambles employed between 1541 and 1580 and the distribution of testators using them indicates that, while the spectrum of beliefs expressed may have been narrower as a result of official pressure, it was certainly not eliminated.

Despite scribal involvement and official pressure, wills can still be used to good effect as a source of information on sixteenth-century lay piety, provided they are analysed with great care and finesse, and with allowances for their complexity. In this light charitable bequests as well as preambles must be examined; the number of preamble categories must be kept as large as possible to maximise the level of detail at which the analysis is conducted; will data should be transcribed as fully as possible to avoid losing detailed information which might be useful at some stage in the analysis; and the sample used in the analysis should be drawn from the population in a way that ensures that it accurately reflects the entire population, and be large enough to produce reliable and representative results.

Appendix B

Results of wills analysis

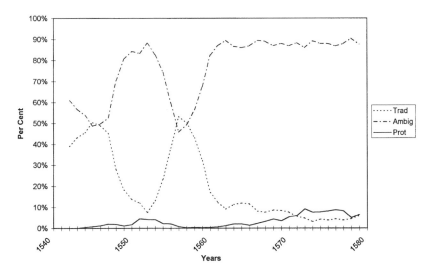

Figure B.1   All non-elite will preambles (three-year rolling average)

Appendix B

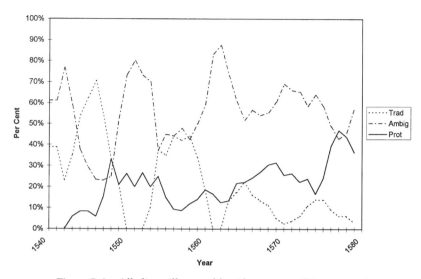

Figure B.2 All elite will preambles (three-year rolling average)

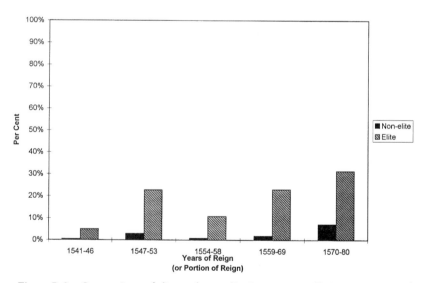

Figure B.3 Comparison of elite and non-elite Protestant wills (as percentage of total of each social category)

Table B.1. *Non-elite Gloucestershire will preambles by category*

	Count				Per cent		
Year	Traditional	Ambiguous	Protestant	Total	Traditional	Ambiguous	Protestant
1541	10	20		30	33	67	
1542	21	27		48	44	54	
1543	25	40		65	39	61	
1544	23	24		47	49	51	
1545	63	67	1	131	48	51	1
1546	40	31	1	72	56	43	1
1547	20	27	1	48	42	56	2
1548	7	20	1	28	25	71	4
1549	3	29		32	9	91	
1550	6	22		28	21	79	
1551	7	46	2	55	13	83	4
1552	3	43	4	50	6	86	8
1553	1	38		39	3	97	
1554	15	39	2	56	27	69	4
1555	15	22	1	38	39	58	3
1556	25	25		50	50	50	
1557	96	70	1	167	57	42	1
1558	90	113		203	44	56	
1559	23	90	1	114	20	79	1
1560	10	55		65	15	85	
1561	6	45		51	12	88	
1562	4	41	1	46	9	89	2
1563	5	60	1	66	8	91	1
1564	8	29	1	38	21	76	3
1565	5	40	1	46	11	87	2
1566	4	58		62	7	94	
1567	5	55	3	63	8	87	5
1568	5	50	3	58	9	86	5
1569	6	55	2	63	10	87	3
1570	6	72	2	80	8	89	3
1571	5	66	8	79	6	84	10
1572	1	53	3	57	2	93	5
1573	5	78	10	93	5	84	11
1574	1	69	4	74	1	93	5
1575	4	58	4	66	6	88	6
1576	2	34	7	43	5	79	16
1577	2	66	5	73	3	90	7
1578	3	60	3	66	5	90	5
1579	4	55	2	61	7	93	3
1580	4	48	7	59	7	81	12
Totals	588	1,940	82	2,610	—	—	—

Source: GRO Gloucestershire Wills.

Appendix B

Table B.2. *Non-elite preambles by reign and general category*

Reign[a]	Traditional	Neutral	Protestant	Totals	Per cent Traditional	Neutral	Protestant
Henry	182	209	2	393	46.3	53.2	0.5
Edward	47	225	8	280	16.8	80.4	2.9
Mary	241	269	4	514	46.9	52.3	0.8
Elizabeth(1)	81	578	13	672	12.1	86.0	1.9
Elizabeth(2)	37	659	55	751	4.9	87.7	7.3
Totals	588	1,940	82	2,610	—	—	—

[a] The early years of Elizabeth's reign have been divided into two segments in this and subsequent tables: 'Elizabeth (1)' refers to 1559–69; 'Elizabeth (2)' refers to 1570–80.

Source: GRO Gloucestershire Wills.

Table B.3. *Non-elite ambiguous preambles by reign and general category*

Reign	Women			Men		
	Ambiguous	Totals	Per cent	Ambiguous	Totals	Per cent
Henry	77	148	52.0	132	245	53.9
Edward	111	138	80.4	114	142	80.3
Mary	132	263	50.2	137	251	54.6
Elizabeth (1)	313	362	86.5	265	310	85.5
Elizabeth (2)	371	414	89.6	288	337	85.5
Totals	1,004	1,325	—	936	1,285	—

Source: GRO Gloucestershire Wills.

Table B.4. *Non-elite preambles by reign and region*

Reign	Cotswolds	Forest	Gloucester	Vale North	Vale South	Totals
Henry	131	49	27	102	84	393
Edward	99	46	17	40	78	280
Mary	190	55	24	133	112	514
Elizabeth (1)	208	102	31	154	177	672
Elizabeth (2)	256	118	36	121	220	751
Totals	884	370	135	550	671	2,610

Source: GRO Gloucestershire Wills.

Table B.5. *Traditional, ambiguous and Protestant preambles by reign and region*

Region	Type	Henry	Edward	Mary	Elizabeth (1)	Elizabeth (2)
Cotswolds	Trad. (%)	51.9	16.1	54.7	18.3	8.2
	Neut. (%)	48.1	77.8	44.2	77.4	80.5
	Prot. (%)	0.0	6.1	1.1	4.3	11.3
	Number	131	99	190	208	256
Forest of Dean	Trad. (%)	69.4	17.4	38.2	14.7	1.7
	Neut. (%)	30.6	78.3	61.8	85.3	95.8
	Prot. (%)	0.0	4.3	0.0	0.0	2.5
	Number	49	46	55	102	118
Gloucester	Trad. (%)	51.9	17.6	33.3	6.5	0.0
	Neut. (%)	48.1	82.4	66.7	90.3	86.1
	Prot. (%)	0.0	0.0	0.0	3.2	13.9
	Number	27	17	24	31	36
Northern Vale	Trad. (%)	35.3	27.5	49.6	6.5	1.7
	Neut. (%)	64.7	72.5	49.6	92.9	94.2
	Prot. (%)	0.0	0.0	0.8	0.6	4.1
	Number	102	40	133	154	121
Southern Vale	Trad. (%)	35.7	11.5	37.5	9.0	5.5
	Neut. (%)	61.9	88.5	61.6	89.8	88.6
	Prot. (%)	2.4	0.0	0.9	1.1	5.9
	Number	84	78	112	177	220

Source: GRO Gloucestershire Wills.

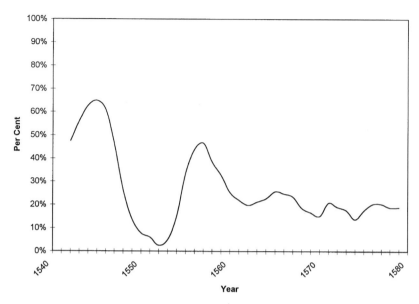

Figure B.4   Per cent parish bequests (three-year rolling average)

Table B.6. *Non-elite parish bequests by reign and sex*

Reign	Women			Men		
	Parish	Totals	Per cent	Parish	Totals	Per cent
Henry	91	148	61.5	146	245	59.6
Edward	22	138	15.9	17	142	12.0
Mary	92	263	35.0	100	251	39.8
Elizabeth (1)	79	362	21.8	77	310	24.8
Elizabeth (2)	66	414	15.9	69	337	20.5
Totals	350	1,325	—	409	1,285	—

Source: GRO Gloucestershire Wills.

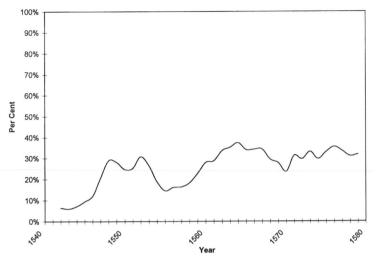

Figure B.5   Per cent bequests to the poor (three-year rolling average)

Table B.7. *Non-elite poor bequests by reign and sex*

Reign	Women			Men		
	Poor	Totals	Per cent	Poor	Totals	Per cent
Henry	13	148	8.8	19	245	7.8
Edward	42	138	30.4	35	142	24.6
Mary	37	263	14.1	41	251	16.3
Elizabeth (1)	107	362	29.6	101	310	32.6
Elizabeth (2)	126	414	30.4	109	337	32.3
Totals	325	1,325	—	305	1,285	—

Source: GRO Gloucestershire Wills.

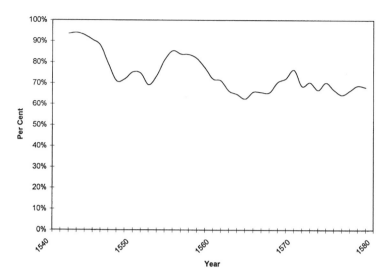

Figure B.6   Per cent no bequests to the poor (three-year rolling average)

Table B.8. *Non-elite wills containing no bequest to poor (by reign and sex)*

Reign	Women			Men		
	No poor	Totals	Per cent	No poor	Totals	Per cent
Henry	135	148	91.2	226	245	92.2
Edward	96	138	69.6	107	142	75.4
Mary	226	263	85.9	210	251	83.7
Elizabeth (1)	255	362	70.4	209	310	67.4
Elizabeth (2)	288	414	69.6	228	337	67.7
Totals	1,000	1,325	—	980	1,285	—

Source: GRO Gloucestershire Wills.

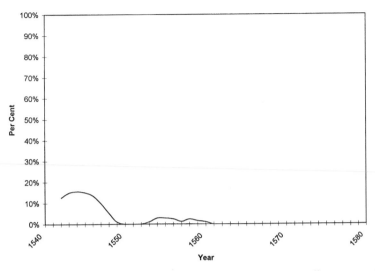

Figure B.7 Provisions for prayers for the dead (three-year rolling average)

Table B.9. *Non-elite wills containing provisions for prayers for the dead (by reign and sex)*

Reign	Women			Men		
	Prayers	Totals	Per cent	Prayers	Totals	Per cent
Henry	22	148	14.9	34	245	13.9
Edward	1	138	0.7	6	142	4.2
Mary	4	263	1.5	7	251	2.8
Elizabeth (1)	1	362	0.2	3	310	1.0
Elizabeth (2)	0	414	0.0	0	337	0.0
Totals	28	1,325	—	50	1,285	—

Source: GRO Gloucestershire Wills.

Appendix C

Parish finances

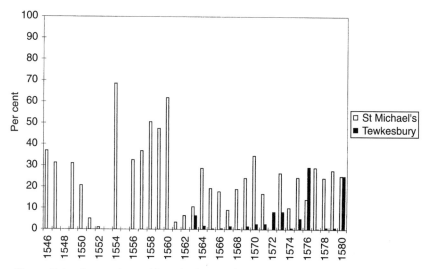

Figure C.1   Comparison of liturgical expenditures as percentage of total annual
expenses

Table C.1. *St Michael's total annual revenue by category of income (stated in old pence)*

Year	Seat	Easter	Rents	Sales[a]	Misc.[b]	Totals
1546	234	138	632		20	1,024
1547	176	78	632		152	1,038
1548						
1549	165		512		172	849
1550	193		512		6	711
1551	159		512	6,510	800	7,981
1552	212		512	6	2	732
1553						
1554			512	60		572
1555						
1556	288	204	516	16	52	1,076
1557	196	170	516	960	690	2,532
1558	192	168	516		252	1,128
1559	180	124	516		2,015	2,835
1560	132	652	516		40	1,340
1561	132	624	708	2,147	326	3,937
1562	160	726	324		621	1,831
1563	186	888	516		500	2,090
1564	156	600	516		24	1,296
1565	200	930	532		144	1,806
1566	218	965	532		120	1,835
1567	244	1,042	532		116	1,934
1568	208	1,052	532		89	1,881
1569	168	1,020	532	132	244	2,096
1570	198	1,036	532		40	1,806
1571	192	1,034	532	240		1,998
1572						
1573	216		564		40	820
1574	196		844			1,040
1575	209		272		120	601
1576	196		564		18	778
1577	209		564		53	826
1578	208		564		68	840
1579	192		564		320	1,076
1580	193	223	564		144	1,124
Totals	5,808	11,674	16,692	10,071	7,188	51,433

[a] 'Sales' refers to receipts from the sale of church goods.

[b] 'Misc.' revenues includes receipts from church rates and debts owed to the parish, and for lights, knells, gravestones, burials, churchings of women, etc.

Source: St Michael's Churchwardens' Accounts, GRO P154/14 CW 1/1–1/31.

Table C.2. *St Michael's total annual expenses by category*
(stated in old pence)

Year	Fabric	Liturgy	Visitations	Misc.[a]	Totals
1546	374	386	2	283	1,045
1547	705	434	4	245	1,388
1548					
1549	303	169	2	71	545
1550	653	171			824
1551	6,348	341		113	6,802
1552	2,000	22	30	195	2,247
1553					
1554	729	2,142		254	3,125
1555					
1556	1,407	721	16	62	2,206
1557	577	373	26	35	1,011
1558	654	741	21	49	1,465
1559	584	630	40	72	1,326
1560	635	1,054	7	6	1,702
1561	6,672	238	65	19	6,994
1562	1,713	120	9	20	1,862
1563	874	202	94	738	1,908
1564	502	222	16	32	772
1565	1,809	515	82	259	2,665
1566	988	248	116	43	1,395
1567	2,066	225	119	79	2,489
1568	424	120		90	634
1569	991	523	589	59	2,162
1570	1,447	844	51	98	2,440
1571	1,588	340	52	54	2,034
1572					
1573	647	481	47	644	1,819
1574	3,261	386	53	159	3,859
1575	843	324	82	78	1,327
1576	2,100	394	72	262	2,828
1577	718	351	32	112	1,213
1578	929	363	122	88	1,502
1579	432	230	68	100	830
1580	571	276	112	142	1,101
Totals	43,544	13,586	1,929	4,661	63,520

[a] 'Misc.' expenses include payments for obits, subsidies, priests' wages, writing the accounts, paper, pentecost money, repairs of rental houses, etc.

Source: St Michael's Churchwardens' Accounts, GRO P154/14 CW 1/1–1/31.

Table C.3. *Tewkesbury's total annual revenue by category of income*
(stated in old pence)

Year	Seat	Ales	Rents	Sales[a]	Misc.[b]	Totals
1564	216		76		1,248	1,540
1565	228		366		3,169	3,763
1566	192	2,760	310		2,960	6,222
1567	148	1,640	585		2,960	5,333
1568	239		532		864	1,635
1569	214	2,112	541		247	3,114
1570	210	3,251	557		328	4,346
1571	210	3,251	557		328	4,346
1572	200	1,164	537		169	2,070
1573	198	1,164	536		168	2,066
1574	486		655		149	1,290
1575	172		564		694	1,430
1576	1,314		678	326	423	2,741
1577	76	2,280	596	116	824	3,892
1578	226		634		298	1,158
1579	226		634		298	1,158
Totals	4,555	17,622	8,358	442	15,127	46,104

[a] 'Sales' refers to receipts from the sale of church goods.

[b] 'Misc.' revenues includes receipts from church rates and debts owed to the parish, and for lights, knells, gravestones, burials, churchings of women, etc.

Source: Tewkesbury Churchwardens' Accounts, GRO P329 CW 2/1, pp. 1–72.

Table C.4. *Tewkesbury's total annual expenses by category (stated in old pence)*

Year	Fabric	Liturgy	Visitations	Misc.[a]	Totals
1563	975	81	46	161	1,263
1564	2,173	35	48	71	2,327
1565	3,756	10	12	87	3,865
1566	5,673	26	47	249	5,995
1567	1,618	26	47	249	1,940
1568	1,682	2		192	1,876
1569	634	10	25	67	736
1570	1,031	32	40	199	1,302
1571	1,031	32	40	199	1,302
1572	1,571	160	29	207	1,967
1573	1,571	160	28	207	1,966
1574	1,137	8	22	204	1,371
1575	1,359	108	106	607	2,180
1576	1,164	906	332	700	3,102
1577	849	4	37	1,375	2,265
1578	1,338	14	95	551	1,998
1579	1,338	14	95	551	1,998
1580	571	276	112	142	1,101
Totals	29,471	1,904	1,161	6,018	38,554

[a] 'Misc.' expenses include payments for obits, subsidies, priests' wages, writing the accounts, paper, pentecost money, repairs of rental houses, etc.

Source: Tewkesbury Churchwardens' Accounts, GRO P329 CW 2/1, pp. 1–72.

BIBLIOGRAPHY

MANUSCRIPT SOURCES

BRITISH LIBRARY

Cotton MS, Appendix 9   Charter of Foundation for the diocese of Gloucester, 3 September 1541.

Harleian MS 594   Ecclesiastical Returns of 1563 for the diocese of Gloucester.

CORPUS CHRISTI COLLEGE

MS 114   Parker Collection.

DR WILLIAMS'S LIBRARY

Morice MS 31L/3   'A True Copy of Bishop Hooper's Visitation Booke, Made by Him. AD 1551, 1552.'

GLOUCESTER CITY LIBRARY – GLOUCESTERSHIRE COLLECTION

Hockaday Abstracts   Transcribed extracts from various records pertaining to the diocese of Gloucester, its parishes and parishioners. (Sources include Gloucester Diocesan Records, Prerogative Court of Canterbury Wills and Letters of Administration and Exchequer Records.)

Hockaday Collections   Transcribed extracts from various records pertaining to the diocese of Gloucester, its parishes and parishioners. (Sources include records of the dioceses of Gloucester and Hereford.)

Smyth of Nibley Papers   Assorted lists and documents pertaining to the history of Gloucestershire and the Berkeley Hundred (4 vols.).

GLOUCESTERSHIRE RECORD OFFICE

Gloucestershire Wills, 1541–1581.

Gloucestershire Dispersed Wills, 1535–1580.

D48/Z2   'Indenture of Agreement' concerning the chancellorship of the diocese of Worcester.

D327   Furney MS, 'History of Gloucester'.

D837	Gloucestershire Muster Rolls, 1539.
D2688	Giles Geaste's Charity Accounts, 1564–1580.
Furney MS B	Transcription of various documents now lost pertaining to the history of the diocese of Gloucester.
GBR B2/1	Gloucester Corporation Records, 1535–1580.
GBR B3/1	Gloucester Corporation Records, 1535–1580.
GBR F4/3	Gloucester Chamberlain's Accounts, 1535–1580.
GDR vols. 1–45	Gloucester Diocesan Records consisting of consistory court act books, episcopal and archiepiscopal visitation records, and bishops' registers, 1541–1580.
P124 CW 2/4	Dursley Churchwardens' Accounts, 1566–1580.
P154/6 CW 1	St Aldate's, Gloucester Churchwardens' Accounts, 1564–1580.
P154/14 CW 1	St Michael's, Gloucester Churchwardens' Accounts, 1545–1580.
P154/14 IN 1/1	St Michael's, Gloucester Parish Registers, 1553–1580.
P197 CW 2/1	Lechlade Churchwardens' Accounts, 1557–1580.
P217 CW 2/1	Minchinhampton Churchwardens' Accounts, 1555–1580.
P329 CW 2/1	Tewkesbury Churchwardens' Accounts, 1563–1580.
P329 IN 1/1	Tewkesbury Parish Registers, 1559–1580.
P329 MI/1	Tewkesbury Abbey Royal Ministers' Accounts, 1539.
TBR A1/1	Notes concerning the purchase of the abbey by the town and parishioners of Tewkesbury (compiled in eighteenth century).
TBR B2/1	Tewkesbury Borough Records, 1575–1580.
TBR D1/1	Tewkesbury Cordwainers' Guild Records, 1562–1580.

HEREFORD AND WORCESTER RECORD OFFICE

	Diocese of Worcester Wills, 1500–1541.
802 BA 2764	Bishop Bell's Visitation Book, 1540.

INNER TEMPLE LIBRARY

Petyt 538	Miscellaneous Ecclesiastical Records.

LAMBETH PALACE LIBRARY

	Lambeth Registrum Cranmer.
	Lambeth Registrum Pole.
	Lambeth Registrum Parker.
Carte Miscellanee XII/7	Returns from a survey of the clergy of the diocese of Gloucester, probably conducted in the summer of 1584.

PUBLIC RECORD OFFICE

E331	Exchequer, Various Accounts
PROB 11	Prerogative Court of Canterbury Wills, 1540–1600
Req	Court of Requests

SP 10   State Papers Domestic, Edward VI
SP 11   State Papers Domestic, Mary
SP 12   State Papers Domestic, Elizabeth I

SUFFOLK RECORD OFFICE, IPSWICH

FC 62/A6/23   Cratfield Churchwardens' Accounts, 1554

PRINTED PRIMARY SOURCES

Acts of the Privy Council of England, ed. J. R. Dasent, new ser., 32 vols. London, 1894.

A Brieff Discours off the Troubles Begonne at Franckford in Germany Anno Domino 1554. STC 25442. Heidelburg, 1574.

Bradford, J., *The writings of John Bradford*, ed. A. Townsend. 2 vols. Cambridge, 1853.

Bruce, J., ed., 'Extracts from Accounts of the Churchwardens of Minchinhampton, in the County of Gloucester, with Observations Thereon', *Archaeologia*, 35 (1853), 432–3.

Calendar of Patent Rolls, Elizabeth. 9 vols. London, 1939.

Calendar of Patent Rolls, Philip and Mary. 4 vols. London, 1939.

'Campion the Martyr to Cheney, Anglican Bishop of Gloucester', *The Rambler: a Catholic Journal and Review*, new ser., 8 (1857), 61–2.

'The Charter of the Diocese of Gloucester', ed. and trans. R. Atkins, in *The Ancient and Present State of Glostershire*, R. Atkins. 1712; reprint, Wakefield, 1974, 44–5.

The Commission for Ecclesiastical Causes within the Dioceses of Bristol and Gloucester, 1574, ed. F. D. Price. Bristol and Gloucestershire Archaeological Society, Records Section, vol. X, Gateshead, 1972.

Cranmer, T., *Miscellaneous Writings and Letters of Thomas Cranmer*, ed. J. E. Cox. Cambridge, 1846.

The Remains of Thomas Cranmer, ed. H. Jenkyns. Oxford, 1833.

Deighton, J., 'Martyrdom of Edward Horne at Newent in 1558', in *Narratives of the Days of the Reformation*, ed. J. G. Nichols. Camden Society, vol. LXXVII. London, 1859, 69–70.

Documentary Annals of the Reformed Church of England, ed. E. Cardwell. 2 vols. Oxford, 1839.

The First and Second Prayer Books of Edward VI. Everyman's Library, 1910; reprint, London, 1960.

Grindal, E., 'Articles to be Enquired of Within the Province of Canterbury', in *The Remains of Edmund Grindal*, ed. W. Nicholson. Cambridge, 1843, 156–77.

Halle, E., *Chronicle; Containing the History of England During the Reign of Henry the Fourth and the Succeeding Monarchs to the End of the Reign of Henry the Eighth.* 1548; reprint, London, 1809.

Hooper, J., *The Early Writings of Bishop Hooper*, ed. S. Carr. Cambridge, 1843.

'A Declaration of Ten Holy Commandments of Almighty God', in *Early Writings*, ed. S. Carr. Cambridge, 1843, 249–430.

Later Writings of Bishop Hooper, ed. C. Nevinson. Cambridge, 1852.

Jones, P., *Certaine Sermons Preached of Late at Cicester . . . upon a Portion of the First Chapter of the Epistle of James.* London, 1588. STC 14728.

Latimer, H., *Sermons and Remains of Hugh Latimer*, ed. G. E. Corrie. 2 vols. Cambridge, 1845.

Laud, W., *The History of the Troubles and Tryal of the Most Reverend Father in God, and Blessed Martyr, William Laud*. London, 1695.

Leland, J., *The Itinerary of John Leland the Antiquary*, 3rd edn, ed. T. Hearne. 9 vols. Oxford, 1769.

The Itinerary of John Leland the Antiquary, ed. L. T. Smith. 5 vols. London, 1906–8.

The Letter Book of John Parkhurst, Compiled during the Years, 1571–5, ed. R. A. Houlbrooke. Norfolk Record Society, vol. XLIII, Norwich, 1974/5.

Letters and Papers, Foreign and Domestic of the Reign of Henry VIII, ed. J. S. Brewer. 21 vols. 1864; reprint, New York, 1965.

Liturgical Services: Liturgies and Occasional Forms of Prayer, ed. W. K. Clay. Cambridge, 1847.

Louth, J., 'The Reminiscences of John Louth, Archdeacon of Nottingham, Written in the Year 1579', in *Narratives of the Days of the Reformation*, ed. J. G. Nichols. Camden Society, vol. LXXVII. London, 1859, 1–59.

Maclean, J., ed., 'Chantry Certificates, Gloucestershire (Roll 22)', *TBGAS*, 8 (1883–4), 229–308.

Marshall, W., *Prymer in Englyshe*. London, 1534. STC 15986.

Narratives of the Days of the Reformation, ed. J. G. Nichols. Camden Society, vol. LXXVII, London, 1859.

Nichols, J. G., ed., 'Summary of Ecclesiastical Events in 1554', in *Narratives of the Days of the Reformation*. Camden Society, vol. LXXVII. London, 1859, 287–91.

Original Letters Relative to the English Reformation, trans. and ed. H. Robinson. 2 vols. Cambridge, 1846.

A Profytable and Necessary Doctryne, with Certayne Homilies Adjoined . . . for the Instruction and Enformation of the People [the Book of Homilies]. London, 1555.

Raines, F. R., ed., 'A Description of the State, Civil and Ecclesiastical of the County of Lancaster about the Year 1590' in *Chetham Miscellanies V*. Chetham Society, old ser., vol. XCVI, Manchester, 1875.

Records of Early English Drama: Cumberland, Westmorland, Gloucestershire, eds. A. Douglas and P. Greenfield. Toronto, Buffalo and London, 1986.

The Reformation of the Ecclesiastical Laws of England, 1552, ed. J. C. Spalding. Sixteenth Century Essays and Studies, vol. XXIX, Kirksville, MO, 1992.

Ridley, N., *The works of Nicholas Ridley*, ed. H. Christmas. Cambridge, 1841.

Smyth, J., *A Description of the Hundred of Berkeley in the County of Gloucester and of its Inhabitants*, ed. J. Maclean. The Berkeley Manuscripts, vol. III, Gloucester, 1885.

The Statutes of the Realm. 11 vols. 1817; reprint, London, 1963.

Synodalia. A Collection of Articles of Religion, Canons, and Proceedings of Convocations, comp. E. Cardwell. 2 vols. Oxford, 1842.

'The Testament of W. Tracie Expounded by W. Tindall' in *Wyclyffes Wycket: Whyche he Made in King Rycards Days the Second in the Yere of Our Lorde God M.CCC.XLV*. London, 1546. STC 25590.

'The Testament of W. Tracie Expounded by W. Tindall and J. Frythe', in *Uvicklieffes Wicket. Faythfully over Seene and Corrected*. London, 1548. STC 25591.

The Testament of Master Wylliam Tracie Esquier/Expounded both by William Tyndale and Jhon Frith. Antwerp, 1535. STC 24167.

Tracy, R., *The Profe and Declaration of thys Proposition: Faythe only Justifieth*. London, 1543(?). STC 24164.

A Supplycacion to our moste Soveraigne Lorde Kynge Henry the Eight. London, 1544. STC 24165.5.

The Trew Report of the Dysputacyon Had and Begonne in the Convocacyon Hows at London . . . in the Yeare of Our Lord MDLJJJJ. Basel [Emden], 1554. STC 19890.

Tudor Royal Proclamations, eds. P. L. Hughes and J. F. Larkin. 3 vols. New Haven, CT, and London, 1964.

'Two Sermons Preached by the Boy Bishop', in *Camden Miscellany*, vol. VII, ed. J. G. Nichols. Camden Society, new ser., vol. XIV, Westminster, 1875.

Tyndale's Answer to Sir Thomas More's Dialogue etc., ed. H. Walter. Cambridge, 1850.

Underhill, E., 'Autobiographical Anecdotes of Edward Underhill, One of the Band of the Gentleman Pensioners', in *Narratives of the Days of the Reformation*, ed. J. G. Nichols. Camden Society, vol. LXXVII. London, 1859, 132–76.

The Union of the Two Noble and Illustrate Famelies of Lancastre and Yorke. London, 1548. STC 12721.

Visitation Articles and Injunctions of the Period of the Reformation, ed. W. H. Frere and W. M. Kennedy. 3 vols. Alcuin Club Collections, vol. XV, London and New York, 1910.

'The *Vita Mariae Angliae Reginae* of Robert Winfield of Brantham', in *Camden Miscellany*, vol. XXVIII, trans. and ed. D. MacCulloch. Camden Society, 4th ser., vol. XXIX, London, 1984.

Wilkins, A., ed., *Concilia Magnae Britanniae et Hiberniae ab anno MDXLVI ad annum MDCCXVII*. 4 vols. London, 1737.

'William Latymer's Cronickille of Anne Bulleyne', in *Camden Miscellany*, vol. XXX, ed. M. Dowling. Camden Society, 4th ser., vol. XXXIX, London, 1990.

Willis, R., *Mount Tabor, or Private Exercises of a Penitent Sinner*. London, 1639. STC 25752.

The Zurich Letters Comprising the Correspondence of Several English Bishops and Others with Some of the Helvetian Reformers, ed. and trans. H. Robinson. 3 vols. Cambridge, 1842.

SECONDARY WORKS

Alsop, J. D., 'Religious Preambles in Early Modern English Wills as Formulae', *JEH*, 40 (1989), 19–27.

Aston, M., *England's Iconoclasts: 1. Laws against Images*. Oxford, 1988.

'Iconoclasm at Rickmansworth 1522', *JEH*, 40 (1989), 524–52.

Atkins, R., *The Ancient and Present State of Glostershire*. 1712; reprint, Wakefield, 1974.

Attreed, L. C., 'Preparation for Death in Sixteenth-century Northern England', *SCJ*, 13 (1982), 37–66.

Austin, R., 'John and Joan Cooke's Gift to Gloucester', *TBGAS*, 65 (1944), 199–219.

Baddeley, S. C., 'The Holy Blood of Hayles', *TBGAS*, 23 (1900), 276–84.

Baker, A. R. H., 'Changes in the Later Middle Ages' in *A New Historical Geography of England before 1600*, ed. H. C. Darby. Cambridge, 1976, 186–247.

Bannister, A. T., comp., *Diocese of Hereford Institutions, etc.* (AD 1539–1900). Hereford, 1932.

Barnes, J. A., 'Class and Committees in a Norwegian Island Parish', *Human Relations: Studies towards the Integration of the Social Sciences*, 7 (1954), 39–58.

Baskerville, G., 'The Dispossessed Religious of Gloucestershire', in *Gloucestershire Studies*, ed. H. P. R. Finberg. Leicester, 1957, 63–80.

Bauer, W., *Orthodoxy and Heresy in Earliest Christianity*, ed. R. A. Kraft and G. Kodel. Philadelphia, PA, 1971.

Bayne, C. G., 'The Visitation of the Province of Canterbury, 1559', *Historical Review*, 28 (1913), 636–69.

Beaver, D., 'Conscience and Context: the Popish Plot and the Politics of Ritual, 1678–1682', *HJ*, 34 (1991), 297–327

Beecham, K. J., *History of Cirencester*. Cirencester, *c.* 1886.

Bennett, J., *History of Tewkesbury*. 1830; reprint, Gloucester, 1976.

Bennett, J. M., 'Conviviality and Charity in Medieval and Early Modern England', *P&P*, 134 (1992), 19–41.

Blalock, H. M., *Social Statistics*. International edn London, Tokyo, Paris and Singapore, 1981.

Bossy, J., 'The Character of Elizabethan Catholicism', *P&P*, 21 (1962), 36–59.
  Christianity in the West, 1400–1700. Oxford and New York, 1985.
  The English Catholic Community, 1570–1850. London, 1975.

Bowker, M., *The Henrician Reformation: the Diocese of Lincoln under John Longland, 1521–1547*. Cambridge, 1981.

Brigden, S., *London and the Reformation*. Oxford, 1989.

Burgess, C., 'Late Medieval Wills and Pious Convention: Testamentary Guidance Reconsidered', in *Profit, Piety and the Professions in Later Medieval England*, ed. M. A. Hicks. Gloucester, 1990, 14–33.

Burgess, C. and B. Kümen, 'Penitential Bequests and Parish Regimes in Late Medieval England', *JEH*, 44 (1993), 610–30.

Burnet, G., *The History of the Reformation of the Church of England*, ed. N. Pocock. 7 vols. Oxford, 1865.

Butler, R. F., 'Brimpsfield Church History', *TBGAS*, 81 (1962), 73–87.

Camden, W., *Britannia: or a Chorographical Description of Great Britain and Ireland*, trans. and ed. E. Gibson. 4th edn, 2 vols. London, 1772.

Cameron, E., *The European Reformation*. Oxford, 1991.

Capp, B., 'Will Formularies', *LPS*, 14 (1975), 49.

Carlson, E., 'The Origins, Functions and Status of the Office of Churchwarden, with Particular Reference to the Diocese of Ely', in *The World of Rural Dissenters 1520–1725*, ed. M. Spufford. Cambridge, 1995, 164–207.

Chambers, E. K., *The Elizabethan Stage*. 4 vols. Oxford, 1923.

Chester, A. G., *Hugh Latimer: Apostle to the English*. Philadelphia, PA, 1954.

Clark, P., 'Early Modern Gloucester, 1547–1720', in *The History of the County of Gloucester*, vol. 4, ed. N. M. Herbert. London, 1988.
  English Provincial Society from the Reformation to the Revolution: Religion, Politics and Society in Kent 1500–1640. Hassocks, Sussex, 1977.
  '"The Ramoth-Gilead of the Good": Urban Change and Political Radicalism at Gloucester 1540–1640', in *The English Commonwealth, 1547–1640*, ed. P. Clark, A. G. R. Smith and N. Tyacke. Leicester, 1979, 167–87.

Clutterbuck, R. H., 'Bishop Cheyney, and the Recusants of the Diocese of Gloucester', *TBGAS*, 5 (1880–81), 222–37.

Collinson, P., 'Andrew Perne and his Times', in *Andrew Perne. Quartercentenary.* Cambridge Biographical Society Monograph No. 11, Cambridge, 1991, 1–13.

Archbishop Grindal, 1519–1583: the Struggle for the Reformed Church. London, 1979.

'The Elizabethan Church and the New Religion', in *The Reign of Elizabeth I*, ed. C. Haigh. 1984; reprint, Basingstoke and London, 1991, 169–94.

The Elizabethan Puritan Movement. 1967; reprint, Oxford, 1990.

'Episcopacy and Reform in England in the Later Sixteenth Century', in *Studies in Church History*, vol. III. ed. G. J. Cuming. Leiden, 1966, 91–125.

The Religion of Protestants: the Church in English Society, 1559–1625. Oxford, 1982.

'William Tyndale and the Course of the English Reformation', *Reformation*, 1 (1996), 72–97.

Collinson, P. and J. Craig, ed., *The Reformation in English Towns.* Basingstoke, 1998.

Cooke, J. H., 'The Great Berkeley Law-suit of the 15th and 16th Centuries', *TBGAS*, 3 (1878), 305–24.

Cooper, C. H. and T. Cooper, *Athenae Cantabrigienses 1500–1609.* 2 vols. Cambridge, 1858–61.

Coppel, S., 'Wills and the Community of Tudor Grantham', in *Probate Records and the Local Community*, ed. P. Riden. Gloucester, 1985, 71–90.

Craig, J. and C. Litzenberger, 'Wills as Religious Propaganda: the Testament of William Tracy', *JEH*, 44 (1993), 415–31.

Cressy, D., *Bonfires and Bells: National Memory and the Protestant Calendar in Elizabethan and Stuart England.* London, 1989.

'Kinship and Kin Interaction in Early Modern England', *P&P*, 113 (1986), 38–69.

Cross, C., 'Northern Women in the Early Modern Period: the Female Testators of Hull and Leeds 1520–1650', *Yorkshire Archaeology Journal*, 59 (1987), 83–94.

'Parochial Structure and the Dissemination of Protestantism in Sixteenth Century England: a Tale of Two Cities', in *The Church in Town and Countryside*, ed. D. Baker. Studies in Church History, vol. XVI, Oxford, 1979, 269–78.

'Wills as Evidence of Popular Piety in the Reformation Period: Leeds and Hull', in *The End of Strife*, ed. D. Loades. Edinburgh, 1984, 44–51.

Cuming, G. J., *A History of Anglican Liturgy.* 2nd edn London, 1982.

Cunich, P., 'The Dissolution of the Chantries', in *The Reformation in English Towns*, ed. P. Collinson and J. Craig. Basingstoke, 1998.

Darby, H. C., *A New Historical Geography of England before 1600.* Cambridge, 1976.

Davis, N. Z., 'Some Tasks and Themes in the Study of Popular Religion', in *The Pursuit of Holiness in Late Medieval and Renaissance Religion*, ed. C. Trinkaus and H. A. Oberman. Leiden, 1974, 307–36.

Davis, J. F., *Heresy and Reformation in the South-East of England, 1520–1559.* Royal Historical Studies. London, Atlantic Highlands, NJ, 1983.

Dickens, A. G., *Lollards and Protestants in the Diocese of York, 1509–1559.* 1959; reprint, London, 1982.

'The Early Expansion of Protestantism in England 1520–1558', *Archiv für Reformationsgeschichte*, 78 (1987), 187–222.

The English Reformation. 2nd edn London, 1989.

The Dictionary of National Biography, ed. S. Lee. 22 vols. London, 1885–1900.

Dowling, M., 'Anne Boleyn and Reform', *JEH*, 35 (1984), 30–46.

    'Introduction', in 'William Latymer's Cronickille of Anne Bulleyne', in *Camden Miscellany*, vol. XXX, Camden Society 4th ser., vol. XXXIX, London, 1990, 27–44.

Duffy, E., *The Stripping of the Altars: Traditional Religion in England, c.1400–c.1580*. New Haven, CT, and London, 1992.

Elton, G. R., *Reform and Reformation: England, 1509–1558*. Cambridge, MA, 1977.

Emden, A. B., *A Biographical Register of the University of Oxford, AD 1501 to 1540*. Oxford, 1974.

Emery, F. V., 'England *circa* 1600', in *A New Historical Geography of England before 1600*, ed. H. C. Darby. Cambridge, 1976, 248–302.

Evans, N., 'Inheritance, Women, Religion and Education in Early Modern Society as Revealed by Wills', in *Probate Records and the Local Community*, ed. P. Riden. Gloucester, 1985, 53–70.

Finberg, H. P. R., 'The Genesis of the Gloucestershire Towns', in *Gloucestershire Studies*, ed. H. P. R. Finberg. Leicester, 1957, 54–60.

    ed., *Gloucestershire Studies*. Leicester, 1957.

Floud, R., *An Introduction to Quantitative Methods for Historians*. 2nd edn 1973; reprint, London and New York, 1986.

Foxe, J., *The Acts and Monuments of John Foxe*, ed. G. Townsend. 8 vols. London, 1846.

Freeman, T. S., 'Research, Rumour and Propaganda: Anne Boleyn in Foxe's "Book of Martyrs"', *HJ*, 38 (1995), 797–819.

Fullbrook-Leggatt, L. E. W. O., 'Medieval Gloucester', *TBGAS*, 66 (1945), 1–47.

Gairdner, J., 'Bishop Hooper's Visitation of Gloucester', *EHR*, 19 (1904), 98–121.

Gardiner, H. C., *Mysteries End: an Investigation of the Last Days of the Medieval Religious Stage*. New Haven, CT, 1946.

Garrett, C. H., *The Marian Exiles: a Study in the Origins of Elizabethan Puritanism*. 1938; reprint, Cambridge, 1966.

Greenblatt, S., *Renaissance Self-Fashioning from More to Shakespeare*. London and Chicago, IL, 1980.

Griffiths, P., *Youth and Authority: Formative Experiences in England 1560–1640*. Oxford, 1996.

Haigh, C.,'The Church of England, the Catholics and the People', in *The Reign of Elizabeth I*, ed. C. Haigh. 1984; reprint, Basingstoke and London, 1991, 195–220.

    'The Continuity of Catholicism in the English Reformation', *P&P*, 93 (1981), 37–69.

    English Reformations: Religion, Politics and Society under the Tudors. Oxford, 1993.

    'The Recent Historiography of the English Reformation', *HJ*, 25 (1982), 995–1007.

    Reformation and Resistance in Tudor Lancashire. Cambridge, 1975.

    ed., *The English Reformation Revised*. Cambridge, 1987.

    ed., *The Reign of Elizabeth I*. 1984; reprint, Basingstoke, 1991.

Hall, J. M., 'Haresfield: Manor and Church', *TBGAS*, 19 (1894), 279–373.

Hannam-Clark, T., *Drama in Gloucestershire*. Gloucester and London, 1928.

Hardwick, C., *A History of the Articles of Religion*. London, 1904.

Hart, C. E., *The Commoners of the Forest of Dean*. Gloucester, 1951.
    The Free Miners of the Forest of Dean. Gloucester, 1953.
    The Industrial History of Dean. Newton Abbot, 1971.
    Royal Forest: A History of Dean's Woods as Producers of Timber. Oxford, 1966.
Hay, D., *Polydore Vergil: Renaissance Historian and Man of Letters*. Oxford, 1952.
Heal, F., *Of Prelates and Princes: a Study of the Economic and Social Position of the Tudor Episcopate*. Cambridge, 1980.
Hearne, W. C., 'Flaxley Grange', *TBGAS*, 6 (1881), 284–305.
Henry, A., ed., *Biblia Pauperum: A facsimile and edition*. Ithaca, NY, 1987.
Holt, R. A., 'Gloucester in the Century after the Black Death', in *The English Medieval Town: a Reader in English Urban History, 1200–1540*, ed. R. A. Holt and G. Rosser. London and New York, 1990, 141–59.
Houlbrook, R., *Church Courts and the People during the English Reformation 1520–1570*. Oxford, 1979.
    'The Protestant Episcopate 1547–1603: the Pastoral Contribution' in *Church and Society in England, Henry VIII to James I.*, eds F. Heal and R. O'Day. London, 1977, 78–98.
Hutton, G. and O. Cook, *English Parish Churches*. London, 1976.
Hutton, R., 'The Local Impact of the Tudor Reformation', in *The English Reformation Revised*, ed. C. Haigh. Cambridge, 1987, 114–38.
Ingram, M., *Church Courts, Sex and Marriage in England, 1570–1640*. Cambridge, 1987.
Jeayes, I. H., comp., *Descriptive Catalogue of the Charters and Muniments at Berkeley Castle*. Bristol, 1892.
Jurica, A. R. J., 'Churches and Chapels', in *The History of the County of Gloucester*, ed. N. M. Herbert. London, 1988.
Kennedy-Skipton, H. S., 'The Berkeleys at Yate', *TBGAS*, 21 (1896–7), 25–31.
Kirby, I. M., comp., *Diocese of Gloucester, a Catalogue of the Records of the Bishop and Archdeacons*. Gloucester, 1968.
Knowles, D., *The Religious Orders of England*. 3 vols. Cambridge, 1959.
Kurtz, L. R., 'The Politics of Heresy', *American Journal of Sociology*, 88 (1983), 1085–115.
LaRocca, J. J., 'Time, Death and the Next Generation: the Early Elizabethan Recusancy Policy, 1558–1574', *Albion*, 14 (1982), 103–17.
Le Neve, J, comp., *Fasti Ecclesiae Anglicanae*. 3 vols. Oxford, 1854.
Lindkvist, K., 'Approaches to Textual Analysis', in *Advances in Content Analysis*, ed. K. E. Rosengren. Sage Annual Reviews of Communications Research, vol. IX, London and Beverly Hills, CA, 1981.
Litzenberger, C., 'The Coming of Protestantism to Elizabethan Tewkesbury', in *The Reformation in English Towns*, ed. P. Collinson and J. Craig. Basingstoke, 1998.
    'Local Responses to Changes in Religious Policy Based on the Evidence from Gloucestershire Wills', *Continuity and Change*, 8 (1993), 417–39.
    'Local Responses to Religious Changes: Evidence from Gloucestershire Wills', in *Religion and the English People, 1500–1640: New Perspectives/New Voices*, ed. E. J. Carlson. Kirksville, MO, 1998.
    'Richard Cheyney, Bishop of Gloucester, an Infidel in Religion?', *SCJ*, 25 (1994), 567–84.
    'St Michael's, Gloucester (1540–1580): the Cost of Conformity in Sixteenth

Century England', in *The Parish in English Life 1400–1600*, ed. K. French, G. Gibbs and B. Kümen. Manchester, 1997.

ed., *Tewkesbury Churchwardens' Accounts, 1563–1624*. Gloucestershire Record Series, vol. VII, Gloucester, 1994.

Loades, D. M., *Two Tudor Conspiracies*. Cambridge, 1965.

MacCaffrey, W. T., *Exeter, 1540–1640: the Growth of an English Town*. Cambridge, MA, 1958.

MacCulloch, D., *Suffolk and the Tudors: Politics and Religion in an English County, 1500–1600*. Oxford, 1986.

Thomas Cranmer, a Life. New Haven, CT, and London, 1996.

Maclean, J., 'The Armory and Merchants' Marks in the Ancient Church of Cirencester', *TBGAS*, 17 (1892–3), 268–87.

'Manor of Tockington, Co, Gloucester and the Roman Villa', *TBGAS*, 12 (1887), 123–69.

Maclean, J. and W. C. Heane, eds., *The Visitation of Gloucestershire Taken in the Year, 1623*. London, 1885.

Maitland, F. W., *The History of English Law before the Time of Edward I*, 2nd edn 3 vols. 1898; reprint, Cambridge, 1968.

Manning, R. B., 'The Crisis of Episcopal Authority during the Reign of Elizabeth I', *JBS*, 11 (1971), 1–25.

Hunters and Poachers: A Cultural and Social history of Unlawful Hunting in England 1485–1640. Oxford, 1993.

Religion and Society in Elizabethan Sussex: a Study of the Enforcement of the Religious Settlement, 1558–1603. Leicester and Bristol, 1969.

Marchant, R. A., *The Church under the Law: Justice, Adminstration and Discipline in the Diocese of York, 1560–1640*. Cambridge, 1969.

Marcombe, D., *English Small Town Life: Retford 1520–1642*. Oxford, 1993.

Marsh, C., '"A Graceless and Audacious Companie": the Family of Love in the Parish of Balsham, 1550–1630', in *Voluntary Religion*, ed. W. J. Sheils and D. Woods. Studies in Church History, vol. XXIII, Oxford, 1986, 191–208.

'In the Name of God? Will-making and Faith in Early Modern England' in *The Records of the Nation*, ed. G. H. Martin and P. Spufford. Woodbridge, 1990, 215–49.

Marshall, P., 'The Rood of Boxley, the Blood of Hailes and the Defence of the Henrician Church', *JEH*, 46 (1995), 689–96.

Matlock Population Studies Group, 'Wills and their Scribes', *LPS*, 8 (1972), 55–7.

Mayhew, G. J., 'The Progress of the Reformation in East Sussex 1530–1559: the Evidence from Wills', *Southern History*, 5 (1983), 38–67.

Tudor Rye. Hove, 1987.

McClendon, M. C., '"Against God'sWord": Government, Religion and the Crisis of Authority in Early Reformation Norwich', *SCJ*, 25 (1994), 353–69.

McGrath, P., 'Gloucestershire and the Counter-Reformation in the Reign of Elizabeth I', *TBGAS*, 88 (1969), 5–28.

'Elizabethan Catholicism: a Reconsideration', *JEH*, 35 (1984), 414–28.

McIntosh, M. K., *A Community Transformed: the Manor of Havering 1500–1620*. Cambridge, 1992.

Newinson, C., 'Biographical Notices', in *Later Writings of Bishop Hooper*, ed. C. Newinson. Cambridge, 1852, vii–xii.

Oates, J. C. T. , 'Richard Pynson and the Holy Blood of Hayles', *The Library*, 5th ser., 13 (1958), 269–77.

Owen, D. M., *A Catalogue of Lambeth Manuscripts 889 to 901, Carte Antique et Miscellanee*. Gateshead, 1968.

Oxley, J. E., *The Reformation in Essex to the Death of Mary*. Manchester, 1965.

Palliser, D. M., 'Popular Reactions to the Reformation during the Years of Uncertainty, 1530–70', in *The English Reformation Revised*, ed. C. Haigh. Cambridge, 1987, 94–113.

Peile, J., comp., *Biographical Register of Christ's College, 1505–1905*. 2 vols. Cambridge, 1910.

Percival, A., 'Gloucestershire Village Populations', *LPS*, 8 (1972), 39–47, unpaginated attachment.

Perry, R., 'The Gloucestershire Woollen Industry, 1100–1690', *TBGAS*, 66 (1945), 49–137.

Pettegree, A., 'Nicodemism and the English Reformation', in *Marian Protestantism: Six Studies*, ed. A. Pettegree. St Andrews Studies in Reformation History, Aldershot, Hants, and Brookfield, VT, 1996, 86–117.

Pogson, R. H., 'The Legacy of Schism: Confusion, Continuity and Change in the Marian Clergy', in *The Mid-Tudor Polity c. 1540–1560*, ed. J. Loach and R. Tittler. Basingstoke, 1980, 116–36.

'Revival and reform in Mary Tudor's church' in *The English Reformation Revised*, ed. C. Haigh. Cambridge, 1987, 139–56.

Powell, K. G., 'The Beginnings of Protestantism in Gloucestershire', *TBGAS*, 90 (1971), 141–57.

'The Social Background of the Reformation in Gloucestershire' *TBGAS*, 92 (1973), 96–120.

Price, F. D., 'The Abuses of Excommunication and the Decline of Ecclesiastical Discipline under Queen Elizabeth', *EHR*, 225 (1942), 106–15.

'Bishop Bullingham and Chancellor Blackleech: a Diocese Divided', *TBGAS*, 91 (1973), 175–98.

'The Commission for Ecclesiastical Causes for the Dioceses of Bristol and Gloucester, 1574', *TBGAS*, 59 (1937), 61–184.

'Elizabethan Apparitors in the Diocese of Gloucester', *The Church Quarterly Review*, 134 (1942), 37–55.

'An Elizabethan Church Official – Thomas Powell, Chancellor of Gloucester Diocese', *The Church Quarterly Review*, 128 (1939), 94–112.

'Gloucester Diocese under Bishop Hooper', *TBGAS*, 60 (1938), 51–151.

Primus, J. H., *The Vestments Controversy: an Historical Study of the Earliest Tensions with the Church of England in the Reigns of Edward VI and Elizabeth*. Amsterdam, 1960.

Prior, M., 'Wives and Wills, 1558–1700' in *English Rural Society, 1500–1800*, ed. J. Chartres and D. Hey. Cambridge, 1990, 201–25.

Raines, F. R., ed., 'A Description of the State, Civil and Ecclesiastical of the County of Lancashire about the Year 1590', in *Chetham Miscellanies V*. Chetham Society, old ser., vol. XCVI, Manchester, 1875.

Ramsay, G. D., 'The Distribution of the Cloth Industry in 1561–1562', *EHR*, 57 (1942), 361–9.

Redworth, Glyn, *In Defence of the Church Catholic: the Life of Stephen Gardiner*. Oxford, 1990.

Reinburg, V., 'Liturgy and the Laity in Late Medieval and Reformation France', *SCJ*, 23 (1992), 526–47.

Richardson, R. C., 'Wills and Will-makers in the Sixteenth and Seventeenth Centuries: Some Lancashire Evidence', *LPS*, 9 (1972), 33–42.

Rollinson, D., *The Local Origins of Modern Society, Gloucestershire 1500–1800.* London and New York, 1992.

Rowlands, M. B., 'Recusant Women, 1560–1640', in *Women in English Society, 1500–1800*, ed. M. Prior. London, 1985.

Sacks, D. H., 'The Demise of the Martyrs: the Feasts of St Clement and St Katherine in Bristol, 1400–1600', *Social History*, 11 (1986), 141–69.

Scarisbrick, J. J., *The Reformation and the English People.* Oxford, 1984.

Schofield, R. S., 'Sampling in Historical Research', in *Nineteenth-Century Society: Essays in the Use of Quantitative Methods for the Study of Social Data*, ed. E. A. Wrigley. Cambridge, 1972, 146–84.

Sheils, W. J., *The Puritans in the Diocese of Peterborough, 1558–1610.* Northampton Record Society. vol. XXX. Northampton, 1979.

A Short Title Catalogue of Books Printed in England, Ireland and Scotland, and English Books Printed Abroad, 1475–1640, comp. A. W. Pollard and G. R. Redgrave, ed. W. A. Jackson, F. S. Ferguson, and K. F. Pantzer. 3 vols. London, 1976.

Skeeters, M. C., *Community and Clergy: Bristol and the Reformation c. 1530–c. 1570.* Oxford, 1993.

'The Creation of the Diocese of Bristol', *TBGAS*, 103 (1985), 175–8.

Smeeton, D. D., *Lollard Themes in the Reformation Theology of William Tyndale.* Kirksville, MO, 1986.

Smith, A. H., *County and Court: Government and Politics in Norfolk, 1558–1603.* Oxford, 1974.

Smith, D. M., *Guide to Bishops' Registers of England and Wales: a Survey from the Middle Ages to the Abolition of Episcopacy in 1646.* London, 1981.

Spufford, M., 'The Scribes of Villagers' Wills in the Sixteenth and Seventeenth Centuries and their Influence', *LPS*, 7 (1971), 28–43.

Strype, J., *Annals of the Reformation and Establishment of Religion.* 4 vols. Oxford, 1824.

Ecclesiastical Memorials, Relating chiefly to Religion and the Reformation of it. 3 vols. Oxford, 1822.

The History of the Life and Acts of Edmund Grindal. 2 vols. Oxford, 1821.

The Life and Acts of Matthew Parker. 3 vols. Oxford, 1821.

Takahashi, M., 'The Number of Wills Proved in the Sixteenth and Seventeenth Centuries. Graphs, with Tables and Commentary' in *The Records of the Nation*, ed. G. H. Martin and P. Spufford. Woodbridge, 1990, 187–213.

Tann, J., 'Some Problems of Water Power – a Study of Mill Siting in Gloucestershire', *TBGAS*, 84 (1965), 53–77.

Gloucestershire Woollen Mills. Newton Abbot, 1967.

Thirsk, J., 'The Farming Regions of England', in *The Agrarian History of England and Wales. 4. 1500–1640*, ed. J. Thirsk, 5 vols. Cambridge, 1967, 1–112.

Thomas, K., *Religion and the Decline of Magic.* 1971; reprint, Reading, 1978.

Tittler, R., *The Reign of Mary.* London and New York, 1983.

'Seats of Honor, Seats of Power: the Symbolism of Public Seating in the English Urban Community, *c.* 1560–1620', *Albion*, 24 (1992), 205–23.

Todd, M., *Christian Humanism and the Puritan Social Order.* Cambridge, 1987.

Tudor, P., 'Religious Instruction for Children and Adolescents in the Early English Reformation', *JEH*, 35 (1984), 391–413.

Urdank, A. M., *Religion and Society in a Cotswold Vale: Nailsworth, Gloucestershire, 1780–1865*. Berkeley, Los Angeles, CA, and Oxford, 1990.

Vann, R. T., 'Wills and the Family in an English Town: Banbury, 1550–1800', *Journal of Family History*, 4 (1979), 347–67.

Venn, J. and J. A. Venn, comps., *Alumni Cantabrigienses Part I, to 1751*. 4 vols. Cambridge, 1922–7.

Verey, D., *Buildings of England: Gloucestershire*. 2 vols. 2nd edn Harmondsworth, 1976.

Cotswold Churches. 1982; reprint, Gloucester, 1991.

Walsham, A., *Church Papists: Catholicism, Conformity and Confessional Polemic in Early Modern England*. Royal Historical Society Studies in History, no. 68, Woodbridge, 1993.

Wark, K. R., *Elizabethan Recusancy in Cheshire*. Chetham Society, 3rd ser., vol. XIX, Manchester, 1971.

Watt, T., *Cheap Print and Popular Piety, 1550–1640*. Cambridge, 1991.

West, W. M. S., 'John Hooper and the Origins of Puritanism', *The Baptist Quarterly*, 15 (1954), 346–68; 16 (1955), 22–46, 67–88.

White, F. O., *Lives of the Elizabethan Bishops of the Anglican Church*. London, 1898.

Whiting, R., ' "For the Health of my Soul": Prayers for the Dead in the Tudor South-west', *Southern History*, 5 (1983), 68–94.

The Blind Devotion of the People. 1989; reprint, Cambridge, 1991.

Willan, T. S., *The Inland Trade: Studies in English Internal Trade in the Sixteenth and Seventeenth Centuries*. Manchester, 1976.

Williams, G., *The Welsh Church from Conquest to Reformation*. rev. edn, Cardiff, 1976.

Wood, A. A., *Athenae Oxonienses: an Exact History of all the Writers and Bishops who Have Had their Education in the University of Oxford*. London, 1813.

Fasti Oxonienses: Annals of the University of Oxford, ed. P. Bliss. London, 1815.

Wrightson, K. and D. Levine, 'Death in Wickham', in *Famine, Disease and the Social Order in Early Modern Society*, ed. J. Walter and R. Schofield. Cambridge, 1989, 129–65.

Zell, M. L., 'The Prebendaries' Plot of 1543: a Reconsideration', *JEH*, 27 (1976), 241–53.

'The Use of Religious Preambles as a Measure of Religious Belief in the Sixteenth Century', *The Bulletin of the Institute of Historical Research*, 1 (1977), 246–9.

UNPUBLISHED SECONDARY SOURCES

Holt, R. A., 'Gloucester: an English Provincial Town During the Later Middle Ages', University of Birmingham, PhD (1987).

Kemp, J. K., 'Laurence Humphrey, Elizabethan Puritan: His Life and Political Theories', West Virginia University, PhD (1978).

McClendon, M. C., 'The Quiet Reformation: Norwich Magistrates and the Coming of Protestantism, 1520–1575', Stanford University, PhD (1990).

Moore, F. A., ' "The Bruised Reed" (Is. 42:3): a Study of the Catholic Remnant in England, 1558–1603, with Special Reference to Gloucestershire', University of London, MPhil (1990).

Newcome, D. G., 'The Life and Theological Thought of John Hooper, Bishop of Gloucester and Worcester, 1551–1553', University of Cambridge, PhD (1990).

Price, F. D., 'The Administration of the Diocese of Gloucester 1547–1579', University of Oxford, BLitt (1939).

Saunders, C. R., 'Social Mobility in the Forest of Dean *c*. 1550–1650', Oxford Polytechnic, PhD (1989).

Wabuda, S. R., 'The Provision of Preaching During the Early English Reformation: with Special Reference to Itineration, *c*. 1530 to 1547', University of Cambridge, PhD (1991).

West, W. M. S., 'John Hooper and the Origins of Puritanism'. Dr Williams's Library, MS P. 4851. (Extracts from University of Zurich, PhD (1954).)

INDEX

Cambridge Studies in Early Modern British History

Titles in the series